W9-BPP-077

THE PRINCIPLES OF CHRISTIAN ETHICS

THE PRINCIPLES OF CHRISTIAN ETHICS

ALBERT C. KNUDSON
Dean Emeritus, Boston University
School of Theology

ABINGDON PRESS
New York • Nashville

THE PRINCIPLES OF CHRISTIAN ETHICS

Library of Congress Catalog Card Number: 43-16331

J

SET UP, PRINTED, AND BOUND BY THE PARTHENON PRESS, AT NASHVILLE, TENNESSEE, UNITED STATES OF AMERICA

TO

EDGAR SHEFFIELD BRIGHTMAN
ELMER ARCHIBALD LESLIE
EARL BOWMAN MARLATT

FRIENDS AND ASSOCIATES THROUGH THE YEARS

PREFACE

THIS book is a systematic and critical exposition of Christian ethics in the light of its history and of present-day thought. Special attention, as its title indicates, is devoted to the fundamental principles of the Christian ethic. But it also contains a general introduction to the more important problems of individual and social ethics, and concludes with a chapter on the validity of Christian ethics. Those who are acquainted with English literature in this field will recognize the need of some such introductory work as this.

During the past forty-five years I have been a teacher of theology in several institutions. Thirty-seven of these years have been spent at the university with which I am still connected. So far as my professorial and administrative duties as dean permitted, I have during these years endeavored to put into book form the conclusions I have reached in the three main divisions of systematic theology. In the field of apologetics two books have been written, *The Philosophy of Personalism* and *The Validity of Religious Experience.* In the field of Christian doctrine two volumes also have been written, *The Doctrine of God* and *The Doctrine of Redemption,* to which *The Religious Teaching of the Old Testament* and *Present Tendencies in Religious Thought* may be regarded as introductory. The present volume completes the series by covering the field of Christian ethics. These books as a whole have emphasized the historical and philosophical approaches to the problems of theology and, so far as possible, have sought to solve these problems in the light of a thoroughgoing and consistent Christian personalism. It is the latter fact, if any, that gives a certain distinctiveness to my life work.

PREFACE

Dr. Edgar S. Brightman and Dr. L. Harold DeWolf have kindly read the manuscript of this volume and given me the benefit of their highly valued judgment on many points—a service for which I am deeply grateful to them.

I also owe a special debt of gratitude to Miss Gertrude L. Allison, librarian at Boston University School of Theology, and Dr. Jannette E. Newhall, assistant librarian at Andover Harvard Theological Library, for their generosity in placing at my disposal large numbers of books needed in the preparation of this volume and for assisting me in other ways.

ALBERT C. KNUDSON

CONTENTS

PART I. INTRODUCTION

CHAPTER I

CHAPTER II

PART II. PRESUPPOSITIONS

CHAPTER III

CONTENTS

PART V. CONCLUSION

CHAPTER XIV

PART I

INTRODUCTION

CHAPTER I

THE PROVINCE OF CHRISTIAN ETHICS[1]

It is customary to distinguish "Christian" or "theological" ethics from "general," "natural," or "philosophical" ethics. This distinction owed its origin to the double stream of speculative thought in the Western world. Since the rise of Christianity philosophy and theology have moved along through parallel channels more or less independently of each other. Each of these streams of thought has produced its own type or system of ethics. These two systems have to some extent overlapped; but they have had distinctive features, and hence different titles have been given them.

This bifurcation of ethics, however, has not been universally accepted. Some object to it on the ground that there can be only one valid science of ethics, just as there can be only one valid science of botany, of chemistry, or of physics. For science is by its very nature unitary and in its own particular field comprehensive. It recognizes only one standard of truth. To have two types of ethics, covering virtually the same field and with two distinct standards or norms, is therefore out of harmony with our modern intellectual or scientific ideal. There is no place for both a philosophical and a Christian ethics. One or the other ought to be eliminated, or one ought to be absorbed by the other. Both of these methods of restoring unity to modern ethics have been advocated.

The prevailing view, however, is still favorable to the tra-

[1] If the reader is not interested in the academic question with which this chapter deals, I suggest that he begin with Chapter II.

ditional distinction between Christian and philosophical ethics. But there is considerable difference of opinion as to how this distincton should be defined. The general tendency is to think of Christian ethics, not as a rival of philosophical ethics, but as supplementary to it. There are, however, various ways of conceiving the latter relationship, and a brief account will be given of some of these and also of the monistic theories referred to in the preceding paragraph.

This survey of the more important types of thought with respect to the relation of Christian and philosophical ethics to each other will serve a double purpose. It will acquaint the reader with the present status of Christian ethics and with the different theories concerning its specific province, and will also introduce him to its fundamental and distinctive problems. The theories to be considered in this survey may be divided into three classes: elimination theories, absorption theories, and supplementary theories.[2]

Elimination Theories

We begin with the elimination theories. Of these there are naturally two types: one which seeks to discredit Christian ethics and another which seeks to discredit philosophical or natural ethics.

The first has taken various forms. It is, for instance, argued by Schopenhauer that Christian morality is based on the divine will but that in order to determine what the divine will is in any particular case it is necessary to appeal to ethical considerations. Moral insight is thus made the basis of our knowledge of the divine will, while at the same time it is claimed that the divine will is the source of our moral insight. In this way Christian ethics moves, and moves necessarily, in a vicious circle.[3] Then, too, it is charged that Christian ethics, in basing

[2] The most comprehensive and thorough discussion of these theories with which I am acquainted is that by Anders Nygren, professor in the University of Lund, *Filosofisk och Kristen Etik* (1923).

[3] *The Basis of Morality*, pp. 12f.; cf. H. Höffding, *Ethik*, pp. 11-19.

the moral life on the divine will, is heteronomous, and hence out of harmony with the autonomy of true morality. It is the self-determination of the will that makes an act moral. Submission to the will of another is not in itself truly ethical. It is, as von Hartmann says, "heteronomous pseudo-morality."[4] A further objection to Christian ethics is that it is otherworldly, egoistic, and eudaemonistic. It lays chief stress on the life to come and so cripples the moral energies of men which are primarily concerned with the present life. It emphasizes also the idea of reward and punishment, and so misses the genuine moral spirit which consists in devotion to virtue for its own sake.

A still more radical criticism was passed upon the moral teaching of Christianity by Friedrich Nietzsche (1844-1900), who denounced its ethic of love as a "slave morality," as a product of the selfish desires of the poorest, weakest, and meanest members of human society. To it he opposed the ethic of power, the "master morality," the morality of the "superman."[5]

Another reason for rejecting Christian ethics has been urged by historical relativists. They have maintained that the ethical teaching of Jesus was adapted to the social, political, and cultural conditions of his own day, and that it consequently cannot be authoritative for the altered circumstances of modern life. The relativity of history rules it out.

A protest against the idea of a scientific Christian ethics has also been voiced by some representatives of the dialectical or transcendental theology. Karl Barth, for instance, has said that "a system of ethics which pretends to know and to establish the commandment of the Creator usurps the throne of God, poisoning the sources of faith. It is more devastating for Christian life than all the cinemas and dance halls put together!"[6] This utterance was of course directed, not against the Christian ethic

---

[4] *Phaenomenologie des sittlichen Bewusstseins* (1879), pp. 88, 92.

[5] Cf. *The Twilight of the Idols; Beyond Good and Evil; Thus Spake Zarathustra; Antichrist.*

[6] Quoted by Adolf Keller, *Religion and Revolution,* p. 87.

as such, but against what Barth regarded as the presumption involved in the idea of a systematic Christian ethics. Man's religious knowledge, he holds, is too limited to warrant such a science.

Efforts to discredit philosophical or natural ethics, on the other hand, have been less common. As an illustration of such an attempt we may take the able and stimulating work by Emil Brunner entitled *The Divine Imperative*.[7] Brunner has been the most influential of Barth's associates in the development and exposition of "the dialectical theology" or "the theology of crisis," as it was at first called. But on the question of a Christian ethics he has parted company with his friend Barth and has himself produced one of the most important books on the subject that has appeared in the past quarter of a century. He has sought to do what no one before him has done. He has tried to deduce theological ethics from the center of the evangelical faith, that is, from the doctrine of justification by faith alone.

In this work Brunner draws a sharp line between Christian and natural morality, and points out what he considers the weaknesses of the latter. The ideal moral life, he insists, is life as interpreted from the purely evangelical standpoint. Such a life is a life dependent on the Holy Spirit, a life receptive of the divine grace, a life that has its initiative in God, not in man. It is a life qualitatively different from the natural life. The latter in its highest or religious form is, it is true, a life directed toward God. It is a quest after him, a search for him, a striving after the ideal; and as such it is from the common human standpoint commendable. But it is nevertheless a self-centered life. It derives its initiative from human rather than divine sources and, as it becomes more strenuous, tends to widen rather than narrow the breach between man and God. The only way to find God is to be found of him. This is the Christian way. The whole Christian moral life has its roots in

[7] The original German edition bears the title *Das Gebot und die Ordnungen* —"The Commandment and the Orders" (1932; Eng. trans., 1937).

him and has no other rootage. This is the ground of its uniqueness and its perfection.

By way of contrast with this Christian ideal the moral ideal of natural or philosophical ethics is, we are told, anthropocentric, legalistic, and self-righteous. Natural ethics lays the stress on human ability; it sets up a moral law which man is declared to be able to obey in his own strength. It thus assumes a false independence of God, out of which grow self-righteousness and all the moral evils associated with man's sense of self-sufficiency. Indeed, it is in this independent attitude toward God that the essence of sin is to be found, and so Brunner tells us that "moralism with its legalism and self-righteousness is at all times the worst foe of true morality."[8] In natural morality we have, consequently, not a lower form of the moral life but rather a type of life antithetical to the Christian ideal. Instead of being ethical, it is rather unethical, a sinful life, such a life as the traditional doctrine of original sin attributes to the natural man.

Along with this radical criticism of natural morality goes a similar criticism of natural ethics. The latter, according to Brunner, is incapable of being developed into a consistent and coherent system. It is, as history makes clear, torn asunder by inner contradictions that cannot be reconciled. There is a conflict between the idea of duty and that of the good, a conflict between freedom and necessity, a conflict between individualism and universalism, a conflict between what is and what ought to be. These conflicts cannot be resolved on the plane of natural ethics, no matter how highly spiritualized it may be. They are inherent in the very structure of the natural conscience. So long as the self asserts any degree of independence over against God, so long as it feels the call of duty and seeks to obey it in its own strength, there is no way of overcoming them. They are involved in the very idea of "ought" as interpreted by the common conscience, and hence natural or philosophical

[8] *Ibid.*, p. 57 (Ger. ed., p. 44).

ethics is necessarily condemned to inner discord and to ultimate disintegration. Indeed, it is already "a field of ruins."

The only way, according to Brunner, to escape this consequence is through such a renunciation of man's moral independence as is implied in the doctrine of justification by faith. This doctrine is or should be basal in Christian ethics. It assumes, we are told, the absolute sinfulness of man and his consequent inability to do any good thing of himself. He has no metaphysical freedom. His moral redemption is completely dependent on God, and can, so far as he himself is concerned, be achieved only through faith. Faith, consequently, with the Christian takes the place of moral effort. It is not his own independent act; it is a divine act within him, a pure gift of God. Hence there is in it no sense of "ought" or of personal achievement. It is all of grace.[9] And this means that the old ethical antinomies are at an end. They have lost their meaning. The divine will has taken the place of the ideas of "duty" and "the good," and with the denial of man's metaphysical freedom

[9] In a later work, called *Man in Revolt,* published in German in 1937 and in English in 1939, Brunner makes an elaborate attempt to harmonize the doctrine here expounded with the idea of freedom and responsibility. Historic Calvinism has always affirmed both, but without ever arriving at a satisfactory synthesis of the two. Such a synthesis or at least a closer approach to it Brunner seeks to effect in his *Man in Revolt* or "Man in Contradiction," as the German title would more precisely be rendered. He here continues to speak of man's very being as "defined by sin" (p. 116), of the impossibility of his "not being a sinner" (p. 271), and of "the sole power of the grace of God" (p. 538). He also rejects "synergism" and says that "God alone does everything" (p. 538). Yet he denies the "sole causality" or "sole operation" of God and declares that faith is a free and responsible act on man's part (p. 541). He tries repeatedly and ingeniously to interpret freedom and responsibility in such a way as to make them fit into a monergistic or Calvinistic framework, but with indifferent success. The net result is an irrational "paradox" (p. 117), "mystery" (p. 540), or "dualism" (p. 541). Most of Brunner's difficulties would have been avoided if he had been able to renounce his Calvinism and accept the synergistic conception of freedom as a freedom of contrary choice. But this he has been unable to do. The center of gravity of his thinking remains Calvinistic. His apparent concessions to Arminianism impress one as efforts to make his fundamental Calvinism more palatable to the modern mind. *Man in Revolt* does not, it seems to me, represent any important change in his theological position, nor does it seriously affect the underlying conceptions or principles of his ethics. The abstract and illicit antithesis between the Law and the Gospel, fundamental in his earlier works, still dominates his thinking (p. 515).

the antithesis between freedom and necessity and between what is and what ought to be has been overcome. A unity is thus achieved in Christian ethics that is impossible in philosophical ethics. But it has been achieved only through the establishment of a radical difference between them. Brunner looks upon Christian and philosophical ethics, not as supplementary, but as antithetical to each other. With him Christian ethics is exclusively an ethics of grace; and grace he regards as the negation, not the perfection, of nature. An ethics based on nature cannot, therefore, stand in any positive relation to Christian ethics, either as an introduction to it or as a part of it. The two exclude each other. It is only on the ruins of philosophical ethics that Christian ethics can be erected. The truly Christian ethic transcends and nullifies the underlying principles of natural ethics.[10]

Absorption Theories

The absorption theories differ from the elimination theories in that they are based on the kinship of Christian and philosophical ethics to each other rather than on their disparity or mutually exclusive relationship. It is because they so closely resemble or so completely involve each other that the attempt has been made to absorb Christian ethics in philosophical ethics or the reverse. Of these two methods the former has naturally been the more common, for it is philosophical rather than Christian ethics that is as a rule taken for granted.

The most distinguished theological representative of the incorporation of Christian ethics in general ethics is Wilhelm Herrmann (1846-1922), who spent most of his life as professor at the University of Marburg and exercised a profound influence on theological thought in England and America as well as in Germany. His systematic treatise on ethics is a relatively small book, which unfortunately has not been translated into English.[11] In this book and elsewhere Herrmann argues

[10] For a more extended exposition and criticism of Brunner's ethics see my article "The Barthian Ethics," *Crozer Quarterly*, October, 1935.

that religion presupposes in man an independent moral nature. Man does not need to be religious in order to be moral, but he could not be truly religious if he were not first of all moral.[12] Morality is the birthplace of religion. It is the inherent demands of the moral nature, when taken seriously, and the difficulty, if not impossibility, of realizing them that give rise to religion. These demands and our inability fully to obey them create within us an impasse, and the only way out is that furnished by religion. Religion is not a logical deduction from morality, as Kant held; but morality is the *conditio sine qua non* of its origin. If it were not for the inner tension and sense of need created by the moral nature of man, religion would not arise. Moral experience is the psychological presupposition of religious experience.

There is also, according to Herrmann, a further difference between morality and religion. The former is universal. It is rooted in the common human reason, and in this respect is universally valid. Religion, on the other hand, is more distinctly an individual matter. It does not have the same universal and necessary character as morality. It cannot, therefore, furnish a basis for the latter. Should morality be made dependent on religion, it too would become individual and lose its universality. And this in turn would have an adverse effect on the status of religion. It would deprive religion of such power of universal appeal as it at present has. For religion, though individual in character, does make an appeal to all men; but it does so only through the medium of their moral nature. It is the universality and independence of the moral nature that gives religion its point of contact with men everywhere. There is, therefore, no apologetic advantage in trying to make the moral judgments of men dependent on religious beliefs and in thus seeking to find an independent basis for Christian ethics. Rather does the advantage lie the other way. The independence

[11] *Ethik* (1901; 6th ed., 1921).
[12] This position is elaborated and ably supported by Edgar S. Brightman, *Religious Values*, pp. 32-69, and *Moral Laws*, pp. 264-76.

of the moral nature and of philosophical ethics furnishes the best basis for a sound Christian apologetic. It is because of this independence that Christianity is able to make a world-wide appeal. The universality of morality gives universality to religion. There are, to be sure, distinctive elements in the Christian moral life, but they can best be treated within the limits of general ethics.

In support of this conclusion it is further argued by Herrmann that the Christian moral ideal is in principle identical with the formal subjective ethics of Kant. Stress is here laid on the good will as the essence of the moral life and on the principle of autonomy. Only that act is morally good which is recognized by the individual to be such and which is performed for this reason. Mere outward obedience to a moral law is not a moral act. Truly moral conduct is rooted in the will and grows out of inner moral conviction. It is the purity and freedom of the will that alone make a person a truly moral being. These Kantian ideas are identified by Herrmann with the principle of inwardness as taught in the New Testament. This principle he regards as basal in the Christian life, and from it he deduces the social principle of love. From his standpoint there is, therefore, nothing fundamentally new or distinctive in the Christian moral ideal. Its content is substantially identical with that of the Kantian type of philosophical ethics.[13] What is new in the Christian moral life is its dynamic, its inspiration, the power it imparts to men to realize the moral ideal. This, it is true, is an extremely important factor in the moral history of mankind and should receive more adequate treatment than it has heretofore received in general ethics. But no special or separate science of Christian ethics is needed for

[13] This was also Friedrich Paulsen's view. Kant's relation, he said, to the vital Christianity of the common people was "close and intimate. Indeed, one may say that his morality is nothing but the translation of this Christianity from religious language to the language of reflection." *Immanuel Kant, His Life and Doctrine,* p. 339. Nietzsche expressed virtually the same idea by speaking of Kant as "a Christian in disguise."

that purpose. All that is needed is an enlargement of the scope of general or philosophical ethics.

The contrary procedure, the absorption of philosophical ethics by Christian ethics, seems at first sight a rather bold and dubious venture. But it has nevertheless had not a little currency in theological circles as a reaction to the position championed by Herrmann, and for an obvious reason. It tends to magnify the Christian ethic and to bring out more clearly and emphatically its fundamental, distinctive, and universal character. It also tends to subordinate the moral to the religious and to make the Christian religion the source, ground, and norm of our Western morality rather than a mere appendix to it.

As representatives of this tendency in theological ethics we may with Nygren[14] name Emil W. Mayer (1854-1927) and Arvid Runestam (1887-——). The former was professor of systematic theology at the University of Strassburg from 1893 to the close of the first World War, when he transferred to the University of Giessen. Runestam held the same chair at the University of Upsala from 1922 until he became a bishop a few years ago. While these two men represent the same general view of the relation of Christian and philosophical ethics to each other, they differ in the method by which they arrive at their conclusion. Mayer argues that morality is more dependent on religion than religion on morality. This holds true whether we have in mind the origin of morality or its validity. The moral norms derived their unconditional character from religious sanctions, and it is only in religious faith that they can find their ultimate validation. Philosophical ethics, if it fully understands itself and its implications, must therefore in a Christian land become Christian ethics. This, of course, assumes that Christianity is the highest form of religion; and reasons for this belief are included by Professor Mayer in his *Ethics*.[15] But however that may be, the fate of

[14] *Op. cit.*, pp. 49-56.
[15] *Ethik: christliche Sittenlehre* (1922).

true morality is linked with that of religion, and this for the Christian means that philosophical ethics finds its ultimate ground and completion in Christian ethics.

Bishop Runestam's method of justifying the incorporation of general ethics in Christian ethics is somewhat more general and direct. He recognizes that, if Christian morality is to be identified with morality in general, it will be necessary to broaden the concept of Christianity and narrow the concept of morality. This he does by insisting that morality in its essential nature is subjective and inward, and that Christianity in its essence is also an ethic of moral inwardness. The two in their purity are, therefore, virtually one. The moral as such is embraced in the Christian spirit. It is itself Christian. There is, consequently, no part of the truly moral life that lies beyond the scope of Christian ethics. Just as Christian theology claims to represent religion in its highest and purest form and thus takes up into itself all that is essential and of permanent value in the religious life of mankind as a whole, so it is with Christian ethics in its relation to other moral systems. It represents morality in its highest and purest form and thus stands in a comprehensive relation to the moral life of mankind as a whole. In order to make this clear all that is required is to deepen and spiritualize the concept of morality on the one hand and the concept of Christianity on the other. When this is done, the Christian ethic becomes a universal ethic and there is no longer need of an independent philosophical ethics.[16]

Supplementary Theories

The theories thus far considered have sought to remove the dualism of philosophical and theological ethics by the virtual elimination of one or the other or by the absorption of one in the other. Opposed to these monistic theories are the theories that we call supplementary. The latter retain the traditional dualism, and treat Christian and philosophical ethics as more

[16] See Runestam's essay "Etikens Kristlighet," *Teologiska Studier Tillägnade E. Stave* (1922), pp. 284 ff.

or less independent of each other and yet as essential to the full expression of the Christian moral consciousness. One is necessary as a supplement to the other. This supplementary relation has been conceived in various ways. We shall distinguish four and deal briefly with each.

1. Historically the most important is the theory of the ancient and medieval church which is still dominant in Roman Catholicism. This theory distinguished between nature and supernature. The moral law of nature was regarded as expressed in the four cardinal virtues of the Greeks: wisdom, temperance, fortitude, and justice. These formed the foundation of the moral life, and to them the Christian or theological graces of faith, hope, and love were added as a supernatural supplement. The addition, however, was conceived in two different ways. Augustine (354-430) saw in the three Christian graces a new ethical spirit, best expressed in the idea of love. Love with him was not one virtue along with other virtues; it was the essence of all virtue. Hence it could not be conceived as a mere external addition to the four cardinal virtues. It had to be thought of rather as the organizing principle of the entire moral life, as a new spirit pervading the whole; and this meant that the cardinal virtues must themselves be Christianized. They must be lifted to the Christian level. The Christian supplement to the natural moral law must take the form of an inner transformation rather than an external addition. This, consequently, was what Augustine sought to do. He sought to reinterpret the cardinal virtues as expressions of the Christian principle of love. "Temperance," he said, "is love keeping itself uncontaminated for its object, fortitude is love readily enduring all for the beloved's sake, justice is love serving only the beloved and therefore rightly governing, prudence is love sagaciously choosing the things that help her and rejecting the things that hinder." [17]

---

[17] Quoted by Henry Sidgwick, *Outlines of the History of Ethics* (1886), p. 130. See Augustine, *De moribus ecclesiae catholicae*, I, 25, 15, and note his statement, *"Virtus est ordo amoris."*

Thomas Aquinas (1225?-74?), on the other hand, treated the cardinal virtues as preliminary stages in the moral life which continued to maintain a certain independence of their own and to which the Christian graces stood in a somewhat loose relation. The relation was that of an external supplement rather than that of an immanent spirit. The Christian graces or theological virtues were a kind of upper story resting on an Aristotelian foundation. Between the foundation and its superstructure there was no really organic or interpenetrating bond of unity. But there was also no sharp antithesis. The relation of nature and grace to each other was divinely established, and both had a divine origin. Indeed, they were grounded in a sort of dualism of the divine substance, which revealed its "nature" in the orders of creation and its "supernature" in the realm of grace. This dualism of nature and supernature served as both a bond of union and a ground of distinction between Christian and natural ethics. But with such a metaphysical background a complete system of Christian ethics could hardly be deduced from its own distinctive principle or principles. Natural ethics might be incorporated within Christian ethics as a preliminary stage, but logically it would still continue to have a more or less independent status. Such was its position in the ethics of Aquinas.[18]

2. Another type of supplementary theory is represented by Schleiermacher (1768-1834). The father of modern theology might also be said to be the father of modern Christian ethics. But his work in the latter field was not carried to such a consistent and definitive conclusion as in the field of theology. He made very important contributions to general ethics. Two in particular may be noted: the reduction of the moral consciousness of mankind to three ruling ideas—the good, duty, and virtue—and the presentation of ethics as an ethics of objective values. The latter, says Troeltsch, is "the highpoint of the

[18] Cf. Étienne Gilson, *The Philosophy of St. Thomas Aquinas* and *The Spirit of Mediæval Philosophy;* E. Troeltsch, *The Social Teaching of the Christian Churches,* I, 257-328.

ethics of German idealism."[19] But Schleiermacher did not utilize these contributions to general ethics, as he might have done, in the construction of his Christian ethics. He might have treated the latter as a possible system of concrete specifications within the categorial framework of his moral ideas. Or he might have treated it as a system of objective values within such a larger whole as constituted the subject of his philosophical ethics, a type of moral theory that might more precisely be described as a general ethical philosophy of culture. Both of these conceptions were fruitful and were implied in his general theory of the moral life. But he did not elaborate them in his Christian ethics.

Instead, he accommodated himself to the method adopted in his theology. As he based the latter on the Christian consciousness and thus differentiated it from the philosophy of religion, so he based his Christian ethics on the Christian moral consciousness and thus differentiated it from philosophical ethics. It was this that he was primarily interested in establishing, the uniqueness of Christian morality as well as the Christian religion. But for this purpose he was unable to utilize the medieval distinction between nature and supernature. For him this metaphysical dualism belonged to the past. In its stead he held to an evolutionary view of the world according to which Christianity is the highest expression of man's nature, both moral and religious. Christian ethics thus became for him the crown of natural ethics, but at the same time it retained its uniqueness by being grounded in the unique moral experience generated by the spirit of Christ.[20]

3. A third method of defining the supplementary relation of Christian and philosophical ethics to each other was advocated by Ernst Troeltsch (1865-1923). According to this learned and very able theologian and Christian moralist, philosophical

[19] *Gesammelte Schriften,* II, 566.

[20] See his posthumous work, *Die christliche Sitte, nach den Grundsätzen der evangelischen Kirche im Zusammenhange dargestellt* (ed. L. Jonas; 1843).

ethics is immanental or this-worldly while Christian ethics is transcendental or other-worldly. Of the two, Christian ethics is the higher and more inclusive. It is able by virtue of its ultimate religious goal to take up into itself the lower temporal goals set by the present life and thus give to the moral life as a whole a certain degree of unity. But this unifying process is limited. "Not in all eternity," says Troeltsch, "can the entire range of man's moral activity in the world be deduced from Christian love. Christian ethics must recognize other moral principles alongside of itself." [21] There is thus a fundamental dualism in the moral life. This dualism is due not to sin but to man's metaphysical constitution, to the fact that he is a denizen of two worlds. He stands midway between the temporal and the eternal, and this double relationship gives rise to a dualism of ethical motive. Christian and philosophical ethics are thus necessary as supplements to each other.

Another distinction that Troeltsch draws between philosophical and theological ethics is that between the theoretical, or scientific, and the practical. This corresponds to the distinction he makes between the philosophy of religion and systematic theology. The latter he regards as practical rather than scientific in character, and so he holds it is with theological ethics. Its task is less that of grounding and expounding the Christian doctrine of love than that of permeating existing conditions with its power. Christian ethics is thus a practical as well as a supramundane supplement to the scientific and intramundane ethics that we call "philosophical." [22]

4. A fourth theory of the supplementary type takes its start from the critical philosophy of Kant. It begins with a recognition of the autonomy of man's moral nature. There is what may be called a moral a priori. This a priori stands in its own right. In its fundamental and independent character we have the ultimate basis of the validity of our moral experience. It is,

---

[21] *Politische Ethik und Christentum,* p. 34.

[22] *The Social Teaching of the Christian Churches* (1912) is Troeltsch's great and truly epoch-making work in the field of Christian ethics.

however, only our moral experience in general, its formal structure, that is thus validated; and it is with this problem that philosophical ethics is, or ought to be, primarily concerned. It has the task of analyzing the moral nature and establishing its essential validity; and in this respect its work is presupposed by Christian ethics.

To what extent philosophical ethics has also the function of determining the concrete content of the moral life is a question. The common view would probably agree with that of H. H. Wendt,[23] who holds that there are certain concrete duties implied in the natural conscience or derived from the principle of values to be realized and that the discussion of these duties properly forms an important part of philosophical ethics. These duties, however, are heterogeneous in character and cannot by themselves be reduced to a coherent whole. They need to be supplemented by the Christian principle of love and reinterpreted in the light of the Christian faith. But while thus raised to a higher level and endowed with a new ethical urgency, they still remain as a bond of union between Christian and philosophical ethics.

As against this view it is argued by Anders Nygren, the distinguished Swedish theologian, that philosophical and Christian ethics do not overlap. Philosophical ethics, he holds, is or should be restricted to the formal task of establishing the validity of ethical experience. Concrete ethics lies beyond its domain. Christian ethics, on the other hand, is concrete, and concrete ethics of a unique type. It is an ethics of love and in this respect differs from Nietzsche's ethics of power and Kant's ethics of right. Love or *agape,* as taught in the New Testament, is something new. It differs from the Platonic *eros* in that it is wholly a divine gift and in itself "spontaneous" and "unmotivated," a purely giving or forgiving love.[24] It thus imparts to the

---

[23] *Die sittliche Pflicht,* pp. 149-81.

[24] See Nygren's very stimulating and significant work on the history of the Christian idea of love, translated under the title *Agape and Eros* and published in three volumes. Special attention will be devoted to it in Chapter VI.

Christian moral ideal an entirely distinct character, so that Christian ethics stands apart from all other types of concrete ethics. But this does not bring it into conflict with philosophical ethics. The latter has to do simply with the formal or rational grounding of the moral life as a whole, and as such is a natural introduction to Christian ethics. The two types of ethics thus supplement each other. Neither overlaps or excludes the other. Each has its own distinct field, and neither is complete without the other. This theory of their relation to each other is more distinctive than the one adopted by Wendt and may be taken as the typical representative of what we have selected as the fourth theory of the supplementary type.

Fundamental Problems

The foregoing theories are by no means exhaustive. But they are sufficiently representative to serve as a general introduction to the field of Christian ethics. They are, it is true, primarily concerned with the question as to whether there is a legitimate place for an independent science or philosophy of the Christian moral life. But, along with their diverse answers to this question and the reasons given for them, they reveal other important differences of opinion and thus introduce us to various fundamental problems that suggest a convenient outline for our study of Christian ethics as a whole.

One of these problems has to do with the relation of religion to morality and more specifically with the relation of Christian morality to "natural" morality. Most of the theories we have outlined have some bearing on this question; but the theories of Herrmann, Mayer and Runestam, Brunner, Schleiermacher, and Nygren lay special emphasis on it. It is the underlying problem in Part II, where we discuss the presuppositions of Christian ethics.

A second problem is concerned with the distinctive nature of the Christian ethic, with its principles of love and perfection, and with the ideal moral life. Here the theories of Augustine and Nygren are particularly important. But the other theories also, in so far as they involve a clear distinction between the Catholic and Protestant points of view, need to be taken into account. The main points at issue are discussed in Part III, where we deal with the Christian moral ideal.

A third problem is that of the adjustment of the Christian ideal to the concrete conditions of life and to the necessities of civilization. The theories of Aquinas and Troeltsch devoted special attention to this problem, but no systematic treatise on Christian ethics could avoid it. It is the basal problem in Part IV, where we take up the practical application of Christian moral teaching to the chief phases of our complex individual and social life.

A fourth problem has to do with the norm and validity of Christian morality. This problem has been kept before the church by its own intrinsic importance and also by religious and moral skeptics such as Schopenhauer and Nietzsche, by historical relativists, by theological traditionalists, and by fanatics. It could, therefore, hardly be overlooked by any Christian moralist. All the theories we have above described contain a more or less direct reference to it. We shall deal with it briefly in Chapter II and more at length in the concluding chapter.

Conclusion

These four fundamental problems and others associated with them, such as sin and conversion, belong to theological as distinguished from philosophical ethics. It is this fact that gives to the former its independent status and province. One may in the abstract argue in favor of a monistic conception of ethics; but no matter how plausible these arguments may be, books on ethics will continue to be written from both a theological and a nontheological standpoint, and this will inevitably make a difference between them. Herrmann, for instance, calls his book on morals simply *Ethics;* but, so far as its content is concerned, it is distinctly a theological ethics.[25]

[25] Works on general ethics may, however, adhere to their distinctive field and yet be of value from the religious point of view. Bowne's *Principles of Ethics* and

The relation of Christian to philosophical ethics is essentially the same as that of theology to the philosophy of religion. Between the latter disciplines there is no longer any difference so far as the validation of religious belief is concerned. They both employ the same method. They reject the idea of an external standard of truth either human or divine, and find in the mind itself the only valid standard. All truth, they hold, rests on its power of appeal to the human mind. But while they are agreed on this fundamental point, they differ in their method of dealing with religion. The philosophy of religion has to do with religion in general, while theology approaches the subject from the standpoint of the church. It is primarily concerned with the Christian faith. It concentrates attention on the teaching of the Bible and on the doctrines of the church, and it does so with the avowed purpose of commending the Christian faith to the modern mind in a way that the philosophy of religion would not feel justified in doing. It is thus a servant of the church, and this fact gives to it a content and a character that are more or less distinctively its own.

Practically the same is also to be said of Christian or theological ethics. In its method of validation it does not differ from philosophical ethics. But it emphasizes, as the latter does not, the ethical teaching of Scripture and of the Christian church. It approaches the whole moral problem from the religious point of view, and hence deals with such questions as those above noted in a way and to an extent that would hardly seem fitting in general ethics. Its standpoint is that of the church. It concentrates attention on those moral problems in which the church has been and is primarily interested, and hence is as much entitled to be regarded as an independent discipline as is theology. This conclusion, it is true, has been contested on the ground that Christian morality and Christian doctrine do not stand in the same relation to modern thought. Theology, it is

---

Brightman's *Moral Laws,* for instance, make an excellent introduction to, and background for, the study of Christian ethics.

said, is obviously so different in its content from modern philosophy that it is entitled to a separate existence. But Christian morality has been so largely absorbed by the modern conscience that there is no need of an independent Christian ethics. Modern morality, in other words, has been Christianized and thus unified, while this does not hold true of modern philosophy. There may, consequently, be a cleavage between theology and philosophy, while no such cleavage between Christian and philosophical ethics is warranted. But this idea that a sharp line can be drawn between Christian ethics and Christian theology is gradually disappearing. It is coming to be seen that the two belong together, and hence among unbelievers there is an increasing tendency to repudiate the Christian moral ideal as well as the Christian faith. If there is, therefore, a legitimate place for theology alongside of the philosophy of religion, there is also a legitimate place for Christian ethics alongside of philosophical ethics. The distinctive content and practical function of Christian ethics, as stated above, warrant this conclusion, and no further justification of it is necessary.

CHAPTER II

THE HISTORY OF CHRISTIAN ETHICS

CHRISTIAN ethics may be defined as the science or philosophy of Christian morality. Both Christian morality and the science or philosophy of it have had a long history; and a general survey of this history will be of interest and value as an introduction to a systematic study of Christian ethics. Especially important will be its bearing on one's conception of the norm of Christian conduct.

In a sense it may be said that the permanent element in Christianity is its ethical teaching.[1] Changes have frequently taken place in doctrine and in forms of worship that have disrupted the unity and continuity of the church. But through all these changes the Christian moral ideal has in principle remained the same. This has been due to the fact that it was once for all set forth by Jesus both in word and deed. He laid down moral principles and set up ethical standards that are still valid for all sections of the church. He also embodied these principles and standards so fully in his own life that his example has been a fixed point in Christian history. Earnest Christians everywhere have sought to conform their lives to his. Their attitude toward him has been such that they might all have joined in singing that familiar stanza of one of Whittier's hymns:

> O Lord and Master of us all,
> Whate'er our name or sign,
> We own thy sway, we hear thy call,
> We test our lives by thine.

But while there has been this relatively unchanging element and uniting bond in Christian piety, it would be a serious

[1] So E. F. Scott, *The Ethical Teaching of Jesus*, pp. ix f.

mistake to suppose that the Christian moral ideal is sharply and exhaustively defined in the New Testament, that it has remained static through the ages, that there have been no serious disagreements as to its content, and that there have been no important variations in its interpretation. The fact is that there have been almost as marked changes in the conception of the ideal Christian life as there have been in the fundamental doctrines of the church. These changes have been due to various causes, external and internal, and may be regarded either as departures from the New Testament or as legitimate unfoldings of its essential spirit. In either case they are factors that need to be reckoned with in any attempt to determine the nature and content of the Christian moral ideal.[2]

To understand this ideal and its application to life, it is obvious that we must first know the ethical teaching of the New Testament, especially that of Jesus. But it is also obvious, or should be, that the ethical teaching of Jesus cannot be fully understood in isolation. It must be studied in its relation both to what preceded and to what followed. It must be linked with and supplemented by the teaching of the Old Testament. For, as George Adam Smith put it, the Old Testament "is the Hinterland of the New; part of the same continent of truth, without whose ampler areas and wider watersheds the rivers, which grew to their fullness in the new dispensation, could never have gained one-tenth of their volume or their influence."[3] Jesus' teaching must also be interpreted in the light of the subsequent history of the church. For despite its many shortcomings the church has always in its ideals sought to be a mirror of the mind of Christ. And it is only with the aid of this

[2] The most complete history of Christian ethics written in English is Thomas C. Hall, *History of Ethics Within Organized Christianity* (1910). C. E. Luthardt, *History of Christian Ethics,* I, covering the period down to the Reformation, was translated into English and published in 1889. H. H. Scullard, *Early Christian Ethics in the West* (1907) begins with Clement of Rome and ends with Ambrose. R. A. Tsanoff, *The Modern Ideals of Our Civilization* (1942) contains a comprehensive history of philosophical ethics written from a Christian standpoint.

[3] *Modern Criticism and the Preaching of the Old Testament,* p. 4.

mirror that we can understand his teaching aright. Apart from the perspective of history we should in many instances be at a loss to know what construction to put on his words, and we should be at an even greater loss in our effort to define the moral mission of Christianity. What this mission is can only be ascertained by a critical study of ecclesiastical history. But while emphasizing this fact, we do not in any way detract from the unique significance of the New Testament as the chief source and norm of the Christian ethic.

The Ethical Teaching of Jesus

In our historical survey of the Christian moral life as preached through the ages we begin, therefore, with the ethical teaching of Jesus. That his teaching stood in close relation to that of the prophets and of contemporary Judaism and that it at the same time inaugurated a profound and significant change, is evident to every student of ancient Hebrew and Jewish history and literature. Jesus himself said that he came not to destroy but to fulfill the law and the prophets. He accepted the authority of the Old Testament, and for the most part lived in conformity with the customs and laws of his own day. The official station and function of even the scribes and Pharisees he recognized as legitimate. They, he said, "sit on Moses' seat: all things therefore whatsoever they bid you, these do and observe."[4] His condemnation of them was due to their insincerity rather than to the content of their teaching. So far as the latter was concerned, he to a large extent agreed with them. Indeed, so extensive was the agreement that Wellhausen said of him that he "was not a Christian; he was a Jew."[5] Between his moral teaching and that recorded in the Jewish literature of his day there is a remarkable similarity. "Throughout the Gospels," says Joseph Klausner, a distinguished Jewish scholar, "there is not one item of ethical teaching which cannot be

[4] Matt. 23:2 f.

[5] *Einleitung in die drei ersten Evangelien*, p. 113.

paralleled either in the Old Testament, the Apocrypha, or in the Talmudic and Midrashic literature near to the time of Jesus."[6]

But despite the striking parallelism in the details of their teaching there were important and far-reaching differences between Jesus and his Pharisaic contemporaries. Otherwise there would not have been such a serious conflict between them, nor would Jesus have been crucified. No matter how much alike the formal content of their teaching may have been, the spirit and accent were quite different. There was in Jesus' moral teaching a unity, a depth, and a concentration on essentials that made it a new morality—a morality that threatened to undermine the existing national and religious consciousness and that, if carried to its logical conclusion, would have meant "the end of the law."[7] The Jewish leaders of the day realized this, and so in self-defense they sought to destroy the new morality by putting its author to death. The result was the reverse of what they expected. The new morality did not perish but, after the death and resurrection of Christ, became a more powerful leaven than it had been in the days of his flesh. It extended beyond its original national limits and became a world-wide ferment, bringing about what Nietzsche called a "transvaluation of all ancient values."

In what, we now ask, did this transformation or revaluation consist? The answer is to be found in the fundamental and distinctive moral principles taught by Jesus. None of these was wholly original. If any had been, it would probably have been some eccentric teaching devoid of permanent significance. The basic elements in the moral law are inherent in the human mind and in the structure of human society, and must have been more or less apparent to earnest men in all periods of the world's history. Moral progress consists not so much in the discovery of new principles as in the deeper penetration into

[6] *Jesus of Nazareth,* p. 384.

[7] Rom. 10:4.

the meaning of principles already voiced by seers of the past, and in their more consistent and thoroughgoing application to the changing social order. Indeed, originality, as some one has said, means thinking for oneself, not thinking differently from other people. It is in the light of this truth that the "moral originality" of Jesus is to be understood. It was relative, not absolute. But this does not diminish its importance. It rather implies that there was a point of contact between Jesus' teaching and that of the past, and thus helps in a measure to explain the powerful appeal that his message, despite its novelty, made to the conscience of his day.

What and how many principles should be included in the fundamental ethical teaching of Jesus is a point on which there may be differences of opinion. But there are two concerning which there could hardly be any question. One is the principle of love, and the other the principle of moral inwardness or moral perfection. Later a chapter will be devoted to each of these principles. Here all that is necessary is a brief explanatory word.

Of the two principles logical priority belongs to the principle of moral inwardness, but from the practical or social point of view the principle of love comes first. Jesus himself gave it that rating in its double form of love to God and man.[8] The latter is its strictly ethical, as distinguished from religious, form; and in it, according to Paul, the whole law is fulfilled.[9] This, however, is true only if love is interpreted as inclusive of the moral ideal of holiness or inward purity. The Golden Rule, for instance, might be fully observed among sots and gluttons. Each might do to the other as he would wish the other to do to himself, and yet there might be no change in their general mode of life. To be truly moral, the Golden Rule must be construed as meaning: Do unto others as you *ought* to wish them to do unto yourself. In other words, the moral ideal must condition

---

[8] Luke 10:27; Mark 12:28-31.

[9] Gal. 5:14.

its application. The law of love must be understood to include devotion to holiness of life as well as a benevolent attitude toward one's fellow men. This is everywhere assumed in the New Testament.

It is, however, important to recognize that the principle of inwardness or of moral autonomy with its ethical consequents is distinct from the law of love and presupposed by it. This principle defines the essential nature of a moral act. It is the will, the motive, the free decision that makes an act moral. Apart from the will an act is neither morally good nor morally evil. It is the motive that alone gives moral quality to an act. This absolute inwardness of the moral law is the underlying theme of the Sermon on the Mount and is implied in the ethical teaching of Jesus as a whole. With him the heart was the seat of all virtue and the spring of all truly righteous conduct. This view was not original with him, but the radical way in which he held and proclaimed it had momentous consequences both negative and positive. It led him, on the one hand, to reject the ceremonialism and legalism of contemporary Judaism and thus to break with his own people. On the other hand, it led to a profound emphasis on moral purity and on a lofty moral ideal. It was this fact that transformed love into holy love and that gave to the Christian doctrine of love its moral comprehensiveness.

In addition to these two fundamental principles of love and moral inwardness there were two characteristics of Jesus' ethical teaching that contributed greatly to its inspirational power and popular effectiveness. One was its religious basis. It derived its imperative from the Divine nature and will; it had a divine goal, that of likeness to God; and it made trust in God the root and principle of all goodness. Religious faith with Jesus was the generating and inspiring source of the moral life. Along with this characteristic of his ethic went also its exemplification in his own life. He taught by example even more effectively than by precept. People beheld in his life an incarnation of the moral ideal, which not only clarified its meaning but endowed it with the warmth of personal contagion. Being a Christian came thus to mean to them not simply the acceptance of certain ethical principles and compliance with their demands but loyalty to a Person, in whom these principles and the spirit they represented had received concrete embodiment. In this respect "the history of religion provides no parallel to the personal influence of Jesus."[10]

Ethical Emphases in the Early and Medieval Church

Turning now to the fortunes of the new ethic within organized Christianity, we consider first the early and medieval church as representative of traditional Catholicism. In view of the length of the period and the complexity of the subject matter, we can deal with it only in a very general way. Our method will be to single out three successive emphases in the moral life of the period and then give some account of each and its relation to the moral ideal and moral mission of Christianity. The three emphases are (1) charity, (2) chastity, and (3) penance and military service. These emphases did not necessarily exclude each other. To a considerable extent they were contemporaneous. But in the public attitude of the church a shift in degree of emphasis from one to the other in the order given is observable. For our present purpose, however, no particular importance attaches to the chronological order or to the relative degree of emphasis in each case so long as they are all recognized as at one time or another, if not in the whole period, major ethical emphases.

1. *Charity*

During the first three centuries the church maintained to a large degree its "first love."[11] It continued the New Testament emphasis on the principle of charity or *agape*. Both by word and deed it made love basic and central in the Christian life. It was this more than anything else that differentiated Christians from the "world." The heathen observed it and ex-

[10] H. H. Henson, *Christian Morality*, p. 301.

[11] Cf. Gerhard Uhlhorn, *Christian Charity in the Ancient Church* (1883).

claimed: "See, how these Christians love one another:"[12] This love was more intense, more inclusive, more dominant than anything to which the pagan world was accustomed. But it was not only that. It was not only greater in degree; it was different in kind. It was a self-denying love, a love directed toward the help of the needy. It was a pure love, a love of inwardness and truth, a love that could boldly say with Justin Martyr, in the face of a compromising world, "We will not live with lies."[13] It was an active love, a love that did not lose itself in contemplation but that could proudly say with Minucius Felix, "We do not *speak* great things; we *live* them."[14]

Such a community love was something new in the world, and by way of contrast with it the ancient world, both pagan and Jewish, has been characterized as "a world without love."[15] But its novelty and also its radical requirements made its application to the concrete relations of human life no easy matter. Serious difficulties arose at this point, and the situation was further complicated by the gradual relinquishment of the apocalyptic hope current in New Testament times.

It has been argued by some modern scholars, such as Albert Schweitzer, that the moral teaching of Jesus was an "interim ethic"—a morality applicable only to the brief period before the advent of the Messianic Age.[16] He was himself an apocalyptist. He believed that the present world order would come to an end soon, and believed this so firmly that his ethical teaching was dominated by it. He told his disciples how they should conduct themselves in the intervening period, and did not particularly concern himself with their mode of life thereafter. It turned out, however, that the expected parousia did not come; and hence his ethic, based upon the belief in its imminence, lost its validity. It ceased to be authoritative

[12] Tertullian, *Apologeticus* xxxix.

[13] *First Apology* viii.

[14] *Octavius* xxxviii.

[15] Uhlhorn, *op. cit.*, pp. 2-55.

[16] *The Quest of the Historical Jesus*, pp. 352 ff.; *The Mystery of the Kingdom of God*, pp. 92 ff.

for later ages, dominated by a different outlook into the future.

In this theory there may be some truth. Jesus' teaching concerning property and self-renunciation may in some respects have been conditioned by the apocalyptic hope of his day, and other phases of his teaching may also have been thus affected. But this relativism manifestly does not apply to his fundamental moral principles, to his ideals of love, purity, truth, goodness. These were independent of the current apocalypticism. They apply to all ages and to all moral beings. They are universal and absolute. And it is they that constitute the essential and permanent element in the ethic of Jesus. It is a serious mistake to think of him as a new lawgiver, the author of new rules, of a new moral code for the guidance of men. His moral precepts are to be understood, not as concrete rules of conduct, but as illustrations of fundamental principles to be applied by each one to his own particular situation. The autonomy of the individual was with him a fundamental presupposition.[17]

This distinction between moral rules and moral principles or between a lawgiver and the creator and inspirer of a new moral spirit seems to have been overlooked by those who ascribe to Jesus a mere "interim ethic." They think of him as primarily the author of a new law. This misconception grew up also in the early church. As the early apocalyptic hope faded away and the corresponding religious fervor waned, people began to lose their confidence in the adequacy of "faith working through love."[18] They felt the need of specific commands and so came to think of Jesus as a new lawgiver. Chris-

---

[17] In this conception of moral autonomy there is implied a relative element in the Christian ethic. Jesus recognized it when he said of the Mosaic law of divorce that it was prescribed "for your hardness of heart" (Mark 10:5). The ideal is often incapable of immediate realization, and under those circumstances it is our duty to do the best we can until altered conditions make possible a closer approach to the ideal. In this respect Jesus' ethical teaching and every sensible and practical form of moral idealism is an "interim ethic." Cf. D. C. Macintosh, *Social Religion*, pp. 59-66.

[18] Gal. 5:6.

tian morality thus took on a legalistic character, which tended to obscure the earlier belief in the spontaneity and sufficiency of love as a motive of action.

Along with this legalistic tendency there also went a decline in religious earnestness and an increasing laxity in church discipline. Against this there was a vigorous reaction. The Montanists sought to establish a rigid discipline that would have transformed the churches into churches of saints and that would have put an end to their growing connection with the world. This reactionary movement failed, but it led to a fateful distinction between perfect and imperfect Christians. The latter were allowed to remain in the church, but the result was a double ethic: an increasingly rigid and ascetic type for the "perfect" and an increasingly lax type for the "imperfect"—a type which required of them hardly anything more than participation in the church services.

These two ethical tendencies—the legalistic and the dualistic—had necessarily a deteriorating effect on the Christian principle of love, but the principle itself was never lost sight of in the early church or subsequently. Love or charity is inherent in the very idea of the Christian Church. The latter could not be conceived of without it. And despite the weaknesses and imperfections associated with its application of love to social problems, the results have been such as to constitute the noblest chapter in the history of the race. Says W. E. H. Lecky:

> The high conception that has been formed of the sanctity of human life, the protection of infancy, the elevation and final emancipation of the slave classes, the suppression of barbarous games, the creation of a vast and multifarious organisation of charity, and the education of the imagination by the Christian type, constitute together a movement of philanthropy which has never been paralleled or approached in the Pagan world. The effects of this movement in promoting happiness have been very great. Its effect in determining character has probably been still greater. In that proportion or disposition of qualities which constitutes the ideal character the gentler and more benevolent virtues have ob-

tained, through Christianity, the foremost place. In the first and purest period they were especially supreme.[19]

2. *Chastity*

The second major emphasis in early Christian morality may be introduced by another quotation from Lecky. He says:

> If an impartial person were to glance over the ethics of the New Testament, and were asked what was the central and distinctive virtue to which the sacred writers most continually referred, he would doubtless answer that it was that which is described as love, charity, or philanthropy. If he were to apply a similar scrutiny to the writings of the fourth and fifth centuries, he would answer that the cardinal virtue of the religious type was not love, but chastity. And this chastity, which was regarded as the ideal state, was not the purity of an undefiled marriage. It was the absolute suppression of the whole sensual side of our nature. The chief form of virtue, the central conception of the saintly life, was a perpetual struggle against all carnal impulses by men who altogether refused the compromise of marriage.[20]

This change of emphasis from charity to chastity was not a mere passing fashion, nor was it unrelated to the true genius of Christianity. It had its roots in the past and made a permanent impress upon the church. In the form of monasticism it rendered incalculable services both to the church and to civilization. Indeed, the monasteries became centers of learning and also institutions of charity comparable in importance to the hospitals which began to be established at about the same time.[21]

The new emphasis on chastity or celibacy did not, then, represent a reaction against the earlier emphasis on charity. It was rather a supplement to it, but so powerful a supplement that it transformed the Christian moral ideal. Virginity became for many its very essence. The monastic ideal became the Christian ideal, and this point of view is still influential in

---

[19] *History of European Morals* (1869), II, 107.
[20] *Ibid.*, II, 130.
[21] Uhlhorn, *op cit.*, pp. 339 ff.

Catholic Christianity.[22] The extremes to which the glorification and pursuit of virginity were carried in the early church are almost unbelievable. Not only was the flesh mortified in extravagant and repugnant ways; social ties were ruthlessly severed, and domestic affections brutally stifled, all "for the love of Christ." The inevitable result was that more or less discredit was thrown upon marriage and upon the domestic virtues. "I approve of marriages," said Jerome, "I praise the married state, but only because it produces virgins." [23] In the Gospel according to the Egyptians the Savior is reported as saying, "I am come to suppress the acts of woman." When the consequences of universal celibacy to the race were pointed out, the reply was that God, could, if necessary, provide other means of propagation." [24]

In order to understand the extraordinary hold that the celibate movement acquired upon the ancient church, there are several important facts that need to be borne in mind. For one thing, celibacy did not stand alone. It was part of a broader movement. It stood directly related to the second of the two fundamental principles in the ethical teaching of Jesus—the principle of inwardness, of moral purity, of spiritual perfection. This principle could be realized in the life of the individual only through self-denial. Again and again Jesus laid stress on this fact. It was a basal element in his teaching, but it was an element that could easily be misapplied. Self-denial might in popular thought take the form of poverty, a renunciation of the world; it might take the form of obedience, a renunciation of self-will; or it might take the

---

[22] Catholic scholars, however, would deny that monasticism introduced into Christianity a new morality or a new ideal of perfection. It was and is, they hold. simply a specialized method of seeking the common Christian ideal, adapted and restricted to particular groups. Karl Adam, for instance, says that the "religious or celibate life is objectively the best way and the surest way to realize the Christian ideal," but for the great majority of men "the subjectively best way to perfection . . . . is to live and work in the world" (*The Spirit of Catholicism,* p. 206).

[23] Quoted by C. E. Luthardt, *op. cit.,* p. 217.

[24] Jerome *Against Jovinian* i. 36. Cf. Cassian *Institutes* vii. 3.

form of chastity, a renunciation of the flesh. Of these it was the last that made the most powerful appeal to the imagination of the church after the time of Constantine. Before his time martyrdom had been regarded as the supreme form of self-renunciation. But with the cessation of governmental persecution, religious zeal turned more and more to chastity as the highest and purest expression of the religious life. It thus became the outstanding symbol of self-renunciation and of the quest after moral perfection.

The rise and dominance of this particular type of asceticism was due to two main causes. One was the influence of dualistic modes of thought represented by Neo-Platonism and Gnosticism. Matter was regarded as the source and seat of evil. To suppress the flesh became, consequently, the chief aim of religious discipline; and, because of its extreme inveteracy, primary attention was naturally devoted to the mastery and suppression of the sexual appetite. Other fleshly appetites, however, were also put under the ban; and the religious devotee sought to weaken, if not extirpate, them by fasting and other ascetic practices.

The other main cause of the celibate movement was the growing worldliness of the church that followed its political victory. The church entered the world-state and identified itself with it, leaving it, as Harnack says, "in possession of all except its Gods."[25] The result was such a lowered moral tone within the church and the continuation of such moral laxity without that men and women fled by the thousands from both the church and the world as things unclean and sought for themselves purity and redemption in the solitude of the desert and the forest. This flight from the world both within and without the church was virtually a renunciation of the effort to penetrate the national life with the Christian spirit. It was an abnegation of the world mission of Christianity in the interest of an extreme religious individualism. But

[25] *Monasticism,* p. 28.

despite this fact and despite the fact that the monastic ideal was on the whole approved by the church, the moral mission of Christianity to the world was not lost sight of. It received brilliant expression in Augustine's *City of God,* a work of genius that profoundly influenced not only Christian thought but the course of Christian and European history.[26] According to this great work, the church was "the visible manifestation of the City of God," and as such she was to guide and train the nations; she was to exercise "spiritual dominion over the world"; she was herself to be "a divine City of Righteousness on earth." [27] This was the Christian ideal.

In addition to these two reasons for the rise of monasticism several other factors may be mentioned. There was, for instance, in the inherited Greek philosophy a preference for the contemplative as over against the active life. The legitimacy of a double morality, as we have seen, was also recognized, a distinction between the perfect and the imperfect. Superior merit was, furthermore, supposed to attach to all acts of self-denial, especially those of an unusual character. Then, too, the life hereafter received a one-sided emphasis. All of these and other factors contributed to the rise and development of the ascetic movement. That this movement represented what was generally and sincerely regarded at the time as the highest, purest, and most thoroughgoing form of self-renunciation and spiritual idealism can hardly be questioned.

3. *Penance and Military Service*

At first there may seem to be no connection between the sacrament of penance and military service. This is the modern point of view. But the situation was different in the medieval period. Military service was then, much of it, virtually a part

[26] Cf. T. S. K. Scott-Craig, *Christian Attitudes to War and Peace*, pp. 50-84; Louis Bertrand, *Saint Augustin*, pp. 333-80; H. H. Milman, *History of Christianity*, III, 187-92.

[27] A. Harnack, *op. cit.*, p. 70

of the penitential system. The way it became such was that pilgrimage to some sacred place had become one of the chief forms of penance and that the Crusades were really armed pilgrimages to the Holy Land. To participate in them was a response to the call of the church. It was a service to the church and at the same time an act of expiation for oneself. Through it one acquired merit, the forgiveness of one's sins, and perfect salvation. Soldiery and penance were thus fused together and won for the participant the same ultimate blessings as the practice of charity and chastity. There was, however, this difference that, while charity and chastity might be called private virtues, the performance of penance and military service might in a sense be said to be ecclesiastical virtues. They were cases of obedience to special prescriptions of the church and derived their meritorious character from its authority as an institution rather than from the spiritual content of its teaching. They were accommodations to human weaknesses rather than responses to the ideal demands of the moral nature. But they were nevertheless important factors in the moral life of the church.

Penance is derived from the same root as repentance and originally had the same meaning. Indeed, they are both still used as translations of the Greek word *metanoia* ("penance" in the Douay version of the New Testament and "repentance" in the Authorized Version). This difference is due to the conflicting views that have arisen between Roman Catholics and Protestants with reference to the nature or essence of repentance. Repentance, as understood by Protestants, is a change of mind, a godly sorrow for sin, an inner moral transformation. As such it is a sufficient ground for the divine forgiveness. This seems to have been in the main the New Testament teaching. But as the church gradually lost its early enthusiasm and the Christian life became externalized and legalized, the conviction grew that something more than the subjective state of repentance and faith was necessary as a condition of forgiveness. If the sin committed involved injury to others, true repentance required restitution, so far as possible. This is implied in the New Testament[28] and is an obvious demand of the moral nature. But even where injury to others is not involved, sin calls for expiation. Some sort of punishment is required by the law of justice. According to Christian theology this punishment was borne by Christ for the whole human race. Or at least he made expiation for our sins. But a distinction was made between the eternal and the temporal penalty of sin, and the latter was left to the church to prescribe. It might take the form of fasting, of scourging, of exile, of claustration, of distant pilgrimages, or of painful experiences of almost any kind. The particular penalty imposed by the priest was a condition of forgiveness and became the distinctive element in the sacrament of penance.

The penitential system thus developed had its moral basis in the need of disciplining the rude, untutored, and wayward members of the church. As such a means of discipline, it rendered an immense service to moral culture and to civilization in general. Great masses of people in the church, reared in paganism or barbarism, who were unprepared for the pure moral idealism of the New Testament, came gradually to understand the seriousness of the moral law and its meaning when confronted with specific penalties for its infraction. Some such method of moral training would seem to have been necessary during the long period of Christianizing and civilizing the pagan and barbarous peoples of Europe.[29]

But valuable as the penitential system was as a moral agency, it led to great evils: to externalism and legalism, to an artificial ecclesiastical morality unrelated to social utility, to the sale of indulgences, and to other corrupt practices. The result was a powerful revolt against it by the Protestant Reformers. They rejected the whole principle of penance and substituted for it the doctrine of justification by faith alone. Ideally the latter

[28] Luke 19:1-9.

[29] Cf. O. D. Watkins, *A History of Penance* (1920), 2 vols.

represents a higher moral standpoint, but that the sacrament of penance is still with large numbers of people a potent influence for good can hardly be questioned.

We have explained briefly the relation of military service in the Crusades to the penitential system. But the attitude of the church toward military service in general is a somewhat different story. A number of the early Church Fathers, such as Justin Martyr, Tatian, Irenaeus, Tertullian, Cyprian, and Lactantius, denounced war altogether in what sounds like extreme pacifist terms, declaring that no Christian ought to engage in it.[30] On the basis of these utterances W. E. H. Lecky has spoken of "the almost Quaker tenets of the primitive church," [31] and many other historians have taken essentially the same view. But it is doubtful if the facts as a whole warrant this conclusion. Indeed, there are weighty considerations against the view that the early church was pacifist in the sense that it condemned war and all participation in it as inherently and in principle evil. For one thing, it is clear that the early Christian opposition to war was much of it based on religious rather than moral grounds. What the Christians objected to was in many cases not so much the sinfulness of war itself as the idolatrous worship associated with it. It was the paganism of war, the heathen associations of the soldier's life, against which they revolted and which led them to denounce military service as unchristian.[32] In the next place, it should be noted that war had among the early Christians a measure of divine sanction. The Old Testament has much to say about it. Jehovah was himself a God of war. Wars were waged at his command, and they served a purpose in his government of the world. They were sent upon peoples as a punishment for their sins. Furthermore, in the Christian as well as the Jewish apocalyptic literature, it was predicted that wars

---

[30] C. John Cadoux, *The Early Christian Attitude to War* (1919) ;*The Early Church and the World* (1925) , pp. 116-22; 183-89; 269-81; 402-42; 564-96.

[31] *Op. cit.,* II, 266.

[32] Cf. Georg Wünsch, *Evangelische Ethik des Politischen,* pp 384 ff.; H. B. Workman, *Persecution in the Early Church,* pp. 181 ff.

would continue to the end of the present era. The gradual attainment of a reign of peace was not expected. War was regarded as a kind of fate. There was, therefore, nothing for Christians to do but to adjust themselves to a warring world as best they could. Then, too, the early Christian aversion to military service was in no small part due to the anti-Christian policy of the state. Decisive evidence of this is found in the sudden change of attitude toward such service after the persecution of the church ceased. In 314, for instance, a year after the edict of Milan granting toleration to Christianity, an ecclesiastical council was held at Arles in France, which "condemned soldiers who from religious motives deserted their colors," and which also declared that "those who throw away their weapons in time of peace shall be excommunicated."[33] A friendly government was instinctively recognized by Christians as deserving their military support.

It is thus clear that early Christian pacifism was a mixed affair. It had some basis in ethical idealism but it was due more to the idolatrous associations of army life and to the hostility of the state to the church. After this hostility ceased the church withdrew its protest against military service as such and gradually came to recognize it, not only as necessary to the existence of the state as a divinely ordained institution, but also as a legitimate instrument in the defense and propagation of the faith.

This development has been described as "revolutionary" and as due to the contagion of Mohammedanism. The followers of Mohammed conquered by the sword a large part of the Christian world and threatened all western Europe. In 732 Charles Martel permanently checked their westward advance at the battle of Poitiers; but conflicts with them in Spain and in the East continued for centuries, and we are told that as a result of these conflicts "the spirit of Mohammedanism slowly passed into Christianity, and transformed it into its image."[34]

[33] Scott-Craig, *op. cit.*, p. 144.
[34] Lecky, *op. cit.,* II, 267.

That there is some truth in this statement can hardly be questioned. The Mohammedan menace did have much to do with evoking the militant spirit in Christianity. But it did not create it. There was a kind of militancy in Christianity from the beginning. So pronounced was it that the word "pagan," which meant originally a civilian as distinguished from a soldier, came to mean a non-Christian. Soldiery and Christianity went together. The man who was not a soldier was not a Christian; he was a "pagan." [35] Soldiery was of the essence of Christianity. What was meant was, of course, a spiritual soldiery. The Christian was a soldier of Christ. But this military terminology was so common, and the corresponding heroic spirit so deeply ingrained in the early church, that they naturally expressed themselves in military action when once the existence of Christianity was threatened by an alien foe, as it was by Mohammedanism. It was, so far as we can see, this militarization of Christianity that saved both Europe and the Christian church from falling a prey to the Moslems. "Unwarlike Christianity," says the historian Milman, "would have been trampled under foot, and have been in danger of total extermination, by triumphant Mohammedanism." [36]

But it was not only the native heroic spirit of Christianity and its instinct of self-preservation in the face of the Mohammedan peril that led to its militarization. There is another side to the history of this change. This is to be found in the warlike spirit of the Germanic tribes and the military structure of the feudal system. Here was a part of the natural order, a given element in the moral situation. The church did not create it; the martial spirit was there; and the church's problem was to decide what to do with it. At first it tried to curb it and by the institution of the "Truce of God" did much to repress private wars. But this did not solve the problem. So the church sought to reduce the barbarity of war and to hu-

---

[35] A. Harnack, *Militia Christi*, pp. 68, 92; H. B. Workman, *The Evolution of the Monastic Ideal*, p. 30; Cadoux, *The Early Christian Attitude to War*, p. 167.

[36] *The History of Christianity*, Book IV, chap. v.

manize the warlike spirit, and in this attempt had a measure of success. Chivalry and knighthood were penetrated with not a little of the Christian spirit. But this, too, failed to meet the needs of the situation. Hence the church decided to consecrate and to utilize the martial impulses of its people in its foreign enterprises and in its plans for the world-wide extension of Christianity. This it did in the Crusades. It glorified martial courage and gave it a supreme place in its penitential system. Says Lecky:

> The papal indulgences proved not less efficacious in stimulating the military spirit than the promises of Mohammed, and for about two centuries every pulpit in Christendom proclaimed the duty of war with the unbeliever, and represented the battle-field as the sure path to heaven. The religious orders which arose united the character of the priest with that of the warrior, and when, at the hour of sunset, the soldier knelt down to pray before the cross, that cross was the handle of his sword.[37]

Ethical Emphases in Protestantism

There are two major emphases in the ethical teaching of the Protestant churches that may here be noted. One is the early Protestant emphasis on the sanctity of the common life, and the other is the emphasis of modern Protestantism on the social application of the Christian ethic.

1. The first of these was not new with Luther and Calvin. It had its basis in the ancient prophetic teaching. But in the light of its immediate background it was new, and the insistent emphasis placed upon it gave it a significance that it had not had before. Ever since the invasion of dualistic ideas and the corresponding ascetic practices into the early church, there had been a tendency to disparage the everyday life and toil by way of contrast with the life set apart for specifically religious tasks. Virginity was honored above marriage; the contemplative life was regarded as higher than the active; and ecclesiastical offices, especially those of a monastic character,

[37] *Op. cit.* II, 267 f.

were endowed with superior sanctity. The result was that religion lost its close connection with the common ethical tasks of life. Its interest centered in the church and its services and in those types of conduct that tended to conform to the "supernatural" ecclesiastical ideal.

It was, therefore, a highly significant change when the Protestant Reformers rejected the monastic ideal with its distinction between nature and supernature, and substituted for it an ethical ideal realizable in the ordinary relations of human life. This change introduced a personal, as opposed to a metaphysical, conception of sanctity. It made sanctity consist in a fundamental attitude of the spirit, an attitude of faith and love. This attitude was as possible to a person in secular life as it was to the ecclesiastic or the monk. The traditional distinction between the religious and the secular, or the perfect and the imperfect Christian, with its resulting double ethic, was thus cancelled. The universal priesthood of believers was affirmed. And along with this went a new emphasis on work, on one's calling, on the secular tasks of life. The natural was moralized and made the sphere of the spiritual.

This change democratized the Christian moral ideal, made it obligatory upon all, and thus brought it into closer relation with the workaday world. It substituted for the older "supernatural" asceticism a new intramundane asceticism of work and faithfulness to one's earthly calling, and in this way gave a new ethical and religious significance to the common tasks of life. It introduced into the secular world a new moral dynamic. At least it did so in theory. Actually its effect in many cases, especially in Lutheran countries, was negative rather than positive. It desanctified ecclesiastical and monastic callings without sanctifying secular vocations. It laid at times a one-sided stress on the subjective attitude of the soul, leaving it apparently a matter of comparative indifference whether the outward conduct of Christians was distinguishable from that of non-Christians. It was also restricted in its moral fruitfulness by an extreme doctrine of original sin and the allied doctrine of predestination. These doctrines tended in many instances to dampen moral optimism and enthusiasm and hence to impede moral progress. Nevertheless, despite these limitations in its interpretation and application, the Protestant principle of the sanctity of the common life marked an important stage in the history of Christian ethics.[38]

2. The emphasis on the social application of the Christian ethic is of comparatively recent origin. Earlier Christian thought was predominantly individualistic. It was concerned with the transformation of the individual rather than with the transformation of society. The social order was looked upon as more or less of a fixity. God had established it; and if any important change was to be made, the change must come from him. This was the idea that underlay the ancient apocalyptic hope, and the idea also that persisted in the Western world down to two centuries or so ago. At about that time the belief in social progress began to supplant the older eschatalogical conception of the future. People began to believe that society was plastic, subject to change on human initiative. For this belief the development of modern science was in large part responsible. The new scientific inventions and discoveries led men to envision a more prosperous and equitable social order. But visions alone would not have been sufficient to effect a vital change in men's beliefs. Before such a change could be brought about, there was need of an urgent practical demand for it. And this was supplied by the industrial revolution in England and by the political revolution in France. These two revolutions were quite different in kind; but they both revealed the plasticity of society, and they both were attended by such great evils that the modern conscience was shocked into the conviction that something could and must be done to insure a better economic and political order in the future.[39]

---

[38] Cf. Robert Calhoun, *God and the Common Life;* Georgia Harkness, *John Calvin,* pp. 178-220; E. W. Mayer, *Ethik,* pp. 155-62.

[39] See J. B. Bury, *The Idea of Progress;* A. C. Knudson, *Present Tendencies in Religious Thought,* pp. 51-59, 272 ff.

Out of this conviction there arose the various socialistic, communistic, and other labor movements of the past century that sought to remedy existing evils and to establish better social and political conditions. These movements more and more attracted the attention of thinking people and in the present century were given a tremendous impetus by the first World War. The result has been that the problems of peace and of industrial reconstruction have during the past century assumed an importance in the common thought of men that they never had before. They have become the "hot spots" of human interest, and no one could hope to speak movingly to the hearts of men who did not take account of them. The church has recognized this, and hence despite its own fundamental individualism has with great earnestness sought to make its contribution to their solution. These problems are highly complex, and there is wide difference of opinion as to the bearing of Christian teaching upon them. But to wrestle strenuously with them and to face all the relevant facts frankly is nevertheless one of the most urgent duties confronting the church, regardless of the divergent conclusions to which it may come. If it should fail to do so, it would hardly be able to speak effectively to the conscience of our day.

Theoretical Ethics

In the two preceding sections we have considered briefly some of the outstanding emphases in the moral history of the church. Along with these changing emphases there has also gone a developing science or philosophy of the Christian moral life. The latter we call theoretical ethics. But this does not mean that it is devoid of practical significance. Moral life and moral theory stand in a close relation to each other. Theory is implicit in life, and life is a presupposition of theory. The Christian moral life and Christian moral theory thus involve one another, and the history of both has an important bearing on the question as to the nature of the Christian moral ideal and also on the question as to the application of this ideal to the concrete conditions of human life. These two questions are fundamental in Christian ethics. Different answers to them are reflected in the changing ethical emphases we have described. Similar differences of opinion also appear in the history of Christian theoretical ethics. These differences we shall briefly review, in so far as they represent different stages in the developing philosophical and theological thought of the church.

1. First, however, it should be noted that the formal answer to the two basal questions of Christian ethics has been much the same throughout the history of the church. Christian thinkers have quite generally agreed that love is the essential element in the ideal Christian life, and they have also to a large extent agreed that the key to the problem of the relation of Christianity to the world is to be found in the idea of "natural law." But love and natural law are complex ideas and, taken in the rough, do not go very far toward solving the problems of theoretical ethics. They need to be analyzed, and their precise meaning or meanings within the Christian system need to be defined. To this task a great deal of intellectual labor has been devoted. Only the barest outline of the resulting contributions to Christian ethics is here possible.

The principle of love was inherited from the New Testament. The idea of natural law was derived from Stoicism. It served the same purpose in the development of Christian ethics that the idea of the Logos did in the development of Christian theology. Both were mediating ideas. As the idea of the Logos furnished a philosophical basis for the early Christian messianism and thus served as a bond of union between the Christian faith and Greek philosophy, so the Stoic idea of natural law furnished a philosophical basis for Christian ethics and served as a bond of union between Christian and pagan morality. Natural law, however, was used in two different senses, as absolute and as relative. It was the ideal moral law divinely implanted in human reason, and it was also the actual moral law embodied in the various human codes. It was the latter conception that was chiefly used in the effort to reconcile the Christian moral ideal with the necessities of secular civilization.

2. To the development of these general ideas current in the early church Augustine made two significant contributions. One had to do with the doctrine of love, and the other with the doctrine of the natural man or of original sin. In the history of the Christian doctrine of love there is no more important name than that of Augustine. He made love to God the basal and unifying principle in Christian ethics. This love, he held, expresses itself in contemplative purity of heart and in active brotherly love. It thus embraces the whole moral life, personal and social, "natural" and Christian. The cardinal virtues of the Greeks were reinterpreted as expressions of Christian love and in this way were made constituent factors in Christian morality. This theory in its fundamental conceptions gave direction to Christian thought for a thousand years, and has not yet spent itself.

Very important also was the way in which Augustine modified the idea of natural law by attributing to the fall of man consequences so serious that the natural man was deprived of all independent moral initiative. Sin now became the signature of his being. The result was an augumented pessimism, so far as human nature and the natural world order were concerned, and an increased emphasis on the need and reality of the divine grace. The ideas of sin and grace thus acquired a new significance in Christian ethics.

3. Thomas Aquinas was the great systematizer of medieval ethics as he was also of medieval theology. In his ethical system he availed himself of the earlier conception of natural law. But there was a considerable difference between his and the earlier use of it. In the early church stress was laid on the distinction between the absolute and the relative law of nature. The latter was regarded from one point of view as divinely instituted and from another point of view

as the result of sin and the remedy for it. Of these two views the emphasis fell on the second. In Thomas Aquinas, however, the situation is quite different. Here the distinction between an absolute and a relative law of nature recedes into the background, and stress is laid on the distinction between nature and supernature. Natural law is looked upon as introductory and preparatory to the supernatural state of grace. It is not a result of sin and a means of punishment so much as a divinely established means of healing and of progress. So viewed, the law of nature tended to lose its earlier absolute character. It ceased to be identical with the Christian law of grace and the Golden Age of the Stoics, and became a purely relative conception denoting a preliminary stage in a unified moral development.

It was the idea of a teleological evolutionary morality that constituted the most characteristic and significant element in the ethics of Aquinas. This idea was derived from Aristotle and the Neo-Platonists. It overcame the moral dualism of the early church and furnished a philosophical basis for the medieval ideal of a unitary Christian civilization. According to this theory of a hierarchy of ends, it was possible to retain the absolute ethics of the Gospel as the ultimate goal of the ascending process and yet make place for the imperfect secular institutions. The latter were not inherently sinful. They stood in an organic relation to the moral ideal. The ideal was "potentially" present in them, and because of this fact they were morally justified. They were expressions of relative natural law and hence had divine sanction.

It may also be noted that the absolute ideal, as conceived by Aquinas, was not wholly future. It was present in the church as an institution miraculously endowed with divine grace, and it was also present as the immediate goal of a particular class within the church—the ascetics. It was the function of this class to realize the absolute ideal in their own lives and to do so not only for themselves but vicariously for others. Through their own sacrificial devotion to the ideal they were to maintain it in power and to radiate its influence throughout the church.

Aquinas thus sought to combine the various classes and motives that go to make up human society into a comprehensive architectonic scheme and to do so without sacrificing the individual factors that enter into it. The attempt was, as Troeltsch says, "splendid and brilliant" and to this day remains "the great fundamental form of Catholic social philosophy." [40]

4. The Protestant Reformers accepted the traditional idea of natural law but construed it and its relation to the Christian ideal of love in a different way from that of the medieval church. They rejected the Catholic conception of grace as a mystical miraculous substance imparted through the sacraments and substituted for it a personal and spiritual view that identified grace with the forgiving love of God appropriated by faith. They also rejected the scholastic distinction between nature and supernature and the corresponding theory of a graduated system within which natural law represented a lower stage leading up to the higher stage of supernatural grace. With them nature was the direct act of God, not "a lower degree of his self emptying." The natural order with its various institutions and laws was the order of creation. Why this patricular order should have been established, we do not know. But as Christian believers it is our duty obediently to accept it and patiently to submit to it.

Nature, however, had been corrupted by the fall. Especially was this true of human nature. Man had become a sinner and in his own strength was unable to do any good thing. His one hope lay in the forgiving love of God. This love might also become his own, but only as a divine gift. He could not achieve it for himself. This was true of all men. There was in this respect no difference between them. All stood on the same level. There were no differences of rank among them. The one

[40] *The Social Teaching of the Christian Churches,* p. 277. On the scholastic ethics in general see T. C. Hall, *op. cit.,* pp. 282-364.

basis of hope for all was the divine forgiveness. There was, therefore, no merit in human striving. Whatever of good there was in man was the gift of God. Even the love of God was not a human love, a human craving for God; it was rather the divine love shed abroad in human hearts.

In harmony with the foregoing changes the Protestant Reformers rejected also the double morality of the past and the ascetic idea of perfection. Perfection with them, so far as it was possible, was an inner attitude of the soul realizable in the ordinary relations of human life. It called for no separation from the world. But while the Reformers thus spiritualized, individualized, and naturalized the Christian moral ideal, they still adhered to the "church type" as distinct from the "sect type" of ecclesiastical organization. They regarded the church as an objective institution, not as a voluntary society. The important thing in it was not the moral attainments of the individual but the divine Word, the message of divine grace. It was the Word that gave to it sanctity. The individual members might or might not be obedient to the Word. Their obedience or disobedience did not create or destroy the church. The church was above the individual and did not lose its distinctive character because of the imperfection of its members. Indeed, so sinful were all men that only to a very limited extent could they be delivered from the power of sin in this life. Conversion, it is true, could work wonders; but it, too, was limited in its efficacy. A deep-seated pessimism with respect to the present life was thus inherent in the churchly type of early Protestantism.[41]

5. Modern Protestantism, in so far as it has a distinctive ethical theory, represents a break with the dualism, determinism, and social conservatism of the past. Dualism has been supplanted by the doctrine of the divine immanence, determinism by the autonomy and freedom of the human spirit, and conservatism by a leaning toward social reform and socialism.

---

[41] Cf. Hall, *op cit.,* pp. 468-534.

These changes have been due in part to the increased influence of the "sects," especially in England and America, with their more radical type of Christianity, but more particularly to the Kantian philosophy and to modern idealism and modern socialism. Personal idealism, with its doctrine of the divine immanence, and the Kantian philosophy, with its principle of spiritual autonomy, have altered the traditional conceptions of natural law, of sin, and of divine grace. They have ruled out the vague dualistic-realistic conceptions of moral evil that lay at the basis of much of the ethical and social pessimism of the past; they have ascribed to human freedom a new spiritual significance in connection with the idea of divine grace; and they have given to the Christian conception of the Kingdom of God a present ethical meaning by identifying its coming with the gradual transformation of the moral and social life of mankind. A new philosophical and theological background and a new intellectual atmosphere have thus been created for the study and attempted solution of the problems of Christian ethics.

It is, however, in the light not only of these modernistic developments but of the entire moral history of the church that the study of Christian ethics should be conducted. Such a method will tend to save us from the irrationalism of current dualistic and authoritarian modes of thought, on the one hand, and from the irrationalism of a fanatical idealism, on the other. It will help us to avoid falling into a narrow and superficial biblicism. It will direct our attention to the universal and comprehensive character of the Christian ethic and to both its religious and its philosophical basis. In this way it will tend to heal the unnatural breach between religion, on the one hand, and morality and culture, on the other, and at the same time tend to give to the Christian ethic a unique and independent place in the world.

PART II

PRESUPPOSITIONS

CHAPTER III

THE MORAL NATURE

THE Christian ethic is a religious ethic, and because it is such, it lays special emphasis on the weakness and sinfulness of man and on his need of conversion through the agency of the Divine Spirit. Man is a sinner and hence, if he is to be saved, if he is to attain to moral purity and to holiness of life, must receive divine forgiveness and experience the transforming power of the divine grace. These are fundamental presuppositions of the Christian moral life, and with them we shall deal in the next two chapters. But they are not the only presuppositions of the Christian ethic. Another presupposition, which is equally fundamental and important, is the moral nature of man, his endowment with a native moral capacity. If we were to believe that man has no moral nature in the proper sense of the term and that he is guided in his conduct solely by considerations of prudence, it is obvious that the moral life would for us lose its seriousness. It would be reduced to a mere calculation of consequences, and from this point of view the doctrines of sin and conversion would lose their ethical significance. They might linger as mystical beliefs, but they would lack the vitality and the profound moral earnestness that have characterized them in the past. In their historic form they imply belief in a distinct and authentic moral nature within men. Indeed, this belief is the basal assumption of all true morality. In our study of the presuppositions of Christian ethics we begin, therefore, with it.

THE MORAL NATURE

Meaning of the Moral Nature

By the moral nature of man we do not mean a metaphysical substance of any kind, nor do we mean a separate compartment or "faculty" of the mind, nor do we use the term as a mere general designation of the common modes of human conduct without reference to their causal ground or agency or with the implication that there is no such ground or agency. By the moral nature of man we mean primarily his capacity for moral experience. How he acquired this capacity does not matter so long as it is recognized to be unique and distinctive. It is not something that can be derived from nonmoral or submoral elements. It is itself an elementary power inherent in the human mind. When it first emerged into distinct consciousness, we do not know. But whenever that may have been, it was not the result of a process of intellectual alchemy. It did not consist in the cloaking of prudence with an emotional sanction. It was due to a native capacity of the human spirit, a capacity to distinguish between right and wrong, to form ideals, and to govern one's actions accordingly.

This capacity may be regarded as co-ordinate with the power to know and with the capacity for aesthetic experience and the capacity for religious experience. These capacities belong to the whole mind. It is the whole self that possesses each of them; and in concrete experience one, to some extent, involves the other. Nevertheless, they are distinct from each other. One cannot be deduced from any one, or any combination, of the others. Hence we may speak of man's intellectual nature, of his aesthetic nature, of his religious nature, and of his moral nature, each denoting an original and fundamental capacity of the human mind.

Contrasted with this conception of the moral nature is the theory known as hedonism or utilitarianism. According to this theory, pleasure is the one absolute good. By some it is regarded as the only rational aim of action and by others as the only possible aim of action, but in either case it is the one thing of absolute worth. Virtue and morality are simply means to its attainment. They represent no direct insight of the human mind. They are merely inductions from experience and are as variable as experience. They are wholly dependent on the observation or calculation of consequences. Those lines of action that have pleasurable or beneficial consequences are good, and those that have painful or injurious consequences are evil. And if the consequences vary, the moral judgments also vary. They have no fixity or permanence. What we call the moral nature of man is simply the deposit left by the experience of the past. It is experience that has created the moral nature of man and not the moral nature of man that has made moral experience possible. Moral experience is not unique. It requires no special native insight or capacity for its explanation. It is simply a phase of the universal human quest after pleasure or well-being. And moral laws are merely the rules that in the past have been found useful in this quest. They have no absolute validity. They are all relative. To disobey them may be imprudent, but it involves no guilt.

This theory of the moral life dates back to the ancient Greeks,[1] to the Cyrenaics and Epicureans, and has had wide vogue in modern times. It is obviously skeptical in character. It denies to the moral nature of man the authority and insight commonly attributed to it. Indeed, it denies the very existence of a moral nature in the sense in which we have interpreted it. Conscience is explained away; and in its stead we have a calculation of consequences, which weakens, if it does not extinguish, the sense of duty. Duty becomes prudence,

[1] The famous dictum of Socrates that virtue is knowledge has often been interpreted in a utilitarian sense. Xenophon and Aristippus so understood it. According to this interpretation, knowledge is a means to virtue and hence identical with it, and virtue is utility or pleasure. But the more probable interpretation looks upon Socrates as an intuitionalist and mystic. With him virtue or goodness was "an absolute and emotion-stirring value," and knowledge was "passion and insight, the vision of eternal goodness." So construed, knowledge, like the Hebraic knowledge of God, implies moral obedience and may properly be identified with virtue. Cf. A. K. Rogers, *Morals in Review,* pp. 22-31.

and the distinction between the "moral" and the "natural" tends to disappear. The moral life thus loses its uniqueness and authority and becomes a matter of no more serious concern than the pursuit of pleasure or well-being in general.[2]

Efforts, it is true, have been made, especially in modern times, to dissociate hedonism from its selfish and skeptical consequences. The greatest happiness of the greatest number has been substituted for the agent's own happiness as the goal and standard of the moral life. A qualitative as well as quantitative distinction has also been made between pleasures, giving to those of higher rank an intrinsic value that endows them with a unique moral authority. These developments have appeared in the altruistic utilitarianism of such men as Jeremy Bentham and John Stuart Mill. Then, too, there has been a theological utilitarianism, represented by John Locke, William Paley, and others. These hedonists sought to restore or maintain the authority of the moral law by basing it on the penalties and rewards visited by a just God on human conduct here and hereafter. The moral motive, which they assumed, was self-interest. Paley, for instance, defined virtue as "the doing good to mankind, in obedience to the will of God, and for the sake of everlasting happiness."[3] This was probably the popular Christian point of view in his day, and the appeal at that time to divine sanctions and to the life to come undoubtedly served as more or less of a corrective of the moral skepticism inherent in secular hedonism. The theological type of hedonism, however, did not escape the charge of egoism and selfishness. This criticism came particularly from

---

[2] A striking contrast between the hedonistic and idealistic types of ethics and their historic consequences is drawn by P. A. Sorokin in his recent work *The Crisis of Our Age.* Professor Sorokin might be described as a sociological Karl Barth. His thinking is dominated by the idea of "crisis" and by a sharp antithesis between "sensate" culture on the one hand and the "ideational" and idealistic forms of culture on the other hand. The present world "crisis" is attributed to the disintegration of the "sensate" culture which has been dominant during the past four centuries.

[3] *The Principles of Moral and Political Philosophy,* Book I, chap. vii. Cf. A. K. Rogers, *op. cit.,* pp. 286-99.

the altruistic utilitarians. But they in turn were unable to find a logical basis for their own principle of the greatest good of the greatest number; and when they introduced a fundamental distinction in kind between pleasures, they renounced a basic tenet of hedonism and assumed on the part of the mind an intuitive moral insight. The modern attempts to harmonize moral seriousness with a consistent and thoroughgoing hedonism have thus failed.

Natural Law

Consistent hedonism leads to moral skepticism, just as consistent empiricism leads to intellectual skepticism. For this reason morally earnest people have quite generally rejected the hedonistic or Epicurean theory of morals. The early Christian thinkers did so in favor of the Stoic idea of a moral law of nature or a natural moral law, and their example has in the main been followed by later Christian philosophers and theologians. The idea of a law of nature (*lex naturae*) has played an important role in the history of Christian ethics. Indeed, the only Christian social philosophy or social ethics that has attained general scientific recognition is that based on the idea of natural law. Troeltsch speaks of this idea as a "paragon of wisdom" compared with the modern socialistic interpretation of the Kingdom of God.[4]

The expression natural law did not originally have anything to do with the outer world. It referred to human nature, to the unwritten as distinguished from the written law. Unwritten or natural law at first meant traditional customs and manners, and this meaning persisted throughout antiquity. But in the time of Thucydides (460?-399? B.C.) the term came to be taken in a new sense, that of a law written by the Deity in the human heart. In this sense the "natural" in man was thought of as prior to social conventions and customs and as uncorrupted by them. Natural law came thus to mean the primitive and ideal

[4] *Die Sozialphilosophie des Christentums,* p. 32.

moral law. This use of the term figured prominently in the Stoic ethics. Nature was regarded as an embodiment of reason, and reason in man was interpreted as "God within him." "To live according to nature" became, consequently, the Stoic rule of life. But nature had with the Stoics a double signification. It denoted not only the moral ideal, the original plan of man's life; it denoted also the actual and customary moral life of man. In the latter sense of the term "conformity to nature" was a conservative rule; in the former sense it might well have been a revolutionary principle. To attempt to conform to the ideal might involve a radical break with existing social institutions. But this interpretation of "nature" was kept in the background. The Stoics made no sharp distinction between the rational law of an ideal society and the positive ordinances and customs of their own day. At times they opposed the "natural" to what they regarded as artificial and conventional, but they still retained a reverence for the established social order. The latter as well as the ideal had for them the sanction of "nature." The result was a "fluctuating compromise" between the two. But the idea of natural law remained, nevertheless, one of the most characteristic and significant features of the Stoic ethics.[5]

There is in the New Testament an express recognition of this law. Paul speaks of the Gentiles as doing "by nature the things of the law." They "have not the law" but "are the law unto themselves." There is a "law written in their hearts, their conscience bearing witness therewith." [6] This law takes the place of the written law of the Jews and was evidently regarded by Paul as having to some extent the same ethical content.

The later development of this conception by Christian philosophers and theologians was complex and often confusing. The emphasis was not as a rule placed on its apologetic value. This was rather assumed. The idea of natural law furnished a rational basis for the moral earnestness of Christianity; and in the Stoic

[5] See Henry Sidgwick, *Outlines of the History of Ethics*, pp. 74-80; Rudolf Eucken, *Main Currents of Modern Thought*, pp. 195 ff.

[6] Rom. 2:14 f.

distinction between an absolute and a relative law of nature there was found a justification of Christian teaching with respect to the fall of man and also an explanation of the obvious contrast between the Christian moral ideal and the ordinary morality of people both within and without the church. The Stoic conception of natural law had also the further value from the Christian point of view that it linked religion with morality and made the divine reason, as well as the rational constitution of human nature, the source and ground of the moral law.

But while the idea of natural moral law thus served an apologetic purpose, it was not this but the content of the law and its place in Christian ethics with which Christian thinkers were especially concerned. In the ancient church stress was laid on the distinction between the original and absolute law of nature and the relative law that followed the fall of man. The relative law of nature was embodied in the state and in the social order. It was based on force and in this respect differed from the absolute law of love. But it was not on that account wholly evil. As a natural law it was an expression of reason. It had a remedial and providential purpose. It sought to repress evil and to undo some of the evil effects of the fall. But only to a very limited extent was this possible. The major evils of human life were penalties for sin, and no important change in them could be effected by man's own efforts. Indeed, the relative law of nature was not a law in the strict sense of the term. It was rather a regulative principle, an expression of the idea that the absolute natural law, which cannot be completely obeyed under existing conditions, should be obeyed as fully as possible. It had, in other words, to do with the application of the absolute law to particular circumstances. This application was obviously variable. It differed with different individuals and with different times and places. A certain uniformity, it is true, was observable in the application, and this uniformity might be called the relative law of nature. But the uniformity was not universal. It was limited both in content and in extent, and this introduced a considerable element of uncertainty into the law. Indeed, one important truth underlying the idea of a relative natural law was that of its indeterminateness. What the moral law requires in many circumstances, especially in novel or changing situations, is far from clear. In such instances the individual must decide for himself. The objective and relative law is fluid. It lays down no definite prescriptions.[7]

In the medieval period less emphasis was laid on the distinction between absolute and relative natural law. A new distinction took its place, that between nature and supernature. Both absolute and relative natural law belonged to "nature." "Supernature" was the realm of grace, a realm in which a mystical union with the divine substance of life was sacramentally effected. In this higher realm alone could the perfect Christian life be realized. But between grace and nature there was no sharp antithesis. The ethic of nature was intramundane, while the ethic of grace was supramundane; but the former was introductory and preparatory to the latter. Nature was infused with reason, and through the divinely implanted reason within him the natural man was enabled to receive the divine grace.

In the teaching of the Protestant Reformers the distinction between nature and grace and between the human and the divine was more sharply drawn. But the natural moral law continued nevertheless to be incorporated in Christian ethics.[8] Its precise content, however, was no more clearly defined than heretofore. There was, as in the past, much confusion of thought on the subject. At times the law of nature was regarded

---

[7] These aspects of the natural moral law are elevated by E. S. Brightman into specific moral laws: "the law of the best possible" and "the law of specification" (*Moral Laws,* pp. 156-82).

[8] There has been considerable difference of opinion as to what changes, if any, were introduced by the Reformers into the conception of natural law. In general it may be said that the Protestant tendency was to think of natural law as historical and "irrational" rather than rational, and as such to emphasize it. Luther often substituted for it *Beruf* ("calling") and interpreted it in the latter sense. See Troeltsch, *The Social Teaching of the Christian Churches,* pp. 528 ff.; Wünsch, *Evangelische Ethik des Politischen,* pp. 126 ff.

as consisting of certain general and immutable principles implanted by God in the human mind. At other times it was identified with non-Christian moral codes in general and more particularly with the four cardinal virtues of the Greeks. At still other times it was thought of as expressed in the decalogue and even in the moral teaching of Jesus. This diversity of view was in part due to the ambiguity in the Stoic use of the term natural law, but it also had its source in the difficulty that the human mind has always had in drawing a sharp line of demarcation between the natural and the supernatural. How much, for instance, of our moral insight and moral convictions do we owe to the natural reason and natural conscience; and how much to divine revelation? Did the decalogue and the ethical teaching of Jesus have a natural origin, and were they in their historical form reduplications of the law of nature? Or were they in a unique sense divinely inspired? Or did they perchance have both a natural and a supernatural source in the metaphysical sense of these terms? These questions are not easy to answer from any religious point of view, and especially from the standpoint of the traditional Christian theology with its dualism and its belief in biblical infallibility. Hence arose such differences of opinion as those above noted.

But despite these differences the Christian doctrine of natural law was one of profound ethical significance. We have already referred to the fact that it played a role in the history of Christian ethics comparable to that of the idea of the Logos in the history of theology.[9] As the latter idea gave a philosophical interpretation to the messiahship of Jesus and thus accommodated it to Greek modes of thought, so the idea of a moral law of nature furnished a rational basis for the Christian ethic and thus made it intellectually acceptable in Greek circles. We have also referred to the permanent apologetic value of the idea of a natural moral law. In this conception we have a protection against moral relativism and its disastrous consequences

[9] P. 58.

to the moral life. Then, too, the Christian doctrine of natural law gave religious sanction to the common moral code and to civilization in general. It did not create a passion for social reform; but it did in principle leave the door open to it, and it did quite positively strengthen the moral foundations of society.

It is, however, possible to set the law of nature or of reason up as a rival of historic Christianity, and this was done in the deistic or rationalistic movement of the seventeenth and eighteenth centuries. The movement was a failure as a religion. But it led to a profound and thorough re-examination of man's native moral endowment, and out of this came the Kantian reconstruction of the traditional Platonic-Aristotelian-Stoic theory. The new Kantian theory had from the outset a pronounced effect on Christian thought, and largely under its influence the modern Christian conception of man's moral nature has been built up.

Fundamental Elements

We have already defined man's moral nature as his capacity for moral experience. This capacity involves several elements. First and most fundamental is the ability to distinguish between right and wrong and to recognize one's obligation to do the right and avoid the wrong. This ability does not specify what is right and what we ought to do. It simply gives rise to the consciousness that there is a right, a law that is obligatory upon us. The right or law is purely formal. What it requires of us in the concrete relations of human life we do not know intuitively. In this field experience must for the most part be our guide. But that there is such a thing as right and that we are obligated to do the right is a conviction grounded deep in our nature. It is this conviction, or the capacity for moral distinctions underlying it, that alone makes possible concrete moral experience. The distinction between right and wrong cannot be deduced from earlier nonmoral susceptibilities to pleasure and pain. It is unique and ultimate. And so also is the sense of obligation. It does not owe its origin to social pressure or to the fear of consequences. It is inherent in the moral nature itself and is an essential element in moral experience.

It has been argued by some Christian moralists that the sense of obligation has no place in the Christian moral ideal.[10] The idea of "ought," it is said, is a legalistic conception. It points to a law which we are obligated to obey and through obedience to which we can alone attain peace of mind. This, however, runs counter to Christian teaching. Christian morality is a morality of grace, not of law. It is a gift to us; it is not something that we achieve through our own effort. It is wrought in us by the Divine Spirit, and hence contains no sense of "ought," no striving after obedience to a divine law. The fact that we do at present have this sense of obligation is evidence of our fallen state. It is a form of bondage, and in the perfect Christian life will vanish. Grateful receptivity will take the place of human effort. Only thus can the moral ideal be realized.

According to this theory, so long as we emphasize the idea of "ought," we condemn ourselves to moral failure. For between "what ought to be" and "what is" there is a necessary gulf. "Ought" refers to something which does not exist. If it did exist, there would be no sense of ought in connection with it. The realization of an ought cancels the ought. But this cancellation, so far as our total moral life is concerned, can never be achieved through our own effort. For the legalistic moral ideal, which we seek to realize, always recedes from us. We can never attain it. It thus imposes on us a perpetual sense of obligation, and we are kept in permanent bondage to the "ought."

In this line of reflection there is not a little confusion. The sense of ought does not necessarily imply nonexistence. A thing may be what it ought to be. In this case the sense of ought means simply moral approval. It means a recognition of the moral quality of the act or situation under consideration. If the situation is one that ought not to be, the "ought" clearly refers

[10] Cf. Emil Brunner, *The Divine Imperative*. pp. 34 93.

to a nonexistent standard. But to restrict the term or the idea to such a standard is quite unwarranted. The sense of ought is inherent in moral action as such. Without it there would be neither moral right nor moral wrong. It is the sense of obligation to do the right and avoid the wrong that gives moral quality to an act. There is, therefore, no warrant for the view that there is a necessary antithesis between what is and what ought to be.

Indeed, the moral law presupposes a large degree of compliance with its demands. It does so because it is itself to a large extent based on rules that make for human welfare. These rules have grown up as the result of experience, and what the moral nature does is to place its sanction upon them. They become thus a part of the moral law, and the moral and the natural are fused together. It is a mistake to think of the moral life as extraneous to the natural. The moral is rather the natural lifted to the moral plane. It thus includes the natural. It has to do with what *is* as well as with what *ought* to be, and hence the moral law may itself be said to be a natural law. There are violations of it, but even these violations point to its general observance. Lying, for instance, implies faith in human speech; if it did not, no one would be deceived by it. But such faith would manifestly be impossible if truthtelling were not the rule. It is, then, clear that the moral law with its *ought-to-be* does not exclude, but in large measure includes, that which *is*.[11]

The distinction between right and wrong together with the obligation to do one and avoid the other is the primary element in our moral nature. Without it there could be no moral experience. But the distinction is, as we have pointed out, purely formal. It bids us do the right but gives us no concrete guidance in determining what is right. Nor does our moral nature as a whole give us such guidance. There are, however, three fundamental elements in our moral nature that are not wholly

[11] Cf. Friedrich Paulsen, *A System of Ethics*, pp. 14 ff.

formal and that give a certain general content to the moral law. These are the principle of good will, the conception of a more or less binding human ideal, and the recognition of the sacredness of personality.[12]

These three elements involve or condition each other, but they are nevertheless sufficiently distinct to be treated separately. The principle of good will supplements the bare obligation to do the right by defining the right in terms of the good or of well-being and by adding to the sense of obligation the will or disposition to do what is right or good. It thus gives direction and content to the moral nature. It imposes upon us the duty of a right motive and a right goal. Both are involved in the good will. The will is good only in so far as it wills the good, and the good is morally good only in so far as it is willed by a good will. The good will in the subjective sense of the term comes first, and of it we may say with Kant that it is the only thing in the world "which can be termed absolutely and altogether good."[13] But to be good the will must have a good object; it must seek to produce well-being.

The well-being may include one's own well-being, but in the moral life the primary stress falls on the well-being of others, and hence the principle of good will is customarily regarded as a social principle. It has to do with the interaction of moral beings. And here it is the deepest and only universal law. It holds for all moral beings, human and divine, in so far as they stand in a free personal relation to each other and are capable of mutual influence, and in so far as the sacredness of the moral personality is recognized. Under these normal circumstances the moral nature demands of all moral beings an attitude of good will. The demand stands in its own right. It needs no other support than that of our own native moral

[12] These three "material" elements in our moral nature correspond in a general way to the three "personalistic laws" in Dr. Brightman's system of moral laws: "the law of altruism," "the law of the ideal of personality," and "the law of individualism" (*Moral Laws*, pp. 89 f.: 204 f.).

[13] *The Metaphysics of Ethics* (trans. J. W. Semple), p. 3.

insight. Every normal human being recognizes its validity. Good will is the relation which should exist among all personal beings, and in so far as it does so it serves a function in the moral realm similar to that of the law of gravitation in the physical world. It binds all moral beings together.

In this native principle of good will there is a manifest basis for the Christian law of love. Efforts have been made to define Christian love or *agape* in such a way as to establish a radical distinction between it and the good will of natural ethics.[14] And it is true that Christian love has an explicit religious and metaphysical background that differentiates it from ordinary good will and that gives to it a potency it would not otherwise have. But in its essential nature it must be regarded as rooted in the ethical structure of the human mind. Otherwise it would have no power of appeal to the common human conscience. T. H. Green said that the command to love one's neighbor as oneself is as old as mankind and that the only difference of opinion which has existed with respect to it, has had to do with the question as to who is one's neighbor. The answer to this question has to a large extent been determined by historical circumstances, and in the expansion of the idea of neighborhood Christianity has exerciesd a powerful influence. But the principle of love itself is inherent in the normal interaction of moral beings, and what we have in Christian teaching is simply a religiously intensified, purified, and expanded expression or application of it. Between Christian love and the good will of natural ethics the difference is one of degree, not of kind.

Love and good will, however, is not to be identified with mere good nature. The good, toward which the good will is directed, is a moral as well as a natural good. It includes character as an essential element. No good is truly good that is not consistent with inner worth and dignity. In other words there is in man a moral ideal, an ideal of humanity, which

---

[14] So E. Brunner and A. Nygren.

conditions the application of the principle of good will. If this were not the case, the Golden Rule might be perfectly fulfilled on a merely animal plane. What gives moral character to the Golden Rule is the fact that it is interpreted in the light of the human ideal.[15]

This ideal is not derived from a consideration of consequences. It is inherent in the moral nature itself and may be regarded as even more basal than the law of love. The latter may be said to be implied or included in the moral ideal. We have a certain notion of what we ought to be, and this implies or includes the obligation of good will. But the human ideal has one disadvantage as over against the law of love. It is more vague and complex, and hence more difficult of precise definition and, as a rule, less compelling in the sense of obligation evoked by it. The result is that efforts have been made to simplify the moral problem by limiting the moral life to the social law of good will. But to do so and to disregard the notion of a human ideal obligatory upon the individual is, as we have seen, to deprive the law of good will in no small measure of the sense of direction and also to withdraw from it the support heretofore given it by the human quest after perfection. Both the law of love and the ideal of human perfection are essential elements in the moral nature, and both give more or less definiteness of content to the moral imperative.

In these two ingredients of the moral nature there is implied a yet deeper principle. This is the sacredness of personality. Man is not a means to an end; he is an end in himself. Individual men, it is true, have often not been so treated by their fellow men. But according to the teaching alike of reason and of revelation they ought to be so treated. This conviction is not based on man's love of life and desire to live. If it were, it would be merely a case of wishful thinking. It is based on man's moral task, on the absoluteness of the moral ideal, whose

---

[15] Cf. Brightman, *op. cit.*, pp. 224 f.

attainment constitutes the true end of his being. This conception of the moral ideal is clearly bound up with religious faith. But as an ingredient of this faith it stands in its own right and puts the stamp of sacredness upon the human spirit in so far as it is the bearer of the moral law. It is this sacredness of personality that is also implied in the principle of love. We owe good will to others, and the obligation is absolute because they are beings of intrinsic and infinite worth. We have no right to use them as mere instruments of our own pleasure. They have an inner sanctity of their own; and because of this fact we owe them good will, and not only good will but that reverence out of which good will grows. Kant speaks of the "reverence-arousing idea of personality." This idea lies at the root of the whole moral life, and without it neither the law of love nor the ideal of human perfection would be invested with the absolute obligation that we ascribe to them. It was Jesus who first brought to light the infinite value of every personality in the sight of God, and in so doing he made his profoundest contribution to ethics.[16]

Freedom

In our analysis of man's moral nature we have discovered four fundamental elements: the ability to distinguish between right and wrong and the obligation to do the right and avoid the wrong, the law of good will, the ideal of humanity, and the sacredness of personality. These elements constitute the moral equipment of mankind from the subjective standpoint. They all, however, imply yet another factor, without which no analysis of the moral nature would be complete. This is freedom. Freedom is a presupposition also of the cognitive nature, the aesthetic nature, and the religious nature. Every phase of the human quest after the ideal presupposes freedom.[17] But the necessity of freedom in the moral life is particularly clear. It is

---

[16] Cf. Knudson, *The Doctrine of Redemption,* pp. 77-91.

[17] Cf. I. G. Whitchurch, *An Enlightened Conscience,* pp. 149-83.

implied in the obligation to do the right and avoid the wrong, and in the duty to obey the law of love, to seek the moral ideal, and to respect the sacredness of personality both in oneself and in others. The very idea of moral obligation would have no meaning apart from freedom. If I truly ought to do a thing, I must be able to choose to do it. If no such choice is open to me, there is and can be no rational obligation in the case. And if I have no freedom whatsoever, no ability to act differently from what I actually do, the sense of obligation and responsibility that I have must be regarded as an illusion, as an instinctive feeling that has gone astray.

Nevertheless, many attempts have been made in the history of philosophy and theology to provide a place for a sense of obligation in a deterministic scheme of thought. Determinism is of two distinct types, one naturalistic and the other theological.[18] Naturalistic determinism is based on the idea of universal and impersonal causality. On this basis there can be no freedom of contrary choice. Everything is determined by its antecedents or by its place in the cosmic system as a whole. This applies to human beings as well as to material objects. Human beings, however, act spontaneously, that is, from impulses that arise within them, as "things" do not; and in this sense they may be said to be "free." But freedom from this point of view means simply spontaneity of action. Such spontaneity belongs also to animals. Nevertheless, it is asserted that in the fact of spontaneous action we have the basis of moral responsibility. Man is responsible for what he does, regardless of whether he could have done otherwise. But this obviously runs counter to the moral reason. No one is morally responsible for what he could not have avoided. Responsibility implies freedom. Mere "psychological" freedom is not freedom. As a theory it is a form of naturalistic determinism, and in such a theory there is no rational place for either freedom or responsibility.

---

[18] See Knudson, *op. cit.*, pp. 143-58.

Theological determinism is based on the belief in the absoluteness of the divine grace and in the absoluteness of the divine sovereignty. Of these two pillars of religious determinism the former has played the more important role in the history of Christian thought. What theological determinists have been primarily concerned about has been to make man completely dependent upon the divine grace for his redemption. And this they have thought they could do only by denying to man in his fallen state the power of contrary choice and by identifying true freedom with the inability to sin or with spontaneity in the right direction—a spontaneity, however, which does not belong to our own human nature but which is the gift of God, wrought in us by the Divine Spirit. We ourselves, according to this theory, have no real freedom. We are the slaves of sin. We can do no good thing. Our every act and thought, in so far as it emanates from ourselves, is sinful. We cannot avoid such action, and yet we are responsible for it. It proceeds from our own sinful nature and hence cannot itself be anything else than sinful. From this bondage to sin we can escape only through the aid of the Divine Spirit. Real freedom is the ability to do the right, and this is God's gift to us. We have nothing to do with it ourselves. We are able to do wrong but not to do right. The power of contrary choice does not belong to us. It is not a possession of our moral nature. By nature we are sinful and cannot make ourselves anything else. By grace we may be made free, but the freedom is not the power of alternative action. It is God working in us. And yet despite these strange affirmations, despite our alleged enslavement to sin on the one hand and to the divine will on the other, we are said to be morally responsible beings. An endless amount of equivocation and theological legerdemain has been resorted to in the effort to justify this position, but none of the attempts has ever succeeded or ever will succeed in rescuing the theory from its inherent irrationality. Theological determinism with its so-called "moral" freedom is as fatal to true morality as is naturalistic determinism with its "psychological" freedom.[19]

Without real freedom, without the freedom of contrary choice, there can be no real obligation and no real responsibility. But real or metaphysical freedom does not mean causeless or motiveless action. It means simply self-control, and this power of self-control is obviously limited. There is nothing in it that excludes our need of the divine grace, or that is out of harmony with the uniformities and regularities of human life. It is entirely consistent with both religion and science and is clearly a postulate of our moral nature. Without it the moral life would be in contradiction with itself. A state of perfection in which there was no sense of obligation and no power of alternative action would be neither personal nor moral. If it be true that "Christ and the Devil have no conscience," they both belong to a realm either beyond or below good and evil. God himself as a moral being must distinguish between good and evil and must be metaphysically capable of choosing either. That he invariably chooses the good is not a necessity of his metaphysical nature but the result of the free activity of his will. If it were not so, and if there were no independent response to his goodness on man's part, the divine grace would lose its spiritual character and descend to the level of magic. Freedom in its metaphysical sense is the presupposition of the moral life both of God and man.[20]

---

[19] For a brilliant exposition of the freedomistic argument see Lynn Harold Hough, *Free Men*, pp. 11-50.

[20] Cf. Brightman, *op cit.*, pp. 276-84.

CHAPTER IV

SIN

THE moral nature of man, as we have interpreted it, is a native capacity for moral experience. It implies freedom. It manifests itself in the ability to distinguish between right and wrong and in the feeling of obligation to do the right and avoid the wrong. It recognizes the law of good will, the unique worth of personality, and the duty to seek the human ideal. These different elements constitute what may be called the structure of our moral nature. They are involved in the common moral experience of men, and hence are also presuppositions of Christian ethics. Without them or without the moral nature constituted by them neither Christian nor "natural" morality would be possible. Both presuppose a common moral capacity in men, and in this capacity both find their ultimate philosophical justification. Natural morality comes first; Christian morality is a later and higher development. But there is no radical difference of kind between them. Christian morality is rooted in the moral nature of man and presupposes both it and the lower expression of it in what has been called natural morality.

The bare structure of the moral nature is not itself either good or evil. To be free, to be able to distinguish between right and wrong, to recognize the obligation to do the right and to do it in such concrete forms as loving one's neighbor and respecting his personality—these constitutive factors in our moral nature are in and of themselves neither virtuous nor sinful. They are morally neutral capacities that make moral good and evil possible. They do not predetermine anyone in either direction. Which course any person will take depends primarily on his own free choice. Without freedom there is, strictly speaking, neither moral good nor moral evil. But human freedom is obviously limited, and there is no way of determining by an analysis of our moral nature to what extent we are free.

In the abstract it may be said that "what we ought, we can." The converse would be that "what we cannot, we ought not." As "ought" implies "can," so "cannot" excludes "ought." From this the optimistic conclusion might be drawn that man is by nature endowed with the ability or freedom necessary to meet all the moral demands of life. He is the master of his fate, the captain of his soul. But while theoretically this may be true, the actual situation is quite different, especially in the early stages of the moral life. Guilt in the sight of God is no doubt dependent on man's possession of the power of contrary choice. But this power develops slowly in children; and before it is awakened, pleasure-giving modes of action have already become established that are destined later to be forbidden and that then resist the newly awakened moral will. To overcome this resistance is not easy. The will in its weakness yields, and habits are thus formed that may properly be called evil. These habits are strengthened by the example of others, and as a result of this social contagion and the weakness of the individual will they become so controlling in human life that they seem at times to constitute the very essence of human nature. Certainly they form an important part of "empirical man."

We may, then, distinguish two different conceptions of the moral nature of man. The first is the one outlined in the preceding chapter. According to it the moral nature is an original endowment of the human mind. It is a capacity for moral experience and as such is itself morally neutral. It is neither good nor bad, though it makes it possible for men to be either one or the other or both. According to the other conception, the moral nature is acquired and has a concrete or definite, as opposed to a formal or intellectual, character. It owes its origin in part to man's free will and in part to the conditions that limit his freedom. These limiting conditions make it easier in many instances to do wrong than to do right. What is easy we attribute to nature, and hence we come to think of man's moral nature as inclined toward evil. It is the "broad" way, as distinguished from the narrow and difficult path represented by the moral law. The truly moral life is a life of struggle against the weaknesses of human nature.

This distinction between the moral nature as an original capacity for moral experience and the moral nature as an acquired moral disposition with more or less of an evil bias has, by way of implication, an important bearing on the Christian doctrine of sin and on the Christian conception of the ideal moral state. It implies that the obligation to do the right and avoid the wrong is inherent in the moral life. It cannot be eradicated, nor can it be transcended by a nonobligatory morality. Such a morality would be moral only in name. It is also implied in the very nature of morality that the moral subject is free in the sense that he has the power of contrary choice. The Augustinian idea, that this power is an "accident" of freedom and that "real" freedom excludes the possibility of sinning, is a lapse into determinism and a negation of an essential element in the moral and spiritual life. Furthermore, it is implied in the conception of an acquired moral nature with a bent toward evil that there can be no sinful state or condition or act apart from a free and responsible agent. In other words there is no such thing as original sin in the traditional sense of the term. Sin cannot be inherited or imputed. These are theological fictions. Nor can it be viewed as a necessary element in human finitude or as a necessary consequence of social contagion. Necessitated sin is not sin. Only a freely acquired moral nature can be sinful. To find evidences of man's inherent sinfulness in such essential factors in his moral consciousness as the sense of obligation and self-love is to run counter to the fundamental presuppositions of the truly moral life.

Nevertheless, the doctrine of original sin in one form or another has figured so prominently in the history of Christian thought, and in recent years has been reaffirmed with such vigor in influential quarters, that serious account needs to be taken of it and of its relation to the Christian ethic. We shall, accordingly, deal briefly with some of the main reasons for the widespread belief in the doctrine, give a general survey of its historical development, and then discuss its ethical significance.

The Inherent Sinfulness of Man

Among the reasons for the belief in original sin, or the inherent sinfulness of man, we may first note the universality of sin. That sin is universal is an explicit teaching of both the Old and the New Testament[1] and a presupposition of the Christian doctrine of redemption. It is also confirmed by experience so far as this is possible. But if sin, as we have argued, is by its very nature voluntary, there would seem to be no reason why it should be universal. Its universality would seem to point to a subvolitional principle or tendency in the soul which is itself sinful and which leads inevitably to sinful conduct. To many minds this seems the most satisfactory explanation of the universality of sin. It is in line with the dualistic theory of the origin of evil in general, according to which the various evils of life are referred to an evil cosmic principle or power. But in so far as this evil principle either in the cosmos as a whole or in the individual man is the cause of sin, it destroys the latter's distinctive character. It depersonalizes and demoralizes sin, reducing it to a nonvolitional level. The theory thus defeats its own end. It does not explain the universality of sin; it explains it away. Real sin implies guilt, and guilt excludes the idea of necessitated sin. If sin is universal, the reason for it must be found, not in any necessity of nature or supernature, but in the conditions under which the free moral life develops. These conditions may be and indeed are such that it is extremely difficult for anyone to meet the full requirements of the moral law, so difficult that we are warranted in assuming that all men have sinned. But while it is thus possible to

[1] I Kings 8:46; II Chron. 6:36; Ps. 14:3; Prov. 20:9; Rom. 3:23; I John 1:8.

explain the universality of sin without basing it on the native and inherent sinfulness of man, the latter has seemed to many the simpler explanation and the explanation most in accord with the seriousness of sin as taught in Scripture.

Another reason for grounding sin in the nature of man as well as in his free will is the failure to distinguish between the standpoint of merit and that of the ideal. The perfect ideal manifestly lies beyond us. We can never attain it so long as we remain growing and developing beings. Indeed, the ideal itself grows and continually recedes from us. If, then, the failure in any particular to reach the ideal is sin, it is obvious that we are all necessarily sinners. But sin in this sense is not strictly an ethical term. It denotes a state of imperfection for which we are not and cannot be responsible. It implies, therefore, no demerit or guilt. Yet we do at times condemn ourselves for unavoidable shortcomings. It is even said to be characteristic of "high religion" that "it excludes no action, not even the best, from the feeling of guilt."[2] In this statement there is an element of truth, but it is a question whether in the feeling of guilt referred to there is not more confused thinking than there is high religion. We should, it is true, not be satisfied with any actual attainment or any achievement of our own, and in this sense we may have a feeling of guilt with respect to the very best that we do. Indefinite moral progress is our goal, and we must entertain no feeling of self-satisfaction that would interfere with this fundamental moral task. We must not be content with what we now are or what we have thus far done and seek nothing better. There is an ever-advancing ideal whose claims upon us we cannot disregard.[3] But this does not mean that we are actually guilty of sin because we have not attained this ideal, an ideal that transcends our ability. Guilt is dependent on ability and apart from that has no meaning.

---

[2] Reinhold Niebuhr, *An Interpretation of Christian Ethics,* p. 82.

[3] This is the element of truth in what Niebuhr calls "the relevance of an impossible ethical ideal" (*ibid.,* pp. 103-35).

We may, if we wish, apply the term guilt or sin to our feeling of the inadequacy of our noblest and purest acts. But if we do so, it should be in a loose, rhetorical sense. According to Isaiah 40:2, the prophet was divinely commissioned to say unto Judah that she had received at Jehovah's hand "double for all her sins." This statement was not literally true, nor was it intended to be so construed. It was simply a gracious method of expressing the divine grace. And so we may confess to God sins that are not sins. The confession is not to be taken in strict literalness. It is merely a rhetorical method of expressing the completeness of our dependence upon God. The language used is that of devotion and is not meant to be theologically precise. But unfortunately this has often not been recognized, and the result has been much confused thinking. Sin and guilt have been detached from the free will to which they belong, and have been reduced to the status of a subvolitional entity somehow resident in human nature and exercising more or less control over the will.

A further source of the subvolitional conception of sin has been the traditional dualism of nature and grace or of the human and the divine. Man and nature have been set in antithesis to God and grace. This has not only been a theological theory. It has entered into the very structure of Christian experience. In prayer, for instance, we as Christians spontaneously attribute all that is good within us and in the world to God. We claim no merit for ourselves. We are "miserable sinners." And from this the conclusion has been drawn that we are by nature sinful or that we are of necessity under the control of some evil power. We have no real freedom. But here, too, there has been an unfortunate confusion of the language of religious devotion with that of metaphysical theory. It is one thing for us in the presence of the infinite God to feel ourselves "but dust and ashes" [4] and a very different thing to affirm

[4] Gen. 18:27.

a radical dualism of human nature and divine grace. Yet under the conditions of thought that prevailed in the past the difference was often overlooked, and an uncriticized religious experience was made a basis for a semi-Manichaean doctrine of sin.

A still further reason for the belief in the inherent sinfulness of man or at least in a native bias toward evil is to be found in certain aspects of human life that seem to impose an undue burden upon the moral will. There are, for instance, the unfavorable psychological conditions under which the child begins his moral life: inherited evil tendencies, animal passions, bad habits later formed, and the organized evils of human society. These factors, all of which enter into the formation of what I have called our acquired moral nature, limit our freedom and incline our wills toward evil. They are not themselves morally evil apart from the action of our wills. They are temptations rather than sinful states and, met in the right way, might be turned to our moral advantage. But while this is true, it is also true that bad habits and evil institutions are not, as a rule, deliberately purposed. Often they are formed or grow up without our being fully aware of the fact. Take, for example, the habits of children. Before conscience is awakened within them, pleasure leads to modes of action that are destined later to be condemned. In the meantime these actions are forged into chains of habit which bind the free spirit as it first confronts the call of duty. To break these bonds is no easy thing, and so the child enters upon the moral life with a serious handicap.[5] That he should at first fail in his moral endeavor seems, therefore, almost inevitable —so inevitable that one is tempted with Julius Müller to say of his first sin, "Sin does not now begin to exist in him; it only steps forth."[6] The power of habit is so strong at the dawn of the moral life that it is this power rather than the

[5] Cf. F. R. Tennant's essay on "The Child and Sin," in *The Child and Religion* (ed. Thomas Stephens), pp. 154-84.

[6] *The Christian Doctrine of Sin,* II, 264.

free will of the child that seems the guilty source of his first sin. And so it is frequently with our later sins. They result so directly from our unwilled impulses and passions that the latter rather than our free wills seem to be responsible for them. Hence it is not strange that many morally sensitive and religiously earnest people should have come to the conclusion that sin has at present its source, not in our free agency, but in our native depravity or in a "dark irrational power," which influences, if it does not control, our wills.

The Ecclesiastical Doctrine of Sin

It was in the postexilic period that the sinfulness of man first became an important theoretical problem among the Hebrews and serious attempts were made to solve it. Two solutions were offered. One arose among the apocalyptists. According to it, moral evil had its ground in a hereditary taint, which was attributed by some to the unnatural intermarriage of divine and human beings recorded in Genesis 6:1-4 and by others to the transgression of Adam and Eve related in Genesis 3. In both cases the introduction of the evil tendency into human life was regarded as a "fall." The other solution had its origin in the rabbinic schools and formed part of the official and scholastic theology. According to it, there is in man an evil impulse, called *yezer hara,* which in the English Version of Genesis 8: 21 is rendered an "evil imagination." This impulse is not inherited. It is implanted in everyone at the time of conception or birth, and, despite its evil character, implanted by the Creator. Not even Adam was free from it. It was the evil *yezer* in him that led to his transgression, and so it has been with all his descendants. That this apparently makes God the author of moral evil would for us create a serious problem, but it seems not to have done so in the Jewish Church. The implications of ethical monotheism were not so highly developed with the ancient Jews as with us. Then, too, it may be noted that the rabbis did not distinguish as clearly as we do between a morally neutral and a sinful impulse. An appetite that might under certain circumstances lead to sin was on that account generally regarded by them as itself sinful. We, on the other hand, look upon such an appetite as nonmoral and as belonging to what may be called the raw material of the moral life. It may become either morally good or morally evil, but this depends wholly on the control to which it is subjected by the human will. It is our volitional attitude toward the natural appetites and passions that alone gives to them an ethical character. This fact, however, was largely overlooked in the rabbinic doctrine of the *yezer hara.* According to the commonly accepted form of the doctrine, the "evil impulse" was evil without any reference to the participation of the human will in it.[7]

In the New Testament this doctrine appeared in the teaching of Paul with two or three important modifications. Jesus did not apparently commit himself either to the Fall theory or to the rabbinic conception of the *yezer hara.* Indeed, he seems not to have raised the question as to the ultimate origin of human sin.[8] Sin was to him an obvious fact; it was somehow rooted in the human "heart"; but just how he did not say. What he was intent upon was the practical task of breaking its malevolent power. Theorizing on the subject he left to others. And this we find in its most influential New Testament form in the Epistles of Paul who had probably been predisposed to such speculation by his rabbinic training. He may have learned the *yezer* theory from Gamaliel; but, if so, he freely modified it after becoming a Christian. He combined it with the idea of the Fall of Adam, and by so doing to some extent improved both doctrines. He gave a more definite psychological content to the moral consequences of the Fall by identifying them with the *yezer hara,* which he thus transformed into a hereditary evil impulse. On

---

[7] See N. P. Williams, *The Ideas of the Fall and of Original Sin,* pp. 39-91; also my *Doctrine of Redemption,* pp. 232-39.

[8] There are three of his sayings in the Synoptic Gospels (Mark 7:21 f.; Matt. 7:11; 12:33 f.) that suggest the idea of a sinful disposition inherent in the human soul, but none of them requires such an interpretation.

the other hand, he saved the *yezer* theory from the charge of attributing the origin of moral evil directly to God by making the "evil impulse" the effect instead of the cause of Adam's transgression. He also departed from the traditional rabbinic teaching in that he made the "flesh" instead of the "heart" the seat of the evil impulse.[9] This change may not seem particularly significant in view of the fact that the Apostle included among "the works of the flesh" such sins as enmities, jealousies, and strife. But the substitution of the word "flesh" for "heart" does, nevertheless, suggest that he thought of the *yezer hara* as manifesting itself especially in "sins of the flesh" in the narrower sense of the term.

It may further be noted that Paul was more explicit and emphatic in his ascription of a sinful character to the *yezer hara* than were the Jewish rabbis of his day. Most of them, it is true, thought of the "evil impulse" as evil, not only in the sense that under certain conditions it led to sin, but as also evil in itself. With them, however, these two meanings were not sharply differentiated. The sinfulness of the *yezer* was regarded as dependent on the sins that resulted from it. And this, it is clear, tended to weaken the idea of its independent and inherent sinfulness as did also the fact that it was believed to have been implanted in every human heart by the Creator himself. Paul, on the other hand, by tracing the evil impulse back to the Fall of Adam, exempted God from responsibility for it and so felt free to brand it as "sinful in the extreme." [10] He did not, to be sure, work out a complete and consistent theory of sin. He did not explain how or why the sin of Adam had such disastrous moral consequences for the entire race; nor for that matter has anyone else succeeded in doing so satisfactorily. But he did lay the foundation for the later ecclesiastical doctrine.

---

[9] Note Rom. 5-7, the parallelism between the two Adams in I Cor. 15, and the hostility between the flesh and the spirit in Gal. 5.

[10] Rom. 7:13 (Moffatt).

The teaching of the church with respect to sin has taken two main forms. One has been of a milder and the other of a more extreme type.[11] One was dominant in the early Greek church and hence has at times been called the "Hellenic" theory. But it also has had wide representation in the Western Church in both its Catholic and Protestant branches. Here it has been subdivided into two fairly distinct types; one represented by Pelagianism, Socinianism, and eighteenth-century "rationalism," and the other by semi-Pelagianism and Arminianism. The former or Pelagian type, as it is commonly called, has never been in favor with the church because of the way in which it has minimized the importance of the divine grace in man's redemption. It has laid such one-sided stress on man's moral independence as to make him virtually capable of saving himself through his own effort. The unique redemptive significance of the gospel and the church was thus largely overlooked. Against the Pelagian theory of sin there has, consequently, been an unfavorable reaction on the part of the church as a whole. The theory does, however, emphasize an important truth, that of man's freedom and responsibility. And in the semi-Pelagian or Arminian theory of sin the effort was made to conserve this truth without sacrificing or curtailing the more fundamental religious truth of the divine grace. According to this theory, man's nature was corrupted by the Fall; and as a result his will was weakened and he was left with a native bias toward evil. This native bias has been differently conceived. Some have regarded it as involving guilt, and others not. In any case the emphasis has fallen on man's moral responsibility rather than on his hereditary or imputed guilt. And the modern tendency among semi-Pelagians and Arminians has been to detach the idea of guilt from that of an original or

[11] N. P. Williams, *op. cit.*, pp. 169, 207, 317 ff., attributes the first of these to the "once-born" and the second to the "twice-born." But it is probable that these two types of doctrine owed their origin quite as much to differences of philosophy as to differences of religious experience. Certainly in modern times the "twice-born" Methodists have for the most part held the milder form of the ecclesiastical doctrine of sin.

native bias toward evil. This bias is such as to make the divine grace essential to man's redemption, but it is not a ground of the divine condemnation.

The other Christian theory of sin has been associated chiefly with the names of Augustine and Calvin. According to this theory man is not morally *well,* as the Pelagians affirmed, nor is he simply morally *sick,* as the semi-Pelagians taught; he is morally *dead.* He has no independent spiritual vitality. He can of himself do no "good" thing. He is absolutely dependent upon the divine grace for his salvation. He cannot in his own strength co-operate with God in the work of redemption. God does everything. Monergism, not synergism, is the true Christian theory of man's relation to God. This theory has some basis in the teaching of Paul. But it was Augustine who first gave it an established place in Christian theology. Since his time it has exercised either positively or negatively a profound influence on Christian thought. The Roman Catholic Church accepted it but in such modified form that its own teaching may be described as semi-Pelagian or semi-Augustinian rather than Augustinian. The strict Augustinian doctrine was revived by the Protestant Reformers and made basal in their theology. And in our own time we have had a vigorous revival of the Reformation doctrine by Karl Barth and his followers.

In its Barthian form the traditional doctrine of original sin and divine grace has in one respect undergone a significant change. It has been detached from its connection with the fall of man considered as an historical event. Modern biblical criticism, which the Barthians accept, has made it necessary to treat the account of the Fall in Genesis 3 as legendary or mythical. The story of Adam and Eve is not to be interpreted literally. But it is a symbol of a profound religious truth. Man is a "fallen" creature. He has rebelled against his Creator. This is a basal fact in his existence. How it came about or why it is so, we do not know. As Christians we simply have to accept it as an ultimate and inexplicable fact. Though made in the image of God we are now sinners, necessarily or inevitably such.

We could not have avoided sinning, and yet we are responsible for it. These two fundamental principles of the Augustinian-Calvinistic doctrine of sin and the accompanying doctrine of the absoluteness of the divine grace are also fundamental in the Barthian creed,[12] and they as well as the other forms of the Christian doctrines of sin and grace have had and still have a profound influence on the Christian conception of the moral life.

Ethical Significance of the Christian Doctrine of Sin

Strictly speaking, sin is a theological term. It has a theistic reference. Its essential nature is defined by one's attitude toward God. One may define it either as unbelief, lack of faith in God, or as hostility to God, lack of love toward Him. But while sin is thus a religious term and denotes an unbelieving or hostile attitude toward God, it has also an ethical meaning. For the Christian conception of God is such that a sinful attitude toward him necessarily involves to some extent a sinful attitude toward one's fellow men and toward the moral ideal. On the positive side this is commonly recognized. One cannot truly love God without loving one's neighbor. But the Christian concept of sin is not so intimately connected with moral evil as the Christian concept of love to God is with moral goodness. Emil Brunner, for instance, says that "in the last resort the fact of being or not being a sinner has nothing to do with the difference between the morally good and the morally evil." [13] A man may be a sinner and yet a "good" man; that is, he may be a sinner from the religious standpoint and yet a good man from the ordinary ethical point of view. This usage is so firmly established that it could hardly be completely avoided. But there is peril in it. There is danger of de-moralizing the idea of sin and also the idea of the divine grace. Sin and grace that have no connection with the moral

[12] Cf. Brunner, *Man in Revolt,* pp. 114-67, and Reinhold Niebuhr, *The Nature and Destiny of Man,* I, 241-300.

[13] *Op. cit.,* p. 154 (Ger. ed., p. 149).

life are dubious objects of human concern. Progress in religion has consisted largely in moralizing its fundamental concepts and in breaking down the traditional antitheses between the moral and the religious. True religion and true morality involve each other. It is, therefore, important not to distinguish too sharply between the religious and the moral aspects of sin. The two are closely related to each other and have a common source in the human heart.

This source, called *yezer hara* by the ancient Jewish rabbis, came to be known in the Christian Church from the time of Tertullian on as "concupiscence." The Latin *concupiscentia* was the translation of the Greek word for desire, *epithumia,* as used by Paul, and expressed about the same idea as the word "libido" in our current psychoanalytic literature. In its theological use, however, concupiscence had various meanings. In its broadest sense it meant putting the love of the creature in the place of the love of God. But doing so meant usually indulging one's physical appetites unduly. Hence concupiscence came to be used in the sense of physical appetite in general, at other times in the sense of inordinate physical appetite, and at still other times in the sense of "lust" or "sexual passion." The last of these uses was common with Augustine and subsequently, as was also the identification of concupiscence with physical appetite in general as distinguished from pride. The result was that the broader use of the term, which made it inclusive of pride, gradually lapsed; and, instead of treating concupiscence as coextensive with original sin, theologians came to divide the latter into pride or arrogance, and concupiscence or sensuality. Concupiscence was thus interpreted as "sinful carnality" and pride as "sinful spirituality." The former was a false self-degradation, and the latter a false self-exaltation.[14] Together they were regarded as constituting the essence of both original and actual sin.

There has been considerable discussion of the question as to

---

[14] H. Martensen, *Christian Ethics,* p. 108.

the relation of sensuality and pride to each other. Is one derived from the other? And if so, which is the more fundamental? Is sin primarily sensuality? Or is it primarily pride and self-love? The two elements might, it is true, be regarded as co-ordinate and mutually complementary, one to some degree involving the other and yet neither derivable from the other. Much may be said in favor of this point of view. But the tendency in the history of Christian thought has been to subordinate one of the two basal forms of sin to the other. In both Christian and non-Christian cultures sensuality has as a rule received the severer condemnation. It is a more obvious evil, and then, too, there is more of pure animalism in it. Pride, no matter how evil it may be, belongs to the higher side of man's nature. It is more spiritual, more distinctively human. It has a less direct relation to "matter." This was probably the chief reason why the Greek Fathers such as Clement of Alexandria, Origen, Gregory of Nyssa, and other Platonists accepted the common view of sensuality as the root of sin and took an ascetic attitude toward the sexual life. Matter with them was inherently evil, and hence the sins of the flesh were looked upon as primary and independent expressions of the principle of sin.

Over against this Hellenistic view, however, the prevailing tendency in the church has been to make pride or selfishness the basal form of sin and to treat sensuality as a derivative from it or a consequence of it. This was in accordance with the teaching of Paul in Romans 1:26-30, and an implication of Augustine's ethical system as a whole. In the latter love to God was the basal and supreme virtue, and by way of contrast the basal sin was hostility to God, or pride. All virtues were derived from the love of God, and in the same way all vices or sins were traced back to pride or disobedience. It was the disobedience of the first man that had as its fruit or penalty the passions of the flesh and the sin of sensuality. This theory passed on to the Augustinians and semi-Augustinians generally and was adopted by Aquinas.[15] It was also in keeping with the teaching of Jesus, in so far as he visited his severest condemnation, not on the common sins of the flesh, but on the pride and selfishness of the Pharisees. Still there is a question whether a less strictly monistic view of sin, such as that above referred to, would not come nearer the truth. The attempt to interpret all sins as expressions of one underlying principle, whether that of sensuality or pride, seems to me artificial and strained, as is also the corresponding attempt to deduce all virtues from the love of God, on the one hand, or the love of neighbor, on the other.[16] Both sensuality and selfishness are in my opinion better viewed as fundamental and more or less independent ingredients of the sinful life.

The traditional doctrine of sin has had to do chiefly with sin in its personal and human form, but it has not been limited to the individual. It has recognized a superindividual evil, represented by evil spirits and embodied in nature and organized society. Superhuman evil spirits have little or no place in the modern thought world. They have been exorcized from nature by the physical sciences and to a large extent from human life by psychology and ethics. But of late some theologians seem to have felt that this phase of modernism involved an ethical loss and that there was need of reaffirming the objectivity of sin. They have, consequently, begun to speak of "cosmic evil" and of a "demonic" element in human society, especially in the economic sphere.[17] In so far as these expressions are merely figurative descriptions of certain phases of our natural and social environment that seem particularly evil from the human standpoint, there is, of course, no objection to them. Whatever be our belief as to the existence

---

[15] Cf. Niebuhr, *op cit.*, I, 228-40.

[16] Cf. my *Doctrine of Redemption,* pp. 239-49.

[17] Professor Paul Tillich is commonly credited with having introduced this conception into theological literature. See his very suggestive essay "*Das Dämonische*" (English translation in his *Interpretation of History,* pp. 77-122) and his *Religious Situation,* pp. 77, 162, 178. Cf. Brunner, *Divine Imperative,* p. 663.

of the Devil, we need, as Bowne used to say, to retain him for rhetorical purposes. But no real contribution is made either to ethics or metaphysical theology by terms borrowed from demonology.

As regards organized society there has been an increasing tendency to ascribe to it an ethical or unethical character. We have heard not a little of late about "immoral society" and its sins. The social, political, and economic evils of the day have been treated as instances of "collective sin," and on the basis of this idea of collective sin a new social theory of original sin has been developed. The new theory agrees with the older individualistic and hereditary theory in that both affirm the necessity of sin and yet our responsibility for it.

The chief criticism to be passed on all such theories of sin is their inherent inconsistency. The necessity of sin and its guilt do not go together. That their combination is logically "absurd," that it is incapable to being "fully rationalized," and that it cannot be even "grasped by thought" is freely conceded by recent advocates of the doctrine of original sin.[18] Yet serious attempts are being made to render the doctrine less obnoxious to reason. A favorite device at present is to call the doctrine a "paradox" and to say that it is to be understood from the "dialectical" standpoint, on the apparent assumption that these euphemistic terms may obscure, if they do not justify, the stark irrationality of the doctrine. More seriously Emil Brunner, in *Man in Revolt,* as we have previously pointed out, tries to reinterpret responsibility and freedom in such a way as to harmonize them with the Reformation doctrine of divine grace without sacrificing their ordinary ethical meaning. As for freedom he holds to the "moral" conception, according to which true or perfect freedom consists in the inability to sin, or the ability to obey the divine will. Such freedom is not attainable in its fullness on earth. In this life we necessarily remain sinners. But forgiveness is possible. This, however, we

[18] Niebuhr, *op. cit.,* pp. 243, 262 f.; Brunner, *Man in Revolt,* p. 117.

cannot achieve through any effort of our own. It is a gift of divine grace which we can appropriate through faith alone. And faith also is a divine gift. But if so, do we have the independent ability to exercise faith? Is it within our own power to accept or to reject the divine grace? This is the crucial question. If we answer it in the affirmative, it is clear that we ascribe to man the power of contrary choice in the profoundest religious and moral act of his life; and with that the theoretical problem of his moral responsibility is solved. If we, however, answer the question in the negative, there is no way of escaping theological determinism. In the book above referred to, Brunner in a few instances seems on the verge of adopting the metaphysical conception of freedom;[19] but if he had actually done so, it would have been out of harmony with the main purpose of the book as a whole.

Responsibility he interprets as constituted by man's loving response to the divine grace. It is in and through this relationship that man becomes a truly responsible being. Love to God and man means responsibility. This is no doubt true. It is only in the relation of love that the sense of responsibility arises within us in its highest and purest form. But this does not mean that in true responsibility there is no feeling of obligation. Without the idea of "ought" and the implied ability to fulfill the "ought," responsibility would not be truly ethical. There is no way of detaching moral responsibility from metaphysical freedom and of finding for it an independent basis in the experience of the divine grace. This line of argument against all attempts to justify the traditional doctrine of original sin seems to me decisive.

Another objection to the doctrine is its condemnation of "concupiscence" in the narrower sexual interpretation of the term as sinful. This has tended toward a monastic conception of the Christian ideal and has cast a moral shadow over human life in its common and natural form.

---

[19] Pp. 486, 540 f.

Yet another stricture to be passed upon the doctrine is the pessimistic conclusions that have been drawn from it. Theoretically the ascription of sinfulness to human nature both in its individual and collective form might have been a stimulus to moral endeavor. It might have led to a more earnest and strenuous effort to perfect one's own life and to improve social conditions. But actually the result has often been the reverse. Sin has been conceived, not as an obstacle to be overcome, but as a chain that binds both the individual and organized society, as a fate to which they must both submit. Ultimately sin must, of course, from the Christian point of view be overcome, but in this life there is but little hope of it. Here we must be saved, if saved at all, *in* our sins rather than *from* our sins.[20] And even more hopeless is the situation with respect to organized society. So deeply is sin ingrained in its very structure that there is little ground for believing that its basic ills will ever be outgrown or suppressed. Such has been to a considerable degree the feeling created by the doctrine of original sin. The doctrine has been a moral opiate rather than a moral stimulant.

A still further defect in the doctrine has been the support it has given to an unspiritual sacramentarianism. It has been interpreted as meaning that infants are infected with original sin and that baptism is, consequently, necessary for their salvation. The result was the rise of the superstitious and magical belief in baptismal regeneration.

But despite these moral drawbacks the traditional Christian doctrine of sin has tended to invest the moral life with a new seriousness, a new humility, and a new reverence. The various ideas of a primitive Fall, of hereditary or racial guilt, and of total depravity may be dismissed as unwarranted speculations. But back of them lay the indubitable fact that the moral task of life is an extremely difficult one. The altruistic tendency in human nature, as compared with the egoistic and sensual tend-

---

[20] On the relation of the doctrine of sin to perfectionism see Chapter VII.

encies, is weak; and hence the moral life is necessarily a struggle, a struggle against powerful odds. Many have no doubt made the idea of original sin an excuse for moral pessimism and indifference. But that was not its original motive. Its purpose was to impress men with the gravity of the moral situation that confronted them, a situation so serious as to call for the utmost concern and the highest endeavor. But the extreme difficulty of the moral task, symbolized by the idea of original sin, is not only a challenge to earnest and heroic effort; it is also a bar to self-complacency. So exacting are the demands of the moral law that we find ourselves unable to meet them. The ideal recedes from us, and we are morally baffled, frustrated. There is no longer any place for pride and self-sufficiency. The only proper attitude in the presence of life's obligations is one of humility. But it is not only moral seriousness and humility that are awakened within us by the moral handicaps of life and by our own moral failures; there is also quickened within us a new reverence for the moral law. This law, we come to see, is not of our own making. It is a divine law. This is implied in the idea of sin. In its essential nature sin is sin against God, and it is such because the moral law which it violates is his law.

The Christian doctrine of sin thus enhances the sanctity of the moral law. At the same time it points the way to the solution of the moral problem. The solution can be found only in religion. Only through the divine grace can sin be forgiven, and only through faith in the divine redemptive power can the will be made strong enough to meet the moral tests of life. In the fact of sin, as interpreted by the Christian conscience, we consequently have a conditioning factor of profound significance in the Christian ethic, and one of its most characteristic features. Nicolai Hartmann speaks of it as "the specially revolutionizing factor in Christian ethics."[21]

[21] *Ethics,* I, 55.

CHAPTER V

CONVERSION

FROM the religious point of view there is danger in thinking both too highly and too meanly of our moral nature. If we think too highly of it, there is danger of self-sufficiency and spiritual pride. If we think too meanly of it, there is peril either of moral indifference or of pessimism and despair. Both tendencies are native to the human mind, and for each Christianity professes to have the cure.

As a remedy for the feeling of moral self-sufficiency the Christian church throughout all its history has laid emphasis on human sinfulness. Men have failed to fulfill the demands of the moral law. They have been disobedient to the divine will. In countless ways they have gone astray. This has been characteristic of the entire human race. All men have sinned and come short of the glory of God; and they have done so because sin has somehow penetrated their very nature. How it did so, and in what way and to what extent it now abides within them, is a question on which, as we have seen, Christian thinkers have differed, and still differ widely. Some have affirmed that human nature was completely corrupted by the Fall and that men have no real freedom and can of themselves do no good thing. Others have been less extreme and have attributed to human nature simply weakness of will or a bias toward evil. This weakness or bias has been variously regarded as a result of the Fall, as due to man's animal inheritance or "the inertia of nature," as belonging to his original endowment by the Creator, or as a "cultural lag." Some have attributed guilt to it, and some not. But, however that may be, man is at present a sinner. His conscience is more or less burdened with the sense of guilt, and his will is more or less enslaved by biological and social heredity and by evil habits. This is a universal human experience. Hence men have no valid ground for spiritual pride. They are unable through their own self-centered efforts to solve their moral problem. They cannot save themselves. Their proper attitude toward the moral task of life is, therefore, one of humility.

Such is the Christian method of dealing with the common human tendency toward moral self-sufficiency and the consequent notion that one can get along without God. Man has a measure of freedom but not enough to set himself up in complete moral independence. Whether he likes it or not, he is morally as well as otherwise a dependent being. Of this his sinfulness is convincing evidence. But the extent of this dependence may easily be exaggerated. The exaggeration appears in both Christian and secular thought. In one case it takes the form of theological determinism, and in the other that of naturalistic determinism. Both forms of determinism deny human freedom and, if logically adhered to, leave the individual without responsibility for his present character and conduct and without the ability to change his will or mend his ways. Such a change might conceivably be wrought either by God or by nature. But that it will actually come through either of these sources, no one can know. There is, to be sure, greater probability that God will bring about such a change than that nature will. But in neither case can there be certainty. From the theological standpoint a number of individuals might be "elected" to salvation, but of his own inclusion in that number no one can be sure. The logical result of theological as well as naturalistic determinism is thus a feeling not only of moral irresponsibility but of complete uncertainty as to the outcome of an earnest quest after the moral ideal. On either theory there would be a strong temptation to pessimism and despair on the part of all who have not yielded to the spirit of moral indifference.

Over against this pessimistic tendency to exaggerate the sinfulness or helplessness of man Christianity in its doctrine of redemption has laid stress on the capacity that human nature has of being changed into something higher and better. Men need not be slaves of sin. They may be liberated from their bondage. They may undergo a new birth. Conversion to a new and higher life is possible. This is the good news of the gospel. This is its message of hope, a message to all men. The message in its ecumenical Christian form is not restricted to any race or class nor to "elect" individuals from different races and classes. It is universal. Conversion is an experience possible to men everywhere. The experience is not self-induced. It is wrought by the Divine Spirit. But it is a work in which the human and the divine co-operate. The experience itself would be impossible if there were not a native capacity for it in the human spirit. On the other hand, the capacity would not come to fruition apart from divine aid.

Meaning of Conversion

Conversion in its Christian usage is thus a religious term. It implies a divine factor. But it has also a broader meaning. It is not limited to Christian experience nor even to religious experience. It is applied to experiences on the secular or natural plane. These different types of conversion experience have all been the subject of extended study from the psychological standpoint during the past half century. Special interest has naturally centered in conversions of the Christian and particularly the "evangelical" type. But the whole field has been carefully investigated by competent scholars. Some have tried to find in the Christian conversion experience a unique divine element that cannot be accounted for by natural law. Others have sought to prove the contrary, that there is nothing in Christian "conversions" which cannot be paralleled in other religions and also that religious conversions in general have nothing distinctive in them. They can all be explained by psychological laws and hence have no evidential value. Both of these groups of scholars have been mistaken in their aim. Their arguments are beside the mark. Neither the positive nor the negative conclusion is warranted. Psychology does not and cannot decide questions of objective validity. These questions belong to philosophy and theology. Nevertheless, the psychological study of conversion has been of great value. For the most part the study has been conducted in a genuine scientific spirit, and as a result important contributions have been made to the understanding of religious experience.

It is sometimes said that "human nature never changes." But the reverse is nearer the truth. It is rather characteristic of human nature that it does change. "Human nature," as W. E. Hocking says, "is undoubtedly the most plastic part of the living world, the most adaptable, the most educable."[1] It does not come into the world complete, nor does it realize its goal through merely mechanical processes. It achieves its true end only through effort, through free and purposive endeavor. Only by rising above nature, only by overcoming its prescriptive power, only by becoming something other and more than it was by nature, can it fulfill the law of its own being. Purposive and significant change is thus inherent in its very structure and in the plan of its own unfolding life. There is, therefore, nothing in human nature that excludes such an experience as conversion. Rather does such a change fit in with the conditions under which the normal moral development of mankind takes place.

Conversion has been defined as "the unification of character, the achievement of a new self" and as "the inner unity of perfect moral selfhood."[2] It has also been defined as "a reaction taking the form of a psychological surrender to an ideal, and issuing in moral development."[3] In these two definitions no specific account is taken of the religious factor. Stress is laid on the inner unity achieved through conversion and on the moral nature of the change. The "ideal" referred to in the second definition might be conceived as religious, but not necessarily so. The reference might be to an abstract

---

[1] *Human Nature and Its Remaking*, p. 9.

[2] J. B. Pratt, *The Religious Consciousness*, pp. 123, 130.

[3] A. C. Underwood, *Conversion, Christian and Non-Christian*, p. 258.

moral ideal. So interpreted the conversion there defined is a purely ethical conversion. That there are such conversions is not to be denied. Individuals here and there have been and are awakened to new lives of heroic moral devotion without any conscious religious belief on their part. Patriotism, social passion, and personal affection have wrought such changes. "But as a fact the great power for the transformation of life that dwarfs all others combined is religion."[4] And in those cases where the religious factor is apparently absent, the probability is that it is subconsciously present. Religion is so pervasive an element in human life that no person has been or could be completely dereligionized. And even when men are themselves unaware of it, their moral idealism is not improperly an outcome of religious faith.

But usually conversion is consciously linked with religion. It is not, however, all religions that call for, or give rise to, conversion experiences. Religions of tradition are concerned with external rites and practices. They have no distinctive doctrines, no missionary message. Their religious life is lived on the natural plane. Their only sanctity is that of custom. Even here, it is true, there may be different degrees of strictness and devotion. But the differences are hardly sharp enough to suggest the need of conversion. Conversion is primarily concerned with the inner life, and in the religions of tradition this concern does not come to distinct recognition. Interest centers in the cult and in external practices that impose no high or rigorous demands upon the human spirit.

It is in the prophetic religions that conversion has its place.[5] Here we have a new faith. A leader and his followers are fired with a new idea. There is profound dissatisfaction with things as they are and an equally profound conviction that a new way of life has been divinely revealed and is possible to man. In the presence of this new faith a personal

---

[4] Pratt, *op. cit.*, p. 158.

[5] A. D. Nock, *Conversion*, pp. 1-16.

decision is necessary. A choice must be made between the old and the new, between the true and the false. On this decision depends one's ultimate weal or woe. It is this new situation created by prophetic religion that gives rise to the conversion experience. In the light of the newly proclaimed moral and religious ideal men feel the need of a change of heart. The consciousness of this need is new. It is awakened by the very religion whose professed function it is to satisfy the need. But the need is not on that account any the less real. All the higher needs of men are awakened by the agencies that seek to fulfill them. It is so in science and art as well as in religion and morals. The conscious need of redemption is created by prophetic religion, and conversion is the prophetic remedy for the need. But both the need and the remedy are rooted in human nature and have a universal application. Both have their legitimate place in the unfolding moral and religious life of mankind.

Conversion, as ordinarily understood in religious circles, is defined by William James as "the process, gradual or sudden, by which a self hitherto divided, and consciously wrong, inferior and unhappy, becomes unified and consciously right, superior and happy, in consequence of its firmer hold upon religious realities."[6] In this definition two things should be noted. One is that conversion may be either sudden or gradual. It is a common view that the conversion experience is by its very nature intense and more or less abrupt. And it is true that the more striking conversions have been of this type. We need only recall Paul, Augustine, Luther, and Wesley. Then, too, the revival methods current during the past two centuries have led many people to look upon sudden conversions as the normative Christian type. But no matter how common and how historically important such conversions have been, it is obvious to reflective thought that there is nothing in the suddenness of conversion that is essential to

[6] *The Varieties of Religious Experience*, p. 189.

its genuineness or its permanence. This is also abundantly confirmed by experience.

Whether the conversion of any particular person will be gradual or sudden depends largely on temperament and training. It has been customary for some time past to distinguish between the "once-born" or "healthy-minded" and the "twice-born" or "sick" souls.[7] The assumption has been that people are predestined by temperament to belong to one group or the other. In this there is no doubt some truth. But much depends also on training and expectation. Conversion experiences of the sudden type are more frequent in "evangelical" churches, where children are taught to expect them, than in the ritualistic or sacramentarian churches. But whatever may be the cause or causes of the different types of conversion experience, there can be no doubt that the essential thing in conversion is the inner moral and spiritual transformation and that the suddenness or gradualness of the change has no intrinsic importance.

Another element worthy of note in James's definition of conversion is his reference to the consciousness of wrong or sin that precedes conversion. In speaking of this factor he emphasizes it as one that in most cases "almost exclusively engrosses the attention," and endorses the view, expressed by Starbuck, that conversion is "a process of struggling away from sin rather than of striving towards righteousness."[8] That this is a correct description of some conversions is no doubt true. Experiences of the "sick" or "twice-born" type are naturally generated by the traditional doctrine of original sin. But that this experience is characteristic of the majority of conversions in our day is open to serious question. Indeed, it may be confidently said that the tendency in present-day thought and experience is to emphasize the positive rather than the negative side of conversion. It is the quest of the ideal and the

[7] *Ibid.*, pp. 80 ff.; and Harold Begbie, *Twice-Born Men*, and *More Twice Born Men*.

[8] *Op. cit.*, p. 209.

satisfaction of service that engross the attention of the convert rather than the consciousness of sin. The latter is, of course, not wholly lacking. But the emphasis falls on the "striving towards righteousness." It would seem, therefore, that this factor ought to receive clearer recognition than it does in James's definition. Conversion is a change from a divided and inferior state of mind to one that is unified, consciously right, superior, and happy, and it is a change brought about by a firmer hold on religious realities; but the change is also due to an earnest desire for a life of greater usefulness.

The more truly spiritual a religion is, the greater is the contrast between its own ethical ideal and the ordinary moral life of men; and the greater also is its emphasis on the need of conversion. This need is recognized to some extent in all prophetic religions,[9] but in none of the other prophetic religions does it occupy the fundamental and essential place that it does in Christianity. Jesus began his public ministry with a call to "repentance." This word in the Greek *metanoia,* means not merely sorrow for sin but a change of mind, and is thus about equivalent to our word conversion. The first requisite, then, that Jesus laid down was that men change their minds, that they be converted. Only by so doing could they enter the Kingdom of God. Expressed in one form or another this was his fundamental requirement. Whether he himself used the figure of the new birth may be a question. It does not occur in his teaching as recorded in the Synoptic Gospels. But the essential idea conveyed by the figure is there. The Johannine doctrine of the new birth and also the Pauline conception of the Christian believer as "a new creature"[10] represent no deepening of the ethical teaching of Jesus and involve no more radical demands upon the human con-

---

[9] See A. C. Underwood, *op. cit.,* (1925). This is a comparative and psychological study which gives an account of conversion in Hinduism, early Buddhism, Islam, the religions of Greece and Rome, and other religions, besides Christianity.

[10] II Cor. 5:17.

science. It may be that in the Pauline and Johannine views of conversion there is a new mystical, sacramental, or semi-metaphysical element not found in the Synoptic Gospels. But if so, this represents no ethical advance. In the radical inwardness of their moral requirements, Paul and John echo the teaching of Jesus. And it is one of the glories of Jesus' ethical teaching that, while it is religiously grounded, it never loses its distinctly ethical or spiritual character. The change that he required of men was a change of mind, not a change of the substance of the mind. It was a change of personal attitude, a change of the will, a change of consciousness, a change that was practical rather than mystical in character. It consisted of repentance and faith, conscious experiences of the soul, and apart from these new volitional, emotional, and intellectual attitudes had no meaning or value.

Ethical Significance

In the history of the church the ethical conception of conversion or regeneration has often been seriously obscured. Stress has been laid on external rites and on formal submission to the authority of the church instead of on inner moral transformation. But the latter ideal has never been lost sight of, and again and again has been the rallying ground for religious revival and reform. Out of conversion experiences, both sudden and gradual, have come the most powerful streams of moral energy that have entered human history.

We may distinguish three different respects in which conversion or regeneration has profoundly affected the Christian moral life. For one thing it has had a liberating effect. It has brought forgiveness, release from the crippling sense of guilt and from the related feelings of misery and futility. To what extent there is necessarily a disabling conviction of sin previous to conversion, may be a question. But that the moral task of life is a difficult one, that there are frequent moral lapses, and that the morally earnest person often has a feeling of discouragement and futility, is obvious. He has the moral impulse, an enthusiasm for the moral ideal; but he suffers defeat again and again, and this causes a sense of weakness and of bondage to evil. It is at this point that repentance and the new birth exert their liberating influence. They do not create within us the desire for the good life, but they emancipate this desire from the insuperable handicaps with which it is encumbered. They save us from the depressing sense of guilt by bringing us the assurance of the divine forgiveness. They rescue us from the disheartening feeling of frustration and helplessness by generating within us a new moral purpose and by making real within us the consciousness of divine aid. In these and other ways conversion liberates the human spirit from the bondage in which it finds itself because of sin and the vicissitudes of experience, and thus invests the moral life with a new courage and a new hope.

Another contribution that the experience of conversion has made to the Christian moral life is that of endowing it with a new dynamic. The great difficulty in the moral life is not that we do not know what we ought to do. For the most part we know fairly well. But life lacks inspiration. We do not feel that it is worth while making the sacrifice that the moral law requires of us. The result is that many of us fall into comparative moral indifference. We cut down the moral law to fit our own virtually naturalistic view of life, and our whole moral nature sags. At this point the Christian faith comes upon the scene. It puts back of the moral law a view of the world and of human life and destiny that justifies the highest demands of the moral law and makes obedience to them abundantly worth while. If there is such a God as the God and Father of our Lord Jesus Christ and if all men are his children, it is obvious that we have in this world view one of the mightiest motives to high and holy living that ever entered the world.[11]

---

[11] This truth applied to the human world as a whole is developed in an original and impressive manner by Dr. Edwin Lewis in *A New Heaven and a New Earth*. A new earth, he argues, presupposes a new heaven: the ideal controls the actual.

But it is not only the general Christian world view that has given to Christianity its moral dynamic. Over and above this, though implied in it, is the conviction that man is not left alone in the moral struggle of life. The divine help stands ready to respond to his call, and this not only in times of crisis nor as a mere external supplement to human strength. It comes into human life as a new affection with expulsive and transforming power. Man becomes a new creature, and under the inspiration of this redemptive experience has the assurance that he can do all things through Christ who strengthens him.[12] Things that before seemed impossible no longer seem such. For "with God all things are possible."[13] This conscious linking of the human with the all sufficiency of the divine has in it extraordinary moral potency and, supported by the Christian world view as a whole, has given to Christian experience in general and to conversion in particular a moral vigor, a sustained power, and a victorious assurance unparalleled in the history of the world.

Along with this new moral dynamic the conversion experience has also brought with it new moral insight. This is implied in the teaching of Jesus. With him obedience to the common moral law is not enough. There is a higher law, a law of perfection to which he summons his disciples. "Ye therefore shall be perfect," he says, "as your heavenly Father is perfect."[14] It is not enough that they do as other men do. They are expected to do more. "Except your righteousness shall exceed the righteousness of the scribes and Pharisees, ye shall in no wise enter into the kingdom of heaven."[15] The kingdom of heaven or kingdom of God has its own new and higher righteousness, and insight into this righteousness and obedience to it are made possible only through repentance or conversion. Conversion not only gives us new moral energy;

[12] Phil. 4:13.
[13] Matt. 19:26.
[14] Matt. 5:48
[15] Matt. 5:20.

it gives us new moral intuitions. And these intuitions set before us a new moral ideal which is a constant source of inspiration and aspiration.

By its very nature conversion is an individual affair. Its liberating, inspiring, and illuminating effects must be experienced by each one for himself. They cannot by any magical means be transmitted from one to another. They must be born anew in every soul. But this does not mean that conversion is a purely subjective experience and that it has no particular institutional and social significance, as many seem to think. There are large numbers both within and without the church who apparently look upon conversion as too highly personalized and spiritualized an experience to be made the basis of a universal Christian fellowship or who regard it as too exclusively religious or emotional to be an effective instrument of social reform. This has been the case throughout most of the history of the church. Conversion has, consequently, been kept in the background. Its value and scriptural authority have not been denied. But it has for the most part been treated as a specialized religious experience, limited to particular individuals and groups, and too variable in form and content to be made a basis or standard of church membership. It might perhaps serve as such in small sects, but not in an ecclesiastical organization with a world-wide mission. To attempt to set up such a standard for universal Christianity would have seemed sheer fanaticism to the leaders of the church throughout most of its history.

Nevertheless, the ideal of a truly regenerate or converted church has never been lost from sight. And in modern Protestantism conversion as a definite and conscious experience has received special emphasis. This was due chiefly to the Evangelical Revival of the eighteenth century, a movement which not only gave concrete and vital expression to a fundamental New Testament doctrine but translated it into what is coming to be widely recognized as the most potent moral and social agency in the modern Anglo-Saxon world.[16] It was almost entirely through conversion that Wesley and his associates did their work and wrought that moral and spiritual "cleansing of the nation," which led directly or indirectly to the abolition of slavery, "the execrable sum of all the villianies," as Wesley termed it; to the humanizing of the prison system and the reform of the penal code; to the laying of the foundations of popular education; to the inauguration of the Protestant Foreign Missionary Movement with its international sympathy and vision; to the emancipation of industrial England and other social reforms—and which "finally transformed the whole tone and tenor of the national life." [17] If evidence of the transforming power of conversion in the moral life of the individual and of society is needed, it will be found in abundance in the history of the Evangelical Revival.

Despite all this, however, the evangelical churches in England and America have of late been losing some of their earlier enthusiasm for conversion, and with it has apparently gone not a little of their earlier spiritual power. Altered conditions are no doubt to a considerable degree responsible for the change, and it may be that the future will call forth a new type of evangelism better adapted to the new social, political, and religious conditions. But in the meantime the evangelical churches would do well to take to heart the blunt warning of Bishop E. W. Barnes of Birmingham. He declared a few years ago that if these churches do not recapture their lost spiritual power, as represented by the preaching of conversion, "they will die." The processes of conversion, he admits, may seem somewhat vulgar to a more refined, more sophisticated, and more respectable age. This is true of any deep and strong emotion. But, he adds, "churches die of respectability just as they become a nuisance through superstition. Conversion takes a man so fully into the realities of the spiritual world

[16] See the remarkable work by J. Wesley Bready, *England: Before and After Wesley* (1938).

[17] *Ibid.*, p. 289. Pp. 331-451 should be carefully read and studied.

that he ignores respectability and has no need of superstition."[18]

But while acknowledging the pertinence of Bishop Barnes's word of warning and the profound truth of what he says concerning conversion, it is important to distinguish between conversion of the "twice-born" and that of the "once-born" type and to recognize that the latter type is as valid as the former. Not to do so is to be in danger of obscuring the true Christian doctrine of conversion and casting doubt upon it. It is, for instance, frequently argued that the New Testament emphasis on conversion or the new birth is no longer applicable to our day. In New Testament times most of the Christians had been either Jews or pagans, and for them the acceptance of Christianity involved a radical change that was properly described as conversion or regeneration or a new creation. But with us the situation is different. Children are now born and reared in Christian homes, and of them no such radical change is as a rule to be expected. "Conversion" in their case is not necessary. Christian nurture properly takes its place.

A theoretical basis for the universal necessity of conversion or regeneration might, it is true, be found in the doctrine of original sin, especially in its Augustinian form. If men inherit guilt and are by nature totally depraved, baptismal regeneration or some sort of transformation of human nature may seem necessary if they are to be saved. But the extreme doctrine of original sin, while undergoing at present a temporary revival, has little promise of being again widely accepted in Protestant circles. It may now be regarded as outmoded and as incapable of serving any longer as a rational ground for the universal necessity of conversion.

The real need of conversion is to be found in the psychological conditions under which human life in general develops. It is not the temperamental peculiarities of certain people that give rise to the conversion experience. The particular form that the experience in some cases takes may thus be

[18] *Scientific Theory and Religion*, pp. 615-17.

accounted for. But conversion as an ethical transformation is not peculiar to the "twice-born temperament." Its need is grounded in the law that governs the development of our common human nature. We begin on the natural pleasure-seeking plane; and later it becomes our task to moralize our native impulses and to rise to a spiritual and altruistic plane of conduct. To fulfill this task is extremely difficult for every one, and out of the moral struggle involved in it there arises a felt need of a power not of ourselves that makes for righteousness. When this power invades our lives and becomes dominant in us, conversion has taken place. There is now within us a new moral orientation. The ethical ideal is now the ruling principle within us. All things are become new. This change may come about suddenly or gradually; it may be accompanied by an emotional crisis or it may not; but, however that may be, it is not due to any magical rite or to any special technique. Nor does it consist in any sort of detachment from reality. It is not a dream, nor a product of fancy or wishful thinking; it is rather an awakening to a higher order of reality, an awakening that endows the human spirit with new courage, with new hope, with new strength, with new assurance of ultimate victory, and with new joy.

PART III

THE MORAL IDEAL

CHAPTER VI

THE PRINCIPLE OF LOVE

In the Christian moral ideal the principle of love comes first. The Christian ethic is an ethic of love, and it is such because the Christian world is a personal world and a personal world is a social world. If the Christian world were a mere collection of individuals, each with his own private aim and destiny, the fundamental ethical principle of Christianity would be purity or perfection. It would be excellence of character, judged by an individualistic standard. But the Christian world is not such a world. A world of perfect individuals, mutually independent of each other, is an abstraction from the Christian ideal world. The real Christian world is a world of mutually dependent beings. It is a social world, a world of interacting moral beings; and in such a world love is necessarily the basic moral law. It sustains a relation to the moral universe analogous to that of the law of gravitation to the physical universe. It is a universal law. It binds all moral orders together. It is valid for all persons, human and superhuman. The very structure of the moral relation requires such a law.

But it is not only the social character of the Christian world on which we base the view that love is the fundamental principle of the moral ideal. We base it also, and more directly, on the teaching of the New Testament. Here we have utterances on the subject so explicit that there is no mistaking their meaning. Love is clearly the chief of New Testament duties and virtues.

"Thou shalt love the Lord thy God with all thy heart, and with all thy soul, and with all thy mind," and "thou shalt love thy neighbor as thyself. On these two commandments," said Jesus, "the whole law hangeth, and the prophets."[1] In them the whole moral life is summed up. Do them, he said, and you shall inherit eternal life.[2] Paul also tells us that to love one's neighbor as oneself is to fulfill the whole law,[3] and he speaks of love as "the bond of perfectness,"[4] as the power which "binds the virtues into a harmonious whole." According to the Epistle of James,[5] love to one's neighbor is "the royal law," that is, the supreme law. And so one might cite passage after passage to illustrate the transcendent place attributed to love in the New Testament. Love comes first in the list of the fruits of the Spirit,[6] and in his immortal hymn to love Paul puts it above both faith and hope. "Now abideth faith, hope, love, these three; and the greatest of these is love."[7] Love, however, in the New Testament is not simply the greatest of human virtues. It is the inmost attribute of God himself. "God is love."[8] Beyond this identification of love with the very essence of the Divine Being thought could not go in its effort to express the absolute supremacy of love in the moral ideal. With reference to this aspect of the Christian ethic there can, therefore, be no question.[9]

The Fundamental Nature of Love

But love is an ambiguous, indeed *multiguous,* term. There is love to God, love to other men, self-love, God's love both of others and of himself, love independent of any object, craving love, and giving love. The word love is used in all of these

---

[1] Matt. 22:37-40; Mark 12:30-31.
[2] Luke 10:25-28.
[3] Gal. 5:14; Rom. 13:8-10.
[4] Col. 3:14.
[5] 2:8.
[6] Gal. 5:22.
[7] I Cor. 13:13.
[8] I John 4:8, 16.
[9] Cf. James Moffatt, *Love in the New Testament* (1930).

different senses, and in the discussion of the Christian principle of love it is important to bear them in mind. Much confusion has arisen from a failure to distinguish clearly between them.

The basal question with reference to Christian love is as to whether it includes a craving or acquisitive element. A remarkable work,[10] to which we have already referred, has recently been written by Anders Nygren, professor in the University of Lund, in which the attempt is made to prove that the true Christian love or *agape* is a purely *giving* love; that it has nothing to do with desire or craving of any kind; and that in this respect it is sharply distinguished from, and indeed opposed to, *eros* or love as conceived by Plato and by Greek philosophy in general.[11] It is Nygren's contention that the primitive and pure Christian conception of love was early fused or confused with extraneous elements borrowed from the Greek doctrine of *eros* and also from the legalism of the Jews. This synthetic process took various directions under the leadership of such men as Tertullian, Clement and Origen, and Irenaeus, and finally attained what may be regarded as its completion in the work of Augustine.

According to Augustine all human love is acquisitive. It is a craving for something that we do not now possess. It is a quest after happiness, after some good, some *bonum*; and as such it is the "most fundamental and elementary phenomenon in human life." It is universal. All men love. They do so by virtue of their finitude. They are temporal and dependent beings, and hence necessarily seek a good or goods beyond themselves. The very fact that they are created beings, and, therefore, not sufficient in themselves makes desire on their part inevitable,

---

[10] *Agape and Eros,* entitled in the Swedish *Den Kristna Kärlekstanken Genom Tiderna* ("The Christian Idea of Love Through the Ages"). An excellent introduction to this work will be found in Nels Ferré, *Swedish Contributions to Modern Theology,* pp. 95-197.

[11] On the absence of the word *eros* from the New Testament consult Moffatt, *op cit.,* p. 38.

and desire is love. Love is thus a spontaneous and inescapable phase of human life.

But love in this general sense of the term is morally neutral. It is neither good nor evil. It is made one or the other by the object toward which it is directed. If the object is above us and is able to satisfy our highest and deepest need, the love of it is good. If, on the other hand, the object is below us and so is unable to add anything to our being or offer us any abiding good, the love of it is false and hence evil. We all seek the good. This is the universal motive of human action. But there is an everlasting difference between the goods sought: the highest good, on the one hand, and the lower goods of life, on the other. For we become like that which we seek or love. If we love the highest good or God, we become like him; if we love the lower goods, or the world, we become like it. There are thus two kinds of love: the love of God and the love of the world. The former Augustine called *caritas* and the latter *cupiditas*. *Caritas* is love directed upwards, toward the eternal; *cupiditas* is love directed downwards, toward the temporal. The only right love is, therefore, *caritas*. This term may, consequently, be used to designate the synthetic theory of Christian love which we owe to Augustine.

In the Augustinian conception of Christian love as primarily love to God or the quest after him we have a viewpoint in harmony with the *eros* doctrine. Love is man's ascent to God. This conception, according to Nygren, stands opposed to the *agape* doctrine of the New Testament, which teaches that Christian love is primarily God's love. It is a spontaneous and unmotivated love, directed toward his creatures, and in man it appears in its purity as love to one's neighbor. This love does not owe its origin to human initiative. It is a manifestation of the divine love. It is God's gift to man and is itself a purely *giving* love. It takes no account of the merit of its object. Like the sun it shines on both the just and the unjust. It is patterned after the divine love and hence is directed toward one's enemies as well as toward one's neighbors and friends. Such a love seems irrational, and it is such in the sense that it is incapable of rational or ethical justification. It is an "unmotivated" love and has no other ground than the fact that God himself is love in the *agape* sense of the term. It is his very nature to give himself in unmerited favor to his creatures. Beyond this we cannot go. God is himself the ultimate standard and source of Christian love. No other justification of it is needed.

This *agape* type of love is not overlooked by Augustine. It has an important though secondary place in his caritas synthesis. He begins with the idea that salvation consists in ascent to God. But this ascent cannot be achieved by one's own strength alone. Man needs divine aid. He needs the divine grace. Without it he can accomplish nothing. This was a profound conviction with Augustine. It lay at the basis of his doctrine of predestination and was also implied in his doctrine of the incarnation. Man is himself unable to do anything that will merit his own salvation. Saving faith is purely the gift of God. It is the divine grace, the divine love, that is the source of it; and since this love or grace is wholly an act of the divine will, one may regard his own salvation as divinely predestined. The doctrine of predestination is an expression of man's complete dependence on God for his redemption. And indirectly the same is also true of the doctrine of the incarnation. Man could not save himself, and hence a divine descent to earth was necessary. This descent had its root in the divine love. It was a pure act of grace. "God so loved the world, that he gave his only begotten Son, that whosoever believeth on him should not perish, but have eternal life." [12] Man's redemption was thus based on the incarnation, and the incarnation was an expression of God's love. This was a fundamental element in Augustine's teaching and, taken together with his emphasis on predestination or the divine sovereignty, would seem to stamp his ethic as an ethic of pure grace, an ethic in which God's love to man completely overshadows man's love to God.

---

[12] John 3:16.

But such, as a matter of fact, was not the case. While Augustine attributed profound significance to the *agape* idea, the idea of God's unmerited love, he did not regard the divine love as absolute, unmotivated, and irrational. He did not view it as an ultimate mystery to be accepted without question. He looked upon it as having an intelligible place in the divine plan of redemption. Man is confronted with the task of ascending to God through love. But the task is impossible of realization by his own effort. He needs to have his will strengthened by the divine will. He needs an infusion of the divine love. Only by such supernatural aid can he achieve access to God. And this aid has been brought to him through the divine grace and the incarnation. God became man in order that we might become gods. Our ascent to God was made possible through his descent. God has poured out his love upon us in order that our love toward him may be perfected and achieve its goal. The divine love, in other words, is a means toward an end. It does not exist of itself alone or as a more or less arbitrary ground of fellowship between sinful men and God. It serves an indispensible purpose in the questing life of mankind and thus fits into the framework of the *eros* doctrine. According to this doctrine all love is craving love and Christian love is a quest after God. But this quest is doomed to failure without the condescending love of God. The divine grace is the air beneath the wings of human faith and love, which bears them up in their flight toward God. This heavenly flight is the basal thing in Christian love; but its success is dependent wholly on the divine grace. Both man's love of God and God's love of man are the essential elements in the Christian doctrine of love. Such was the teaching of Augustine.

This Augustinian synthesis marks an epoch in the history of Christian thought. It "has exercised incomparably the greatest influence in the whole history of the Christian idea of love. It even puts the basic New Testament view of love in the shade." But, influential as it has been, it is according to Nygren self-contradictory. The *eros* and *agape* motifs, combined in it, are mutually exclusive, and hence it was inevitable that the synthesis should eventually be dissolved. The dissolution was effected by Luther, who ruled out the *eros* motif altogether as sinful and revived what Nygren regards as the pure *agape* motif of the New Testament. This change, we are told, was as important a part of Luther's reforming work as was his doctrine of justification by faith. Indeed, it has been called a "Copernican revolution." But the revolution has had only a limited acceptance. Even Nygren admits that "in Evangelical Christendom up to the present day Augustine's view has been far more determinative than Luther's of what is meant by Christian love."[13]

Self-Love and Duties to Self

There are thus two different theories of the nature of Christian love. Both admit that the giving spirit is an essential element in Christian love. But one affirms and the other excludes the craving or acquisitive spirit. By the craving spirit is meant desire for any sort of good. Some of these goods are essential to human life or to its inner worth and dignity, and hence the desire for them comes to be regarded as a duty. These duties have to do with our own well-being, and, consequently, we speak of duties to self as well as duties to others. But if desire has no place in Christian love, it is obvious that there can be no duties to self. Self-love of every kind is excluded. All Christian love is giving love. It "seeketh not its own."[14]

There is thus an important difference between Christian moralists with respect to self-love and duties to self. They also differ at one point with regard to love to others. Is this love, or should it be, wholly "unmotivated," that is, without any conditioning ground whatsoever within the object loved? Does, for instance, the divine love to sinners exclude the idea that these sinners have themselves any worth or merit? Is God's love and true Christian love wholly free from every

[13] Nygren *op. cit.,* Part II, Vol. II, p. 232 (Swedish ed., II, 253).
[14] I Cor. 13:5.

consideration of moral desert? Nygren and extreme Calvinists in general answer this question in the affirmative. But in doing so they either attribute complete arbitrariness to the divine love or fall into inconsistency. Nygren, for instance, says that *agape* "demands unconditional self-giving" and "pronounces an annihilating judgment on the self-seeking life." [15] But such a judging *agape* is obviously not an "unmotivated" love. Its treatment of men is determined by their attitude toward itself or toward God. If they yield themselves to the divine *agape* to be transformed by it, their future blessedness is assured; but if they resist, the severity of the divine judgment awaits them. Surely such a love is not unconditional. Its judgment is as truly dependent on moral worthiness as would be the case in a legalistic system. Nor could it be otherwise. Moral love is necessarily conditioned love. If it were not, it would not be moral.

We now recur to the question of self-love and duties to self. That self-love or desire for one's own well-being is a fact, is of course obvious. It is involved in the human instinct of self-preservation and is a basic factor in human consciousness. Human life under existing conditions would hardly be possible without it. But whether self-love is, or by a process of sublimation can become, truly ethical is a question on which Protestant theologians are not agreed. Some hold that self love belongs to the natural plane, that in principle it is egocentric, that it cannot be dissociated from selfishness, and hence that it is and necessarily must be sinful. True Christian love excludes all egocentricity, no matter how refined it may be. "To love," as Luther puts it, "is the same as to hate oneself." [16] Self-love has, therefore, no place in the Christian ethic. When Jesus said, "Thou shalt love thy neighbor as thyself," he did not mean to justify and still less to commend self-love. He meant simply that the manner in which we love ourselves, the constancy and the zeal with which we seek our own good, is an example of the way in which we should love others. Self-seeking is sinful, but

[15] *Op. cit.*, Part I, p. 175.
[16] Quoted by Nygren, *op cit.*, Part II, Vol. II, p. 493.

the mastery that it has over us is a pattern of the way in which we ought to be mastered by the love of others. And when the love of neighbor masters us, it will completely dispossess and destroy our native love of self. Self-love cannot be spiritualized or sublimated into *agape*. It is itself wholly evil. There can, therefore, from the Christian point of view, be no talk of duties to self.

A kindred view is represented by the school of philosophical ethics known as "altruism." The name was coined by Auguste Comte and was adopted by his positivistic followers in England as a natural antithesis to egoism. All motives, it is said, are either egoistic or altruistic, but only the latter have moral worth. This idea was developed in an extreme form by Schopenhauer. He added "malice" to "egoism" and "compassion" as a third fundamental spring of human conduct, but this did not affect his main altruistic contention that moral worth is dependent "exclusively on the circumstance that the act is carried out, or omitted, purely for the benefit and advantage of another." Since this is so, egoistic and malicious acts are devoid of all moral value. Egoistic motives which aim at the "weal of the self" may be morally neutral, but they may be combined with malicious motives which desire "the woe of others," and in that case they share in their evil character. It is desire for the weal of others that alone makes an act morally good. Duties are, therefore, limited to our relation to others.[17]

Opposed to these exclusively altruistic theories of the moral life stands the main body of theological and philosophical ethics. The common view is that there are duties to self as well as duties to others, a legitimate self-love as well as a mandatotry love of neighbor This is for the most part the New Testament point of view. Wholehearted love to God is the great and first commandment. Self-love is to be subordinated to it, but it is not to be eliminated. It is to retain a place co-

[17] Schopenhauer, *The Basis of Morality*, pp. 38 ff.: 165 ff.

ordinate with the love of man. No direct command to this effect, it is true, is given. But it is implied in the command to love one's neighbor as oneself. To interpret "as oneself" in such a way as to exclude the right and duty of self-love is strained and artificial and would hardly have occurred to any-one apart from the exigencies of theological theory. Regard for one's own good underlies many of Jesus' promises and exhortations to self-sacrifice and is assumed throughout most of the New Testament.[18] New Testament teaching is not altruistic in the modern sense of excluding egoism.

Love to God and God's Own Love

Love to God is itself a form of self-love in so far as it is a craving after a good, in this case the highest good. And that it is so conceived in the New Testament is obvious. We are to love God with all the heart; that is, he is to be the chief object of our desire. And as such we are to seek him. Seeking is a Christian attitude of mind. "Seek, and ye shall find." "Seek first the kingdom of God and his righteousness." [19] This earnest, striving spirit is everywhere enjoined in the New Testament. The gospel sets before us a goal toward which we are to press on. This goal is in a sense a prize for which we are contending. It is our highest good and is often identified with life itself, with eternal life. The purpose of Jesus' mission was that we might have life and have it more abundantly. This is the fundamental note of the New Testament as a whole. It underlies its oft-repeated doctrine of reward and punishment and its entire eschatology. God is our chief good, and if we love and seek him aright, we shall be rewarded with eternal life. This point of view is generally assumed in the New Testament. But it is not worked out in systematic form. Love to God is not clearly defined in its relation to God's love of us, to our love of our

[18] Matt. 5:3-10; 6:14; 7:1; 19:29; Mark 11:25; Luke 6:38. Cf. E. F. Scott, *The Ethical Teaching of Jesus,* pp. 60 f.; H. J. Cadbury, *The Peril of Modernizing Jesus,* pp. 105 ff.

[19] Matt. 6:33; 7:7.

fellow men, and to self-love. The first three forms of love are plainly and emphatically taught, and the fourth is clearly assumed. But the four are not logically related to each other, and we have, consequently, in the New Testament no coherent and comprehensive theory of Christian love.

It was Augustine who first gave the church such a theory. He saw in love to God the fundamental and essential form of Christian love and from it sought to deduce self-love and love of neighbor. As for God's own love, he explained it in accordance with principles implicit in our love to God. All love, he held, is acquisitive love and, in this sense, self-love. It is desire for a good. But this desire becomes truly Christian only when it is directed toward the highest good. The highest good, however, is God. True Christian love is, therefore, the love of God. But the love of God as the highest good is the truest form of self-love. For we truly or rightly love ourselves only when we seek the highest good. Hence, the more we love God, the more we love ourselves; and the more truly and wisely we love ourselves, the more inevitably do we come to love God. True self-love thus leads to the love of God, and the love of God is self-love in its highest and purest form.

The duty of love to one's neighbor Augustine derived both from love to God and self-love. Men in and of themselves are not worthy of love. They are such only in so far as the divine purpose is embodied in them, only in so far as they are potentially sons of God. In loving them we do not, then, love them in their present unworthiness; we rather love God in them. Love of neighbor is thus a specification under the love of God. The commandment to love God includes the commandment to love one's neighbor. It does so because in loving one's neighbor one is really loving God. It is the divine image in men, God in them, rather than men in their fallen state that we love. Then, too, the true love of others is directed toward their highest good, and this can be attained only by their loving God. If we are, therefore, truly to love others, we must ourselves love God and seek to induce others to do so also.

Love of neighbor thus stands in a double relation to the love of God. It is both a love of God in one's neighbor and an attempt to awaken one's neighbor to the love of God.

Love of neighbor also involves self-love. It does so because all love is craving love. In loving others we at the same time seek our own good in some form. We may distinguish between goods that we are to enjoy (*frui*) and goods that we are to use (*uti*). God is the only good to be "enjoyed" in the full sense of the term. The external or material goods of life are only for "use." Other people may be "enjoyed," but only in a relative way, only "in God." But whether "enjoyed" or "used" the objects of our love sustain some relation to our own well-being. In doing good to others, even in sacrificing ourselves for them, we are not acting without some reference to our own good. This is not merely a psychological fact. It is grounded in the nature of Christian love. God has stamped his image upon us; we are his sons. And hence we are not only justified in loving ourselves; we are obligated to do so. We have duties to ourselves, because selfhood is a divinely given treasure entrusted to our care. We may not do what we please with it. We may not spurn or neglect it. It has eternal value in the sight of God; and this we may interpret as meaning that God is in us or that we are in him. In any case, it is the Godward reference of the self that furnishes a rational ground for the love both of ourselves and of others. As Christians we love ourselves because in doing so we love God, and for a similar reason we are obligated to love others. We begin with self-love; and since this in its purity is really the love of God who is in us and in every human soul, self-love carries with it the duty of love to others. In Christian altruism we love the same God as in Christian egoism, which comes first in the order of time. Love of neighbor has thus its source in self-love, and both it and self-love are ultimately derived from the love of God.

Turning now to God's own love, we find Augustine interpreting it in two different ways. It is, first of all, self-love. Since God is absolute and self-sufficient, he has no unsatisfied desire.

He craves nothing outside of himself. He finds his satisfaction and enjoyment in the perfection of his own being. In this sense he is love. He is love also in the sense that he is the object of all *caritas*, all heavenward love. All true love is directed toward him. He gathers it all into himself. Thus as the object both of his own love and that of others he is himself identified with love.

But along with these egocentric conceptions of the divine love there was in Augustine a profound emphasis on the divine love for sinners. This love might seem to be wholly unmotivated; and at times Augustine spoke of it as an incomprehensible miracle.[20] But at other times he expresses a different view. It was not sinners as such whom God loved. He rather loved the good that was still in them and the perfection they might yet attain. But this present good and possible perfection were not due to themselves. They were due to the Divine Spirit within them; and so in the last analysis what God loved in the sinner was none other than himself. There was thus, according to Augustine, nothing in the Christian doctrine of the divine grace that was inconsistent with the conception of the divine love as self-love.

Moral Worth in the Objects of Christian Love

Self-love and the love of God were, as we have seen, basal in the Augustinian ethics. They were such because human love was regarded as necessarily craving love, a love that found its highest expression in love to God, and because the self-sufficiency of God made his love necessarily a love of self. But back of these reasons or involved in them was the conviction that the object of true love must have personal worth. The worth may not be one's own achievement. It may be a divine gift, or inherent in one's own nature as in the case of God himself. But whatever its source, it must be in some form the possession of every object of true love. This was the reason why Augustine

[20] *On the Gospel of St. John*, CX, 6.

interpreted true self-love and true love of neighbor as in the last analysis a love of God. It was God in men, in oneself and in others, that gave to them their moral worth and made them proper objects of Christian love.

This way of putting the matter does not fit into our modern modes of thought and speech. But the idea underlying it was true and important. Love, to be true love, must have a worthy object—worthy not in the sense of being self-sufficient and self-righteous but in the sense of having been made in the image of God and of having a capacity for a high and noble destiny. Such a person may be a sinner, but he would not be such unless he had been made for God and were capable of fellowship with him. In this sense moral worth must inhere in every object of true love. If it were not so, love would sink to a non-moral plane. Moralized love must take account of the innate capacity and dignity of the human soul. Augustine saw this clearly and, consequently, interpreted true self-love and true love of neighbor in terms of love to God. For the same reason he also construed God's love of sinful men as a form of self-love. With him all true love was a love of the moral ideal, real or possible, and this ideal he identified with God. Hence all true Christian love was for him a love of God, but in this love both love of self and love of neighbor were implied as essential constituents.

In the identification of the moral ideal with God it was implied that love to God did not require the performance of what Kant called "court duties," that is, arbitrary duties in which God had a special interest and which he on that account perhaps valued above duties performed toward others. There are no such duties. As an embodiment of the moral ideal God is not concerned with religious etiquette. There are no special services of this character that we owe him. Loving one's neighbor is loving God, and loving God is loving one's neighbor. But this does not mean that there is no place for prayer and worship. These religious acts are essential to the Christian life. They are natural expressions of our consciousness of a filial relation to God and as such stand in a vital relation to our moral and spiritual life as a whole. Both the love of others and the love of self receive an added inspiration through the love of God and communion with him.

To make craving love and giving love, *eros* and *agape,* antithetical to each other, and to limit Christian love to "unmotivated" giving love on the part both of God and man, is to be guilty of a false abstractionism. In the abstract we may oppose the egoistic to the altruistic, the acquisitive to the receptive, the free to the determined, the human to the divine; but in actual life they are combined. It is the mystery of personality that it unites what seem to be logical opposites. It is not either egoistic or altruistic, either free or determined; it is both. It is free in a sense that justifies the *eros* doctrine, and dependent on God in a sense that justifies the *agape* doctrine. One is not exclusive of the other. From the practical religious point of view the emphasis naturally falls on the *agape* idea; from the theoretical and ethical standpoint the *eros* idea is properly stressed. But both have a place in the Christian ethic. To reject the *eros* idea, to exclude self-love and duties to self as non-Christian, and to limit Christian love to an "unmotivated" love to others is to create an abstract Christian ethic and to fall into a sentimental immoralism. True Christian love presupposes an ethical ideal, obligatory upon all men, which each must seek to realize for himself. And in the ideal self-sacrificing love to others occupies a central place. But self-sacrifice is not the final word in the Christian ethic. It is a means to an end. The Christian ideal is self-realization through self-sacrifice.

Brotherly Love and Its Conditioning Factors

Brotherly love is not, then, an ethical ultimate in the Christian system, nor is its counterpart in the divine love such. It is grounded in the worth of the individual, in the sacredness of personality, and in a universal moral ideal. But with these presuppositions it is the one great Christian principle governing the interaction of moral beings. As such a principle it does not exhaust the Christian moral ideal. It needs to be supplemented by love to God and one's true self. Only in this comprehensive sense of the term is love the fulfillment of "the whole law." But within the limits of human relationships love to neighbor may be said to be the all-inclusive moral law. In it is expressed the essence of the Christian social ideal.

In applying the principle of brotherly love to the concrete problems of human life there are two conditioning factors that need to be noted. One has already been emphasized. It is that love to be truly ethical must be something more than mere good nature, something more than merely doing to others what we would like to have done to ourselves under similar circumstances. It must include compliance with the demands of the moral ideal. It must mean doing unto others what we *ought* to want them to do to us. Without this conditioning "ought" the Golden Rule could be literally fulfilled on a submoral and even immoral level. Mere good will does not suffice. It must first be moralized and idealized before it can become "the royal law" of the Christian ethic. And this means that the Christian moral ideal is not exhausted in what is commonly understood by love. The principle of love must be supplemented by the idea of perfection, with which we shall deal in the next chapter.

The other conditioning factor in the application of the law of love is that due to "the orders of creation." Human nature and the structure of human society interpose obstacles to the realization of the moral ideal that have to be reckoned with. What the law of love would require in a world of angelic beings is one thing; what it requires in our present human world is a very different thing. With people divided into different stages of mental and moral maturity, into different families, into different economic and cultural groups, into different nations, into different races, into different religious faiths, the problem of conduct inevitably becomes highly complicated. What we ought to do in many concrete situations that arise is far from clear. Custom is our usual guide. But it often fails us, and the abstract principle of love does not help us out very much. Under such conditions we simply have to acknowledge the indeterminateness of the moral law and decide for ourselves, as best we can, what we ought to do. The moral ideal lies at present beyond us; and necessarily so because our world is a developing world. It begins on the natural plane and only gradually can be moralized. The process is necessarily a slow one, but progress is being made, and within the developing process the Christian ideal of brotherly love serves as both a guiding star and a spiritual dynamic.

CHAPTER VII

THE PRINCIPLE OF PERFECTION

CHRISTIAN love, as commonly understood, is a composite principle. It includes love of God and love of self as well as love of neighbor. In each of these instances love has a distinctive meaning; and hence if we take account of the various meanings of the term instead of the term itself, it would seem that love could hardly be regarded as the comprehensive and unitary principle of Christian morality as a whole. The unity it gives to Christian ethics is verbal rather than real.

In order to avoid this conclusion, two methods have been adopted by Christian moralists. Augustine argued that all Christian love is reducible to the love of God. What we love in ourselves and in others is not what we and they actually are. All men are in and of themselves sinners and unworthy of pure Christian love. What we as Christians love in them is the divine goodness and the divine purpose embodied in them. In other words, it is God in them and in ourselves that we love. It is so also with the divine love. God is said to be love, but the love which constitutes the essence of the divine being is self-love. Only God is worthy of the divine love. When it comes to the divine love of sinful men, what God loves is not sinful men as such but himself in them. All true love, both human and divine, is thus in the last analysis reducible to the love of God.

The other method of maintaining the unity and comprehensiveness of the Christian principle of love has been to exclude from it self-love and all craving love, even the love of God as commonly understood. Love to God is interpreted as "faith" rather than love, or is regarded as expressing itself in love to one's neighbor rather than in mystic devotion to Deity.[1]

---

[1] Nygren, *Agape and Eros,* Part I, pp. 90-93; Part II, Vol. II, pp. 498, 518 (Swedish ed., I, 92-95; II, 554 f.).

In any case it is God's love of men that constitutes the norm of Christian love. This love is "spontaneous" and "unmotivated" and finds its only proper expression in the love of others. Self-love, duties to self, and the mystic love of God have no place in it. Christian love is thus purely a social principle, and as such constitutes the sole basis of the Christian ethic.

In both of these historic interpretations of Christian love there are elements of truth. The main truth in the Augustinian theory is its recognition of an independent ethical ideal as implicit in Christian love. Love is itself not necessarily Christian. What makes it Christian is its permeation with the Christian ideal of moral perfection. Love itself belongs to this ideal, but only after it has been moralized. True Christian love thus involves a moral supplement, and from the Augustinian point of view it is this supplement that gives to Christian love its characteristic and ideal character. It is not love that makes an act Christian so much as it is the moral quality of the act. In other words, the moral ideal is basal. It comes first and transforms love into moralized and Christian love. It was this insight that led Augustine to place primary stress on the love of God rather than on the love of neighbor. True love with him was the love of the ideal, whether it took the form of the love of self, of neighbor, or of God. And since he identified the ideal with God, he looked upon the true love of self and neighbor as at bottom the love of God. This transformation of self-love and love of neighbor into the love of God seems to us somewhat forced and unnatural, but it served the purpose of linking Christian love indissolubly with the ideal of moral perfection.

In the *agape* theory as expounded by Nygren, on the other hand, there is a closer approach to the New Testament emphasis on the divine love for sinners and on the duty to love one's neighbor. There is also a more distinct recognition of the independent personality of one's neighbor, not as an object of moral worth, but as an object of both human and divine love. God does not, on this theory, love himself in sinful men; he loves sinful men themselves. That is the miracle of divine grace, and it is through this miracle wrought in us by the Divine Spirit that we are able to love even our enemies. It is not God in them whom we are to love. We are to love our enemies themselves as independent beings and so also our neighbors generally. We are not to love them because of their own inherent worth—they have no such worth—but because they are human beings and God loves them. The bare fact of their humanity, of their being created by God, is the ground of his affection for them and should be the ground of ours. This view of human individuality stands closer to modern personalism than does the abstract idealism of Augustine. It may also be noted that the exclusive emphasis on brotherly love as opposed to duties to self is more in keeping with the ethical spirit of the New Testament and with the manifest fact that "social action is the chief part of our life." In this field "good will is the spring of conduct, and the common good the aim."[2]

There is, however, one serious and it seems to me decisive objection to the *agape* theory in its more extreme form. In so far as this theory completely eliminates moral worth from the objects of the divine grace and in so far as it entirely excludes duties to self from the Christian ethic, it de-moralizes and de-personalizes the Christian life. It leaves both the divine grace and the law of brotherly love without a rational basis. Blind faith takes the place of moral insight. We affirm the divine love and the duty of brotherly love, but without any rational ground for either. If the individual has no inherent worth, the affirmation of the divine grace leads to an unmoral predestinationism, and the inculcation of brotherly love leads to an unmoral sentimentalism. If, on the other hand, we acknowledge the worth of others as a basis for our love of them, it is clear that we cannot deny a similar value to ourselves, nor can we deny duties to self. We find it, therefore, necessary to supplement the Christian principle of brotherly love with the Christian ideal of moral perfection. Without either the Christian ethic would be rad

[2] B. P. Bowne, *The Principles of Ethics*, p. 113.

ically defective. Like Christian theology, Christian ethics is not a circle with a centre but an ellipse with two foci.

In the preceding chapter we considered the first of these foci, the principle of love. In the present chapter our task is to consider the second, moral perfection.

Love and perfection do not exclude—they rather include—each other. Indeed, the two terms are at times used synonymously. The reason is this: Moral perfection would seem to be the broader and more inclusive term. But since the time of Augustine, indeed from New Testament times, the tendency has been to make love coextensive with the whole Christian life. Love is not simply one Christian virtue, it is the sum of all Christian virtues. Its possession is itself the perfect moral life. But there are different kinds and degrees of love, and hence it has been customary to speak of "perfect love." Perfect love is moral perfection, and moral perfection is a state of perfect love.

But while love and perfection have thus at times been identified with each other, the identification has never been complete. There has always been a tendency to distinguish between them in some such way as we distinguish between mercy and justice. Mercy is directed toward well-being, while justice is concerned with the abstract moral ideal. In a somewhat similar way love has for its aim the welfare or happiness of its object, while perfection has to do with his moral purity, his freedom from any stain of sin. General well-being is the goal in one case and excellence of character in the other. The two involve each other, as we have repeatedly pointed out. But it makes a considerable practical difference whether the emphasis falls on one or the other. And in an exposition of the Christian moral ideal it is important that account be taken of both. One cannot be completely reduced to the other without doing violence to both. There is a certain moral uniqueness in each. There is a good will in love and a moral rightness in perfection that cannot be eliminated. Both stand in their own right, and both are fundamental factors in Christian morality.

The idea of perfection, while less prominent than the principle of love, receives frequent recognition and is generally assumed throughout the New Testament. Jesus enjoins us to be perfect as our heavenly Father is perfect.[3] This injunction ranks in ethical importance with the commandment to love one's neighbor as oneself. It is implicit in the idea of the Kingdom of God. The Kingdom of God is a perfectionist conception. It stands for the ideal and perfect rule of God.[4] Only those are qualified to be members of it who acknowledge the authority of the divine will and seek to obey it. It was from this point of view that the ethic of Jesus was developed. He set before men a perfect moral standard, a standard which most men would feel lay completely beyond them; and hence his ethic has been called "an ethical teaching for heroes."[5] Indeed, even moral heroes would feel that his ideal of human conduct was beyond their power of realization.

Nevertheless, the ideal was kept before the early church. Paul looked upon perfection as the goal of the Christian life for himself,[6] and for believers generally;[7] and this was also the view commonly held in New Testament times.[8] Perfection was not infrequently applied to love as the basal Christian virtue, but it is clear from the Sermon on the Mount and from the New Testament as a whole that it applied also to purity, truthfulness, and the Christian virtues generally.

The obligation to moral perfection is inherent in the moral law itself. The moral nature requires us to do the right and to avoid the wrong. This requirement is absolute in the sense that it admits of no exception. There are no moral holidays. In the moral realm no one is entitled to a "day off." The duty

[3] Matt. 5:48.

[4] Note the parallelism in the Lord's Prayer, "Thy kingdom come, thy will be done" (Matt. 6:10), and the virtual identification of the Kingdom of God with his "righteousness" (Matt. 6:33; Rom. 14:17).

[5] C. G. Montefiore, *The Old Testament and After,* p. 241.

[6] Phil. 3:12-14.

[7] II Cor. 13:9, 11; Eph. 4:13; Col. 1:28; 4:12.

[8] Heb. 13:21; James 1:4; I Peter 5:10; I John 4:17.

of perfection is an implication of the moral nature itself; and from this point of view it might be said that to violate the moral law at one point is to violate the whole law, the all-embracing law of moral perfection.[9]

Perfection, however, in the New Testament is grounded, not in the nature of the moral law, but in the nature of God. God is perfect, and because of this fact we ought to be such. He is also love, and because of this fact we ought to be loving both in thought and deed. God is thus the norm and ground of moral excellence, and he is also its inspiring source. We are to act in our sphere as he does in his that we may be children of our Father who is in heaven.[10] Kinship to God is the true goal of conduct, and in this fact is to be found the basis of perfectionism. In order to be like God and to have fellowship with him we must share in his perfection. This has been generally assumed in the course of Christian history, and hence one of the most characteristic features of the Christian ethic has been the quest of the perfect life.

This quest has taken various directions. Brotherly love has been included in it and has been one of its chief, if not its chief, objective. But it has also had other objectives that stand more closely related to the self and with which we are here more directly concerned. Those I have in mind are self-renunciation, asceticism, sinlessness, and self-realization. These different aspects of the Christian moral life do not exclude—they rather involve—each other. But they are sufficiently distinct to make a separate consideration of each desirable.

Self-Renunciation

Jesus is reported to have said to the rich young ruler who professed that he had kept all the commandments of the decalogue, "If thou wouldst be *perfect,* go, sell that which thou hast, and give to the poor."[11] Perfection is here apparently made

---

[9] James 2:10.
[10] Matt. 5:45; Luke 6:35.
[11] Matt. 19:21.

conditional on a specific act of renunciation. There is, it is true, a question whether Jesus himself used the word "perfect" in this connection. But whether he did or not, there is no question as to the importance that he attributed to the general principle of renunciation. "If any man would come after me, let him deny himself, and take up his cross, and follow me."[12] "Whosoever shall seek to gain his life shall lose it; but whosoever shall lose his life shall preserve it."[13] "Whosoever would be first among you, shall be servant of all. For the Son of man also came not to be ministered unto, but to minister, and to give his life a ransom for many."[14] By such utterances as these and still more by his own example Jesus put the principle of self-sacrifice at the very heart of the Christian ethic. There is no more characteristic element in the ideal Christian life than the spirit of self-denial.

To some extent the necessity of self-denial has been recognized in all ethical systems. Even extreme hedonists have admitted that some pleasures must be renounced. The conflict of desires and the conditions of our present human existence make this inevitable. Some pleasures exclude others, and none admit of complete realization in this life. Some renunciation is thus required even on a hedonistic basis, but the extent of it is reduced to a minimum. An extreme form of renunciation is represented by Buddhism, which aims at the complete annihilation of desire. Indeed, there is a question whether its goal of nirvana does not exclude consciousness itself.

The Christian doctrine of renunciation occupies a position midway between these extremes. It affirms life, eternal life for the individual, as over against Buddhism, and it conceives this life as lived with the brethren, not apart from them. On the other hand, it draws a sharp line, as hedonism does not, between good and evil desires, and a sharp line also between the relative goods of the temporal life and the absolute good or

[12] Mark 8:34.
[13] Luke 17:33; cf. Mark 8:35; Matt. 16:25; John 12:25.
[14] Mark 10:44 f.

goods of the Kingdom of God. Evil desires and the pleasures toward which they are directed must be renounced as contrary to the divine will. It may not always be easy to distinguish them from good or indifferent desires and pleasures. On questions of this kind opinions vary. But when the distinction has once been made by the Christian conscience, the obligation is imperative to surrender all purely selfish and evil pleasures. Contrasted with such pleasures are those derived from the relative and permissible goods of life. These goods are essential to our existence. God knows that we have need of them. They have a place in the divine economy. But it is a point of special emphasis with Jesus that they should not be allowed to stand in the way of wholehearted devotion to the Kingdom of God. One must be ready to sacrifice material possessions, family ties, and even life itself, if necessary, in the interest of the Kingdom.[15] Loyalty to it must come first.

It is this primary and supreme obligation to the Kingdom of God that makes self-sacrifice necessary. It does so because the Kingdom is at present in a more or less hostile environment. One might, it is true, think of self-sacrifice as having a necessary place in a developing world free from evil. In that case self-denial would be a kind of pedagogical or gymnastic exercise. But on that basis alone it is hardly probable that there would be adequate ground for such an intensified form of the principle of renunciation as we have in the teaching of Jesus. Certainly, in a morally perfect or perfected world there would be no urgent demand for the exercise of this virtue. The emphasis placed by Jesus upon it belongs to his "interim" ethic. In such a world as this with its animal passions and evil desires, with its exposure to the deceitfulness of riches, and with its many forms of self-aggression the importance of self-sacrifice with its curb on our native selfishness and with its ministry to those in need can hardly be overestimated. It is through self-denial that we rise above the animal plane and assert our true spiritual

---

[15] Luke 14: 26-27, 33; Matt. 10:37-39; Mark 8:34-37.

nature; it is through self-denial that we gain insight into the true values of human life; it is through self-denial that we enter into true fellowship with God. The highest goods of life are thus mediated to us through self-denial. We gain life only through losing it. This is the supreme law of the spiritual life in this world and an essential element in Christian perfection.

Asceticism

The word asceticism is at times used in a general sense as a synonym of renunciation or self-denial. But it also has a more restricted meaning, and it is in this sense that I here use it. Renunciation with Jesus had an ethical purpose. It served as a means of self-discipline. If thy hand or foot offend thee, cut it off; and if thy eye offend thee, pluck it out.[16] It also served as a means of help to others. The rich young ruler was bidden not only to renounce his possessions but also sell them and give to the poor. Renunciation for its own sake had no place in the teaching of Jesus. It must accrue to the good of others, or contribute to one's own redemption, or both. Some worthy end it must have. Pearls are not to be thrown away. They are to be sold and the proceeds used to buy the "pearl of great price."[17]

But another type of renunciation arose in the early church and in the form of monasticism became one of the most significant movements in the history of Christianity. This type of renunciation may be described as metaphysically redemptive by way of contrast with the disciplinary and altruistic type represented in the New Testament. These two types did not exclude each other. They intermingled, but the metaphysically redemptive type was basic in historic monasticism and gave to it its distinctive character. It is this type to which the term asceticism is here applied. The philosophy underlying it was

[16] Mark 9:43-47.

[17] Matt. 13:45.

dualistic. It drew a sharp distinction between body and soul, between matter and spirit, between the world and God. Matter was regarded as inherently evil, and hence the only hope of mankind lay in escape from it. It was not the discipline, the training, of the body with which men were to be primarily concerned, but its ultimate extinction. Their task was not the transformation of the world but flight from it. They were not, therefore, to seek the material goods of life but to emancipate themselves from them so far as possible. They were to mortify the flesh and subdue it by all manner of abstinences and inflictions.

That this ascetic mode of life was foreign to the teaching of Jesus is obvious. He nowhere speaks of the material goods of life as sin and of themselves evil. He looked upon them as divine gifts and urged men not to be unduly anxious about them, for "your heavenly Father knoweth that ye have need of all these things." [18] They were for him included in the divine Providence and so he taught his disciples to pray for their "daily bread," for those material things that are needed to sustain life. He did not require of them the ordinary "fasting" of his day. Indeed, he himself was so free from the traditional abstinences of "holy" men that he was charged with being "a gluttonous man, and a winebibber." [19] The ascetic ideal of life manifestly did not appeal to him. He did, it is true, demand sacrifice of his followers. Self-denial was to be their guiding principle in life as a whole, and this self-denial might include all their earthly possessions and even life itself. But if it did, it would not be because these earthly possessions and life itself were evil. It would be due to the fact that under the particular circumstances that had arisen they stood in the way of a higher good. In the interest of this higher or highest good any sacrifice, even the extremest, might, according to Jesus, be demanded of his followers, as it was of himself. But in such cases the motive would not be ascetic.

[18] Matt. 6:32.
[19] Luke 7:34; Matt. 11:19.

Later, however, under the influence of Gnostic and other dualistic modes of thought Jesus' heroic injunctions came to be interpreted in an ascetic sense; and thus gradually there arose the great Christian monastic movement, which has continued, though modified in important respects, down to the present. It has been said of monasticism that it "is the boldest organized attempt to attain Christian perfection in all the long history of the church." [20] It has also been called "a second Pentecost." But the perfection aimed at was not the same as that of the original Pentecost. The ethical and spiritual element in the latter was not excluded, but there was added to it a metaphysical element that gave to Christian perfection a different cast. It became fundamentally ascetic. Emphasis was now laid on the antithesis between the "Christian" and the "natural" life and on the necessity of as complete an emancipation from the latter as possible. It was this emancipation that was the important thing in the quest after Christian perfection. On the one hand were the world, the flesh, and the Devil. These had to be completely renounced if the Christian ideal of spiritual purity was to be attained. Hence the primary requisites of the perfect Christian life were poverty, chastity, and obedience. Poverty meant renunciation of the world, chastity the renunciation of the flesh, and obedience to God or the church the renunciation of the Devil or of self-will. These different forms of self-abnegation were often carried to extravagant and even revolting extremes in the effort completely to destroy the evil material principle within human nature and to attain to "spiritual" perfection. The perfection thus aimed at was fundamentally metaphysical or religious rather than ethical, and from our modern point of view would be regarded as a pseudo perfection. It consisted in the annihilation of "nature" rather than in its moral transformation.[21]

A radical metaphysical dualism thus lay at the root of

[20] R. Newton Flew, *The Idea of Perfection in Christian Theology*, p. 158.

[21] Cf. H. B. Workman, *The Evolution of the Monastic Ideal*, pp. 50-66.

asceticism and the ascetic misinterpretation of the New Testament teaching. This dualism was out of harmony with a consistent Christian theism, and the ascetic type of perfection to which it gave rise was obviously incapable of universal application. If so applied, it would have led to the extinction of the race. The result was the restriction of the ascetic ideal to a special class of religious devotees and the introduction of a double ethical standard into Christianity, one for the monastic and priestly orders and the other for people in general. Of these two standards the monastic was assumed to be the higher. It was the ideal or perfect standard. But since its realization was necessarily limited to a few, it was evident that it could not be regarded as obligatory upon all. People in general were under obligation to obey the "commandments" but not the "counsels," and in so far as they did this they might in a certain sense be said to be "perfect." They avoided things "contrary to charity" though not all the things "that hinder the act of charity . . . . such as marriage, the occupation of worldly business, and so forth." [22] Perfection has, consequently, been declared to be the common goal of all Christians. The ascetics have one way of attaining it, and people in general another way. The difference, however, is simply one of method; the goal of perfection is the same for all, and this goal is "love and love alone." There is no ascetic perfection distinct from Christian perfection in general.

This is the point of view adopted by Karl Adam and other Roman Catholic apologists in their effort to rescue monastic asceticism from the charge of dualism. There is in principle, they say, no distinction between asceticism and renunciation. Asceticism is simply "the methodical practice of renunciation." It is "the methodical training of the will," "the deliberate methodical exercise of self-control." [23] This holds true not only of asceticism in general but of such extreme forms of it

---

[22] Thomas Aquinas, *Summa Theologica,* II—II, Q. clxxxiv, art. 3.

[23] Karl Adam, *The Spirit of Catholicism,* pp. 202-4.

as celibacy and the other monastic vows. Celibacy is not a war on nature. It implies no reflection on the married state. It is simply a renunciation made by priest and monk that they "may be free for the things of God." "A man," says Karl Adam, "cannot be a good apostle and the father of a family at one and the same time." [24] Celibacy makes possible a more whole-hearted service of God. That is its purpose. It is a means to an end, and so also are the ascetic practices in general required by the church. They have no value in and of themselves. They are not metaphysical redemptive agencies. They are disciplinary and have a purely spiritual function.

In this conception of asceticism we have an attempt to Christianize the monastic movement. At its beginning and for centuries thereafter the movement looked upon the sexual instinct as well-nigh "devilish" and upon the body as itself evil or the source of evil. But such a metaphysic is not in accord with a consistent Christian theism.[25] This became increasingly clear through the centuries. Protestantism, consequently, rejected it; and Roman Catholic writers have been gradually accommodating themselves to the modern point of view by trying to shake monasticism free from its dualistic swaddling clothes. Formally Karl Adam would seem to have succeeded in this by making love, the love of God and man, the sole aim of monastic asceticism and by denying superior virtue to celibacy in and of itself. But despite this formal moralization of monasticism one has the feeling that in the Catholic conception of love to God the old dualistic prejudice still lingers. If it did not, one would have difficulty in understanding why Karl Adam should quote with apparent approval the saying of Schopenhauer that "Protestantism by eliminating asceticism and its central belief in the meritoriousness of celibacy, practically rejected the very core of Christianity, and in that respect Protestantism must be regarded

---

[24] *Ibid.*, p. 204.

[25] Cf. B. P. Bowne, *Theism* (1903); E. S. Brightman, *A Philosophy of Religion* (1940).

as a falling away from Christianity." [26] It is here plainly assumed that celibacy has something more than a pragmatic justification, that it is inherent in the essence of Christianity, and that it implies a more or less dualistic view of human nature. Such importance could hardly be attributed to it if it had no other value than a "methodical training of the will." The very fact that so sharp a distinction is drawn at this point between Protestantism and Catholicism is evidence that a dualistic and nonethical element is still implicit in monastic asceticism.

For Protestanism has no objection to a "methodical practice of renunciation." Such asceticism was characteristic of both Puritanism and Methodism and could hardly be completely divorced from earnest Christianity anywhere. There are naturally differences of opinion as to how far ascetic practices should be carried, but it is generally agreed that they should not be carried so far as to involve a defiance of nature. Dualistic asceticism is alien to the spirit of Christianity. The Christian goal is not the suppression of nature but its moralization. It is "conscious life in the full development of all its normal possibilities"; [27] and only in so far as it contributes to this end is the practice of asceticism or renunciation morally obligatory or justifiable.

Sinlessness

In the two preceding subsections we have considered Christian perfection in its relation to "nature." We now turn to a consideration of its relation to sin. Nature is the raw material of the moral life. It is itself nonmoral and hence is not to be repudiated but moralized and incorporated in the Christian ideal. Sin, on the other hand, is inherently evil and hence can have no place in the Christian moral ideal. Christian perfection in the strict sense of the term excludes it. But different degrees of perfection have been recognized, and this has complicated the problem of sinlessness as well as of perfection. A distinction

[26] *Op. cit.*, pp. 205 f.

[27] Bowne, *Principles of Ethics*, p. 69.

is drawn between the absolute perfection of the life to come and the relative perfection possible in this life. A further distinction is also drawn between a relative perfection that involves freedom from only conscious or voluntary sin and a relative perfection that goes deeper and includes the elimination of indwelling or involuntary sin. The latter view usually assumes the doctrine of "original" sin in some form.

That absolute sinless perfection is impossible of attainment in this life is generally conceded.[28] But with respect to a relative sinless perfection there have been and still are wide differences of opinion. Those who have laid primary stress on original sin and human depravity have usually ruled out altogether the possibility of attaining a sinless state in this life. Sin, they hold, is inherent in human nature. It takes the form of self-love, and this cannot be eliminated so long as we remain in the body. The whole quest after sinless perfection should, therefore, be rejected as based on ignorance and as fanatical; and if the idea of perfection be retained, it should be with a definite qualification. We should say with Augustine that "when we speak of the perfect virtue of the saints, part of this perfection consists in the recognition of our imperfection both in truth and in humility." [29]

But over against this negative attitude toward the attainment of sinlessness in this life stand the teaching of the New Testament and a considerable body of opinion in the subsequent history of the church.[30] Paul seems clearly to conceive of the Christian as one who ought to be free from sin,[31] and the author of Hebrews speaks of our laying aside "every weight, and the sin which doth so easily beset us." [32] John is still more explicit.

[28] Mark 10:18.

[29] Quoted in Calvin, *Institutes* (Eng. trans., 1845), II, 412.

[30] See Flew, *op cit.;* W. B. Pope, *Compendium of Christian Theology,* III, 28-99; H. W. Perkins, *The Doctrine of Perfection; Encyclopaedia of Religion and Ethics,* IX, 728-37.

[31] Rom. 6:2, 6, 11, 14, 22; 8:1-17.

[32] 12:1.

He says that "whosoever is begotten of God doeth no sin, because his seed abideth in him: and he cannot sin, because he is begotten of God." [33] There are, it is true, two verses in which John seems to state the direct contrary.[34] In these verses those are condemned who say, "We have no sin," or "We have not sinned." But the reference here would seem to be not to Christians in general but to persons who denied that they had themselves ever sinned. Otherwise there would be a plain contradiction in the text.

In the later history of the church a long list of distinguished names might be cited in support of the view that a relative sinlessness, a sinlessness not inconsistent with growth, is possible on earth. In this list would be included Justin Martyr, Irenaeus, Clement of Alexandria, Origen, Basil, Thomas Aquinas, George Fox, William Law, John Wesley, and many others.[35] Indeed, the theoretical possibility of attaining a relative sinlessness in this life may be said to have been on the whole the prevailing opinion in the church. Certainly it is most in accord with a consistent freedomism. If we are really free, freedom from sin must be within the reach of our powers when inspired and sustained by the divine grace. Otherwise sin would be necessitated and hence not sin in the ethical sense of the term. Opposition to this view has come chiefly from Lutherans, Calvinists, and other Augustinians, who have held to an extreme doctrine of original sin and denied to "fallen" man real freedom. Sin with them has been conceived as in large part subvolitional. We cannot completely avoid it in this life, and to attempt to do so is fanaticism. Perfection with them has, consequently, become a term of reproach.[36]

But despite this theoretical opposition, supported by the

[33] I John 3:9; cf. I John 1:6 f.; 3:5 f.; 2:4, 6.

[34] I John 1:8, 10.

[35] On perfectionism in Germany and America during the past century see B. B. Warfield, *Studies in Perfectionism,* 2 vols.

[36] Reinhold Niebuhr reflects this attitude. See his Gifford Lectures on *The Nature and Destiny of Man,* esp. Vol. II.

moral sluggishness of human nature, the perfectionist doctrine has been the vital faith of many and the professed belief of a large portion of the Christian Church. Special significance was attributed to the doctrine by Wesley. It has been said of him that he "had almost the same epochal relation to the doctrinal emphasis upon holiness that Luther had to the doctrinal emphasis upon justification by faith, or that Athanasius had to the doctrinal emphasis upon the Deity of our Lord." [37] In this statement there is a measure of truth, and there would have been more if Wesley had defined the doctrine of holiness or perfection more precisely and consistently and had grounded it in the essential nature of Christian experience rather than in a specialized and somewhat dubious phase of it.[38] Fundamentally the doctrine as he expounded it was sound and has had a profound influence on Anglo-Saxon Protestantism, giving to it a pronounced activistic and ethical character. But thus interpreted his perfectionism was not new, nor was it sectarian. It "lies not merely upon the by-paths of Christian theology but upon the high road." [39]

In the discussion of sinlessness as a possible ideal for this life there has been much confusion of thought due to mistaken views of sin. Some under the conscious or unconscious influence of a dualistic philosophy have conceived of sin as a kind of substance or energy that has somehow gained lodgment in the human soul and that must be eradicated if men are to be saved. In so far, therefore, as Christians are truly "saved," it is argued, they must have triumphed over an independent principle of sin by eliminating it from their lives. But this impersonal conception of sin is obviously erroneous. Sin has no existence apart from a free personal agent. As an independent substantial or dynamic principle it is a product of the abstracting and uni-

---

[37] Olin A. Curtis, *The Christian Faith*, p. 373.

[38] For an illuminating criticism and appraisal of the Wesleyan doctrine of perfection, see F. J. McConnell, *John Wesley*, pp. 181-216. Cf. James Mudge, *Growth in Holiness*.

[39] R. N. Flew, *op cit.*, p. 397.

versalizing activity of the human mind and has no metaphysical reality corresponding to it. This conception of sin is an instance of both the fallacy of abstraction and the fallacy of the universal.[40] Sin by its very nature is the attitude or act of a free agent, and as such cannot be literally treated as an external substance or force that has invaded human life and that can or cannot be expelled from it.

Equally erroneous is the atomistic view of sin. According to this view sin consists of individual and independent acts that fail to square with an external standard of right. Sinlessness, consequently, consists simply in the avoidance of such acts. But such a view is clearly too passive, too superficial, too external, and too legalistic. Sin has primarily to do with what man is rather than what he does. It is the motive that determines the moral quality of an act. There is and can be no absolute external standard of right. The moral standard must be found within the mind itself and must itself be the product of an active process. It must be arrived at through an evaluation of all the different factors that enter into the problem of personal responsibility such as environment, heredity, intelligence, strength of will, and the divine grace. The resulting standard is in every case complex and fluid, yet it alone is adequate in dealing with the problem of sin and sinlessness. And the emphasis in applying it must be laid on the abiding elements in the moral life, on its general direction rather than on the individual and separate acts that compose it. Sinlessness for instance, as William Law explained in his famous *Practical Treatise on Christian Perfection,* does not necessarily exclude "falling into anything sinful." It is itself "a habit in our minds," "an inward principle of holiness," which maintains itself in spite of an occasional lapse. A man born of God does not commit sin, as the Apostle John says,[41] but only "in such a sense as a man may be said to do that, which it is his constant care and principle to

---

[40] B. P. Bowne, *The Theory of Thought and Knowledge,* pp. 244-59.

[41] I John 3:9.

prevent being done. . . . . And if he finds himself in any sin, it is his greatest pain and trouble, and he labors after holiness with a double zeal." [42]

The quest after sinlessness is, therefore, not an attempt to get rid of the metaphysical "roots of sin," nor does it require complete compliance with all the detailed requirements of an external standard of absolute purity. It is rather such a whole-hearted devotion to the fundamental Christian principles of love and holiness as will save one from deliberate violations of them. Violations may now and then occur, but where they are few and not of a serious nature, the moral quality of the life is determined by its obedience rather than by its lapses, and in such a case we may speak of a relative sinlessness. Such a sinlessness is a constituent element in the Christian moral ideal.

Self-Realization

In a certain sense Christian perfection may be said to consist in self-realization. Self-renunciation, asceticism, and the quest after sinlessness are means to this end. Each human life has its plan and goal, and the Christian's most comprehensive duty is to realize this plan and goal. The Christian emphasis, however, does not fall on the self but on God. It is not what I do but what God helps me to do that is ultimately decisive. This is the religious as distinguished from the philosophical point of view. As Christians we do not stress *self*-realization so much as realization of the *self,* and the latter we attribute to God. He is the ultimate source of whatever approach we make to the realization of the moral ideal. But we ourselves have a necessary part in it. Paul said, "Work out your own salvation." [43] This is the religious method of expressing the duty of self-realization. Self-realization and salvation mean practically the same thing from the ethical point of view. Both are designations of the moral ideal.

[42] Chap. ii, p. 39.

[43] Phil. 2:12.

The reference to the "self" has the value of bringing out the ideas of individual worth and individual responsibility which lie at the basis of the Christian ethic. There has at times been a tendency toward a pantheistic devaluation of the individual. It has, for instance, been argued that the Christian ought to be willing "to be damned for the glory of God." There has also been a pronounced tendency toward determinism with its disastrous consequences to human freedom and responsibility. Both of these tendencies run counter to the true genius of Christianity. Self-renunciation is not and cannot be the last word in the Christian ethic, as it is in Buddhism. The basal idea is self-realization. Freedom and responsibility are fundamental and essental terms in the Christian ethic. But they do not exclude the need of the divine grace. They rather make a necessary and rational place for it. We may, then, define the Christian ideal as self-realization through self-renunciation and through the aid of the Divine Spirit.

In the quest of the perfect life there are obvious perils. There is, for instance, danger of a one-sided subjectivity, of unhealthy introspection, of dwelling unduly on one's mental states and developing a mystical type of experience that spends itself "gazing at its own navel," as Carlyle once said of Methodism. But while there is this peril, there is a protection against it in the other side of the Christian ethic, in its principle of love. Christian love is objective. It is directed primarily toward God and neighbor. Self-love in the ethical sense of the term is secondary. It is implicit rather than explicit. In this respect the Christian ethic differs from the Greek and Indian ethic. Both Greek and Indian philosophy began with the exhortation to "know the self" or "know thyself." This maxim, one might think, would naturally lead to a pronounced personalism. But actually, as C. C. J. Webb has pointed out,[44] the reverse has often been the case. Emphasis on self-knowledge has been followed by the denial of true reality to the self, as for instance

[44] *Contribution of Christianity to Ethics*, pp. 31-33.

in early Buddhism and in various monistic philosophies. Christianity, on the other hand, while directing attention away from self to God and neighbor, created a new faith in the reality and worth of the self and imparted to the soul a new richness of life. The self was thus saved by losing itself. Self-renunciation became the gateway to self-realization in philosophy as well as in life. This is an interesting and significant fact. Self-realization is a by-product of noble living and thinking. It is not to be directly sought. When this is clearly understood and carried into practice, the peril of a barren and unwholesome subjectivity in the perfectionist movement tends to disappear.

Another and perhaps more serious peril associated with historic perfectionism has been that of spiritual pride. The cure for this evil is to be found in the Christian doctrine of divine grace. When a man stands in a free and vital relation to the Divine Spirit, he takes no credit to himself for his own redemption. But many have interpreted the divine grace in such a way as to deny human freedom in the sense of the power of contrary choice. They have affirmed man's responsibility for sin but denied his ability to avoid it. They have said that in his highest aspirations and noblest achievements he is still a sinner, and that his life is corrupt and sinful "on every level of goodness." From this they have concluded that the quest of the perfect life is a spiritual misadventure, that it is indeed itself an exhibition of sinful pride.

In reply to this contention it is sufficient to point out that the attempted synthesis of subvolitional sin and moral responsibility has and can have no rational basis. This is frankly admitted by its leading advocates, and hence in their dilemma they have fallen back upon theological irrationalism and upon the cult of the paradoxical. But the argumentative jungles into which they have thus been led have gotten them and us nowhere. The fact is that the fundamental confusion of thought implied in their bewildering paradoxes and antinomies is for the most part a gratuitous mystification growing out of their subrational and subethical conceptions of sin and freedom.

Furthermore, it may be noted that their theory of original sin runs so counter to the common moral convictions of men that it leads easily to pious hypocrisy, to public and private confessions of sinfulness that are belied by their own Christian consciousness. Excessive self-humiliation is morally quite as perilous as a mistaken zeal for sinless perfection.

In addition to pride and a one-sided subjectivity there are other evils into which the perfectionist movement has at times lapsed, such as a shallow optimism, an excessive individualism, a morbid introspectionism, and a narrow and fanatical provincialism. Of all these evils, however, it may be said that they have been incidental to the movement as a whole, excrescences, not essential elements in it. True perfectionism is simply a challenge to high moral and spiritual endeavor, an endeavor that persists throughout life, free from enslaving bondage to deterministic theories both theological and naturalistic.

CHAPTER VIII

CHRISTIAN CHARACTER

In the two preceding chapters we have discussed the principles of love and perfection. These principles are fundamental and essential elements in the Christian moral ideal. But they are both general and more or less abstract. Perfection is not a concrete virtue, nor is love in the sense in which it has commonly been used in the history of Christian ethics. Both are general characteristics of the Christian moral ideal rather than concrete expressions or ingredients of it. They are not specific and distinct virtues but principles more or less constitutive of all Christian virtue. They do not themselves make up the content of Christian character; they are rather general descriptions of it.

Character is concrete, and it has been the glory of the Christian ethic from the beginning that it has found its ideal not in abstract principles or virtues but in the character of an historical person. Jesus not only taught us what the moral ideal is; he exemplified it in his own life; he bade us follow him. The result has been that the Christian life has been generally regarded as consisting in the "imitation of Christ" rather than in obedience to general rules and precepts. Jesus himself, his example, has been and is the Christian moral ideal.

The Example of Jesus

There is, however, a question as to how far the life of Jesus can be an example for us, and a question also as to how far the details of his ethical teaching can be authoritative in our day. The difficulties connected with these questions are due mainly to two facts. First, Jesus spoke, not to us, but to the people of his own time. He had in mind the conditions under which they lived and thought, and these conditions were so different from those of our day that his utterances on concrete moral questions cannot be accepted as necessarily final and authoritative for us. Moral rules vary with the changing social, economic, and political life of the community, and their intelligent application to particular cases requires a firsthand acquaintance with the special circumstances of each case. No set of rules or regulations can, therefore, serve as an adequate moral guide for subsequent ages. Every generation must rethink its own moral problems and be in a sense its own lawgiver. No comprehensive body of concrete moral laws can have permanent validity in human life, and any serious attempt to give them such validity would lead to social and moral stagnation.

Jesus recognized this and hence did not formulate a moral code. He said many things of a moral character as occasion suggested, and these scattered sayings have at times been gathered together to serve as a kind of vade mecum. But they do not constitute a systematic and coherent whole. In not a few instances they seem to contradict each other, and at times they are so extreme in form as to seem inconsistent with the existence of organized society. Such sayings as these, it is obvious, must be interpreted in the light of his life and teachings as a whole and in the light of the times in which he lived. He shared, for instance, the apocalyptic hope of his day, and in not a few instances his moral judgments were no doubt colored by this fact. His ethical teaching was in part an "interim" ethic. In any case he did not have in mind the complex social and ethical conditions of the modern world. He spoke and acted as a man of his own day, and this makes it impossible for us to accept either his teaching or his example as an infallible guide in dealing with the concrete problems of our time.

A second reason for the difficulty we have in utilizing the example and teaching of Jesus as a moral guide is the fact that he had a unique mission and that he concentrated his attention on what was central in that mission. He did not touch life at all points. He did not seek to have a universal human experience, one that would make him a master in all the main spheres of human activity, in science and art, in commerce and government. Various problems that seem to us highly important did not apparently receive particular attention from him. Such questions as those of labor and capital, of national policy, of peace and war, and the social problem in general seemed to lie beyond his horizons. At least they did not weigh heavily on his mind. He had little to say about them that seems to us pertinent to the complex social and political situations that confront us. Large areas of our present life seem virtually untouched by his teaching and example. His life seems narrow and circumscribed in its interests as compared with ours. The modern mind, consequently, has difficulty in finding in him an adequate moral pattern. It feels the need of a broader and more universal moral ideal.

The difficulty experienced at this point is due to a failure to recognize the limited respect in which Jesus could be an example to us. He had a mission to which there has been no complete parallel in human history, and this necessarily imposed upon him obligations different from those of people in general. It is not our duty literally to imitate him and in this sense to follow "in his steps." We could not if we would, and we ought not if we could. Such a following of Jesus would be more or less external and would lack the inner motive which, according to Jesus, constitutes the essence of every moral act. We can truly follow him only in so far as his motives have a proper place in our own particular spheres of activity and in so far as they are made our own. It is in his motives alone that Jesus can be a universal and authoritative example, and here it is not so much his specific motives that are normative for us as it is the quality or spirit of his life as a whole. This spirit is not easily definable, but we perhaps come as close as we can to its essential content by identifying it with *agape* in the predominant New Testament meaning of this term. It is not merely love of neighbor but such a love of neighbor as God revealed in Christ. It is a mingling of the human with the divine, an attitude of mind that sees human life from the standpoint of the divine holiness and yet beholds it encompassed by the divine redemptive love. Here it is that we have the authentic and authoritative note in the life of Christ. It cannot be reduced to a code of laws; it cannot be incarnated in human form and photographed; but it can be spiritually discerned in the face of Jesus Christ, and this it is that has made him our perfect example and has given to Christianity its unique moral quality. "The vision of God's holy love," as F. R. Barry puts it, "seen through the windows of Christ's mind and mediated by his Spirit, is the differentia of the Christian ethic."[1]

THE NATURAL LIFE

In seeking further to define the ideal Christian character as exemplified in Christ we need to consider briefly its relation to the natural life and to one's secular calling. This subject has to some extent been anticipated. Jesus, we have pointed out, was not ascetic either in theory or practice. He did not renounce nature in itself as evil. He recognized the legitimacy of life on the natural secular plane. But life on this level represented with him a lower degree of moral potency. It was also obviously to a large extent morally imperfect, and in so far as it was such it could hardly have received his approval. Furthermore, it has been questioned whether so-called natural morality has a place in the Christian ethic and whether the so-called natural virtues are constitutive elements in Christian character.

One influential school of Christian thought has argued that man is by nature so totally sinful or depraved that he can of himself do no good thing. Natural morality, therefore, in so far as it has a purely human origin, is not truly moral. The pagan virtues are "splendid vices."[2] Only such motives and acts as are inspired by the Divine Spirit are truly moral and Christian. All true, or Christian, morality is of grace. It has its source in God rather than man. There is thus a sharp cleavage

[1] *The Relevance of Christianity* (Amer. ed. entitled *Christianity and the New World*), p. 102.

[2] These words were not Augustine's, as is at times assumed, but they come near to expressing his real thought. See *The City of God,* XIX, 25.

between Christian and natural morality, and, strictly speaking, the latter is antithetical to the Christian ethic, not a part of it.

But this antithesis between Christian and natural morality is theological rather than ethical. The divine source and divine norm of Christian morality are treated as its differentiating marks. Natural morality is conceived as having no relation to divine causality or the divine will. The distinction between "Christian" and "natural" is thus one of theological theory. It does not have a direct practical or empirical basis. In actual life the difference between natural and Christian morality has been one of degree rather than of kind. This is attested by the relation of Greek to Christian ethics and indeed by the whole history of ethics.[3] Christian ethics is not in its content wholly new. It is built on the accumulated experience of the past. Natural morality is the foundation and raw material of Christian morality. The latter cannot, therefore, be wholly detached from the common moral sentiments of mankind, nor can Christian character in its perfection be divested of all "natural" virtues. Ideal Christian character is a glorification of the natural, not its negation.

This view has an important bearing on the content of the ideal Christian life. There has always been a tendency to oppose the church to the world, and this tendency has generally been regarded as the authentic expression of Christian piety. To conform to the world is to deny the distinctiveness of Christianity and the uniqueness of its values. The Christian church grew up as a protest against a pagan or worldly mode of life, and all through its history many people both in and out of the church have had the feeling that there ought to be some clearly perceptible difference or differences between the life of the Christian and that of the non-Christian. Emphasis has in the course of the history of the different churches and sects

[3] An extended account of the relation of some of "the great notions of moral philosophy" and some of "the persistent problems of ethics" to the teaching of the New Testament and of Christianity in general will be found in G. F. Barbour, *A Philosophical Study of Christian Ethics* (1911).

been placed on various concrete features of the Christian life, such as creedal profession, church membership, sacramental symbols, ascetic practices, emotional experiences, modes of worship, sabbath observance, and even peculiarities of dress and speech. But these aspects of the Christian life are all obviously too superficial or external to constitute or represent its essential or distinctive nature.

The unique element in Christian character is a thing of the spirit. This does not mean that it has a purely divine source as distinguished from natural morality. It is both divine and human in its metaphysical origin. But it has a distinct quality, a unique ethical flavor, that differentiates it from the non-Christian life. Many factors enter into this unique quality or flavor. But there are three of a fundamental character that may be mentioned. One is living faith in God, the God and Father of our Lord Jesus Christ. This permeates the entire ethical life of the Christian. The second is love in its *agape* form. The third is unswerving devotion to the ideal of moral perfection, to the ideal of purity, truth, and right. This moral earnestness together with a loving regard for others and a devout attitude toward God gives to Christian character its distinctive quality.

Christian character is not, then, simple in its structure. It contains the three general factors just mentioned, and in addition to these it has various specific characteristics or qualities that may be called virtues. What these specific Christian virtues are, is a question on which complete agreement could hardly be expected. We may nevertheless venture to single out six that may be called cardinal Christian virtues.

Before, however, taking these up for discussion, we need to be again reminded that the Christian ethic is not restricted to the virtues which received unique emphasis in the New Testament and in the later history of the church. Christianity appeared on the scene with the Old Testament under its arm. Later it sat at the feet of the Greek philosophers and paid tribute to the Roman Empire. It thus became the heir of the moral ideals of the Hebrews, the Greeks, and the Romans.

It did not renounce the Greek and Roman ideal because it was the work of "nature" rather than grace. It did not look upon grace as "the cuckoo driving the other bird out of the nest," to use one of von Hügel's favorite figures of speech.[4] It saw in the cardinal virtues of the Greeks (wisdom, justice, temperance, and courage) elements of permanent worth. These virtues, more or less transformed, had their place in the Christian ethic. Without them the Christian ethic would have been an incomplete and misleading ideal.

The Hebrew moral ideal was the soil out of which the Christian ideal grew. It had also with Christians a more or less permanent divine sanction and thus served not only as a source of the Christian ethic but as a supplement to it. In other words, it was the background and framework of the ethical teaching of the New Testament without which the latter cannot be correctly or fully understood. The New Testament ethic must be interpreted in the light of the ideals of the Old Testament prophets, priests, and wise men; and these ideals must be regarded as included in the Christian ethic in so far as they were not abrogated by Jesus and his disciples and were not out of harmony with the Christian spirit. The Christian ethic had a great "hinterland," Greek and Roman as well as Hebraic, and much of this hinterland was part and parcel of Christian moral teaching. But here our main concern is not with the ethical inheritance of Christianity nor with the "natural" moral convictions contained or implied in it but with those virtues which are more or less distinctively Christian.

The Christian Virtues

In the New Testament there are several lists of the Christian virtues. In Galatians 5:22-23 the list is: "love, joy, peace, longsuffering, kindness, goodness, faithfulness, meekness, self-control." In Colossians 3:12-13 the list consists of "compassion, kindness, lowliness, meekness, longsuffering; forbearing one

[4] Flew, *op. cit.*, p. 149.

another, and forgiving each other." In II Peter 1:5-7 the list comprises faith, virtue, knowledge, self-control, patience, godliness, brotherly kindness, love. And in Philippians 4:8 there is another list of a somewhat more general character made up of "whatsoever things are honorable, whatsoever things are just, whatsoever things are pure, whatsoever things are lovely, whatsoever things are of good report." In addition to these lists of virtues the description of love in I Cor. 13:4-7 may be noted: "Love suffereth long, and is kind; love envieth not; love vaunteth not itself, is not puffed up, doth not behave itself unseemly, seeketh not its own, is not provoked, taketh not account of evil; rejoiceth not in unrighteousness, but rejoiceth with the truth; beareth all things, believeth all things, hopeth all things, endureth all things." We may also in this connection direct attention to Matthew 5:3-10, where blessing is pronounced on the poor in spirit, on the meek, on those that hunger and thirst after righteousness, on the merciful, on the pure in heart, on the peacemakers, on those that have been persecuted for righteousness' sake.

In looking over the foregoing passages from the New Testament it should be observed that there are direct references to three of the cardinal virtues of the Greeks: "self-control," or temperance; "knowledge," or wisdom; and "things" that "are just," or justice. Indirectly there may also be a reference to courage in the blessing pronounced on those who are persecuted for righteousness' sake and in what is said of things "honorable" and "of good report." But the emphasis manifestly falls on virtues of a somewhat different type: love, purity, humility, patience, fidelity, and hope. These I have called the cardinal Christian virtues, not because they were lacking among the pre-Christian Hebrews and other peoples, but because in their Christian context they had a unique significance and flavor and in large part brought about that "transvaluation of all ancient values" to which Nietzsche referred.

Love properly comes first among the cardinal Christian virtues. We have devoted an entire chapter to the fundamental principle of love and its various interpretations. Here we deal with love in the narrower ethical sense of *brotherly love*. It is doubtful if love in this sense can be completely detached from love to God. If it were, it would rest in the last resort on feeling, not on principle; and feelings are variable. What love to God does to brotherly love is to give to it the note of authority. It transforms the feeling of benevolence into an obligatory principle. The principle may generate anew the feeling of benevolence, but it abides through the changes of affection and sympathy and is thus the basal element in love. Love to God and love to neighbor go together. But their union, as C. C. J. Webb says, is "an intimate association of two principles, not the idle repetition of the same principle twice over." [5] Love to God means love to man, but it means something more, and this additional "something" gives to brotherly love a religious overtone, an authoritative note of immense ethical significance.[6] This is evident in early Christian teaching. It was the First Commandment that gave to the Second its fundamental place in the Christian ethic; and through its emphasis on the bond of union between them Christianity made one of its most important contributions to general ethics. Another contribution of equal, if not greater, importance was the extension of the duty of love beyond its earlier national and racial limits to include all men. This was impressively taught in the Parable of the Good Samaritan. There was, it is true, a universalistic element in the Stoic ethic. But it was based on the participation of all men in a common reason, which was a far less stirring and moving conception than that of a universal need and experience of redemption such as formed the basis of the Christian doctrine of the brotherhood of man.

A further point to be noted in this connection is the command of Jesus that we love our enemies. In this command the idea of neighbor is extended so as to include not only those

---

[5] *Op. cit.*, p. 75.

[6] For the contrary view see Nicolai Hartmann, *Ethics*, II, 267.

separated from us by race and nationality but also those separated from us by the deeper cleavage of personal hostility. This extension of neighborhood is one of the most remarkable things in the ethical teaching of Jesus. Rudolf Eucken saw in it the emergence of a new order of things, an order in which the grace of love was to supplant the ideal of justice based on merit.[7] To love one's enemies is to be actuated by the motive of forgiving grace, not of desert. But such love is not to be understood as a feeling of affection. Feelings cannot be commanded. Loving one's enemies means treating them as though they were our friends. Out of such conduct there may arise an altered feeling toward them. But the essential thing in love of one's enemies is practical good will. In this respect the teaching of Jesus differed from that of the Stoics who encouraged an attitude of indifference toward attacks made upon oneself by others. It called for a positive attitude of benevolence.

As love is the fundamental value of the Christian ethic, so justice was the fundamental value of the ancient Greek ethic. This gave to the Christian ethic a distinct superiority, in so far as universal brotherly love represents a higher moral level than justice. From this, however, we are not to infer that Christian love is independent of justice and might exist without it. Justice is implied in Christian love. If we interpret it as regard for the rights of others, it is simply the negative side of love. If, on the other hand, we understand by it retribution or requital, it is a constituent element in Christian love. For without it love would lose its moral character. What gives to love its superiority over justice is its personal warmth and intimacy, its positive good will, and its redemptive spirit.

Next to the Christian virtue of brotherly love we put *purity*. By purity we mean not so much freedom from the sins of the flesh as sincerity and truthfulness. We might, indeed, define purity as the sincere love of the truth. The pure in heart are those who have no place in their hearts for hypocrisy or false-

[7] *The Truth of Religion*, pp. 391-400.

hood or evil desires. Purity is thus a more subjective and individual virtue than brotherly love. It stands closely related to the Christian principle of perfection, to which we devoted the entire preceding chapter. Perfection is a thing of the spirit, a quality of the inner man. No act can be morally perfect that is not inwardly pure, that is not free "from every admixture of what is false." [8] This, as we have previously emphasized, was one of the fundamental elements in the ethical teaching of Jesus. The true Christian, to quote again the words of Justin Martyr, "will not live with lies." His yea is yea, and his nay is nay. This purity of heart, according to N. Hartmann, was "the primal Christian virtue," more basic and original even than brotherly love.[9]

The third in our list of cardinal Christian virtues is *humility.* Some assign it first place. Said Calvin:

> I have always been exceedingly pleased with this observation of Chrysostom, that humility is the foundation of our philosophy; but still more with this of Augustine, "As a rhetorician," says he, "on being interrogated what was the first thing in the rules of eloquence, replied 'Pronunciation,' and on being separately interrogated what was the second and what was the third, gave the same reply; so should anyone interrogate me concerning the rules of the Christian religion the first, second, and third, I would always reply. 'Humility'." [10]

But humility in this Augustinian and Calvinistic sense is a religious rather than an ethical attitude of mind. It has to do with our relation to God. In the presence of his greatness and goodness we as Christians have properly a deep sense of humility. No matter how completely we may have fulfilled the duties devolving upon us, we still feel ourselves to be "unprofitable servants." And the more extreme our theory of man's impotence and need of the divine grace is, the more inevitable and the

[8] Cf. I Tim. 1:5; II Tim. 2:22.

[9] *Ethics,* II, 212 f.

[10] *Institutes of the Christian Religion,* Book II, chap. ii.

more profound is likely to be our feeling of humility and of absolute dependence upon God.

But Christian humility is not confined to the religious field. Jesus also emphasizes its importance in our relation to our fellow men.[11] Pride and arrogance toward others he condemns as the cardinal sin. Such an attitude cuts one off from one's fellow men and makes it impossible for one to help and serve them. It blinds him to their needs and, as in the case of the Pharisees, tends to pervert his attitude toward God also. "The gaze of the haughty man is directed downward, that of the modest man upward." [12] It was this fact that led Jesus to put such insistent, and what at times may seem like excessive, emphasis on humility or modesty. He was confronted in the Pharisaic movement with a type of arrogance that manifested itself even in piety, and against this his whole nature, religious as well as ethical, revolted. So again and again he expressed himself in praise of humility. "Whosoever . . . . shall humble himself as this little child, the same is the greatest in the kingdom of heaven." "For everyone that exalteth himself shall be humbled; but he that humbleth himself shall be exalted." [13] It is, however, to be noted, that abasement and shame are regarded by Jesus as themselves evil. "Exaltation," not directly sought, is itself a good. To enjoy the respect of others, and to respect oneself is a legitimate object of human desire and endeavor. There is nothing in such desire or endeavor that is inconsistent with Christian humility. Indeed, true humility with Jesus was "only the other side of a lofty self-respect." [14] Respect for oneself, he held, would prevent, self-assertiveness and haughtiness of spirit. For the latter implies a false estimate of oneself and is liable to lead to humiliation and the loss of true self-respect. What we all desire, and legitimately desire, is "to enjoy the feeling of our worth as persons among other persons." [15]

---

[11] Luke 14:8-11; Matt. 18:4; 23:12.
[12] N. Hartmann, *op. cit.,* II, 299.
[13] Matt. 18:4; Luke 18:14.
[14] E. F. Scott, *The Ethical Teaching of Jesus,* p. 104.
[15] Whiting Williams, *Mainsprings of Men,* p. 147.

There are two dangers in the quest after humility. One is that of becoming proud of one's own humility and thus falling into what Ritschl calls an "arrogant humility," which is obviously self-contradictory.[16] The other is the danger of an ascetic misconstrutcion of humility. It has, for instance, been said that "humility is the eye which sees everything except itself." [17] It has also been said that "when humility says 'I am here,' it is gone." [18] Such sayings as these may have value as correctives of a priggish humility, but taken literally they exclude that consciousness of self and of self-integrity which lies at the basis of moral personality. True humility is not blind to its own existence or to its own moral worth. It simply rules out a false or self-centered pride. There is a true pride or self-respect which is humble because it acknowledges the activity of the divine grace in all human worth.

Closely related to humility is *patience,* the fourth in our list of cardinal Christian virtues. Both of these virtues have a religious background. Humility grows out of the belief in the greatness and holiness of God, and excludes the tendency toward self-complacency which was more or less characteristic of Jewish as well as Greek and pagan ethics in general. Patience, on the other hand, has its source in the belief in the divine goodness or providence. If we believe in the guiding hand of God, it is not only possible, it is our duty, to be patient in the midst of the most untoward circumstances of human life. This is a fundamental characteristic of Christian piety. But the patience thus required of the Christian is a patience toward God. It is "that submission of spirit which gladly accepts the will of God, and which waits on in sure and certain hope that life 'means intensely and means good.'" [19] As such a submissive spirit, it saves us from fatalism and despair, on the one hand,

---

[16] *Justificatio*[illegible] *nd Reconciliation,* p. 540.

[17] Quoted *ibid.,* p. 695.

[18] Quoted by R. N. Flew, *op. cit.,* p. 384.

[19] *Enc. Rel. and Eth.* IX, 675.

and from a futile resentment, on the other. It creates within us a spirit of cheerfulness and serenity.

These, however, are the results of patience toward God rather than toward men. No doubt a patient and submissive attitude toward the divine providence in general may at times require a similar attitude toward evils suffered at the hands of men. In the New Testament no sharp distinction is made between these two kinds of patience.[20] But it is obvious that patience in the presence of human injustice becomes an absolute duty only when required by the divine will. To endure evil without resistance and to permit others so to do may easily cease to be a virtue. Passive endurance of suffering may, it is true, at times be necessary and may call for a high degree of courage. Such courage is an outstanding virtue in the New Testament. "Fear not," may be said to be its "very watchword." [21] Faithfulness unto death is its clarion call to all Christian believers in the face of persecution.[22] But passive submission to wrong done both to others and oneself may become an ally of tyranny. This not only has frequently occurred but has been such an enduring phase of human history that Edwin Markham has justly spoken of "the long, long patience of the plundered poor"—a thing, he says, "more awful and obscure" than the starry heaven and the moral law that filled the mind of Kant with wonder and with awe. Facts of this nature make it evident that Christian patience has its limitations. It does not necessarily exclude the resort to force and to social or political revolution. But while under the unjust and troubled conditions of human life circumstances may and do arise when patience ceases to be a virtue, it is still true that in the common and normal relations of life patience is what Chrysostom called it, "the queen of the virtues." Nothing does more to smooth over the ruffled surface of life, to pro-

---

[20] Luke 8:15; Rom. 2:7; 8:25; II Cor. 6:4; I Thess. 1:3; I Tim. 6:11; Heb. 10:36; James 1:3 f.; Rev. 1:9.

[21] Matt. 10:26, 31; Luke 5:10; 8:50; 12:7, 32.

[22] Rev. 2:10.

mote peace, to give the other virtues an opportunity to assert themselves, to transform untoward circumstances into stepping stones to nobler living, to encourage activities that make for social and spiritual progress, and to create conditions under which life neither "jars nor jolts but glides."

Fidelity is the fifth trait of Christian character which we have classed among the cardinal Christian virtues. It is closely related to purity and brotherly love, differing from them chiefly in its object. As purity is devotion to inward holiness and truth and as brotherly love is devotion to one's neighbors, so fidelity is devotion to one's God-given tasks. These tasks are committed to our care. We are appointed stewards over them. As such we owe God unlimited service. But it is not the service we render, it is not the work we do, that he most values. What he regards as most important is the attitude of will that leads one to perform one's duties. Fidelity, to be sure, does fit one for larger responsibilities.[23] It increases one's moral worth.[24] But it is not these contributions to richness of life and character that God most prizes. It is fidelity itself.

For fidelity does not consist in merely keeping one's promises and agreements. It has to do with one's disposition, with one's moral self-identity. If one is unfaithful to his tasks, if one changes lightly his loves, loyalties, and friendships, one destroys the continuity of his own being. It is only through sustained devotion to one's work and to others that one conserves his own personality. It is fidelity that constitutes the very fiber of one's moral character. Without it the moral self disintegrates. It is, therefore, in keeping with the profound insight and moral depth of the Christian ethic that special prominence is given to the virtue of fidelity, or faithfulness.

To the five cardinal Christian virtues already considered we may add another, that of *hope*. Joy and peace are also characteristic traits of Christian character and might be treated

---

[23] Matt. 25:21.

[24] Luke 16:10.

as additional cardinal virtues. But they may be regarded as fruits of hope and hence included in it. We are saved, says Paul by hope.[25] Hope generates peace and joy and other qualities of the redeemed life. It is placed by Paul alongside of faith and love as one of the three Christian graces;[26] and in I Peter[27] so much emphasis is laid upon it that Peter is called the Apostle of Hope as John is called the Apostle of Love and Paul the Apostle of Faith.

Christian hope was at first predominantly eschatological. It had to do with the life to come, but its radiance was shed over the present life also; and this has continued to be more or less the case throughout the whole of Christian history. It has been said that "perhaps the chief differentiation of Paul from the men and women of today is in the high place he assigns to hope. If we were making a list for ourselves, it would hardly occur to any of us to include this quality in it."[28] This statement, however, seems to me rather extreme. It hardly does justice to modern Christian optimism. The eschatological hope was no doubt more vivid in early Christianity than with us, and there was also a more confident expectation and a more common and assured realization of the divine aid in the moral struggle of life. But, on the other hand, the intramundane hope of an improved social order is much stronger with us than with Paul, and the modern Christian is also less burdened than the early Christian with a more or less fatalistic conception of sin as an objective and impersonal power. There are thus special forms or sources of optimism in modern as well as ancient Christianity. And when we compare the Christian spirit of today with the fundamental pessimism of the current materialistic or naturalistic world view, it can hardly be denied that hope still runs strong in the Christian church and that optimism is still an outstanding characteristic of the Christian

[25] Rom. 8:24.
[26] I Cor. 13:13.
[27] 1:3-5, 9, 13, 21; 3:5, 15.
[28] Flew, *op. cit.*, p. 66.

ethic. This ethical characteristic of Christianity not only gives peace and joy to the individual soul; it also imparts a new dynamic to the upward striving of mankind. Both society and the individual are thus being redeemed in our time, as in the past, by Christian hope.

A character constituted by the foregoing virtues—brotherly love, purity, humility, patience, fidelity, hope—is distinctively Christian in the sense that these virtues received in Christianity a new emphasis and a new interpretation. They were not unknown among the Greeks and Romans; no civilized society could exist without them. But the primary importance attributed to them by Jesus and his disciples was an essential factor in bringing about what Friedrich Paulsen has called "the greatest revolution which European humanity experienced." Indeed, in all human history, he says, there has been no occurrence "more astonishing than the conversion of the old world to Christianity." [29]

This conversion, it is true, was fundamentally religious. But Christianity is an ethical religion, and it was this fact that gave to the conversion of the Roman Empire its revolutionary significance in the history of Europe and of the world. As compared with the cardinal virtues of the Greeks, the cardinal Christian virtues, which we have briefly defined and discussed, had several distinctive characteristics. First, they were personal rather than civic virtues. Second, they were ethical in the narrower sense of the term: the good at which they aimed was righteousness, not the harmony or symmetry of man's natural capacities. Their goal was not beauty but the beauty of holiness. Third, they were less intellectualistic and more democratic than the Greek virtues. They laid more stress on love than on knowledge and were more completely within the reach of simple folk. Fourth, they were based on a transcendental instead of a humanistic ideal. They found their norm in the character of God rather than in the needs of civilization. The

[29] *A System of Ethics,* pp. 65, 98.

summum bonum toward which they were directed was divine sonship, not "the perfection of man as a natural being." Human life thus took on a sanctity, and the moral law a divine authority and a universal humane quality, that it had not had before. The individual and his place in the eternal Kingdom of God became the center of interest. A profound personalism supplanted the earlier statolatry. The divine grace overshadowed all earthly goods.

In view of these radical changes of emphasis it is not strange that early Christianity seemed to many by its very nature hostile to the world, hostile to its pleasures, to its wealth, to its culture, to its governmental machinery. Tertullian declared that nothing was "more foreign" to Christians than public affairs, and that the existence of "Christian emperors" was a contradiction in terms.[30] According to Ambrose, "not only wanton jests but all jests" were to be avoided by Christians.[31] Paul looked askance at "the wisdom of this world." Numerous illustrations of these anti-intellectual, antipolitical, and antinatural tendencies in the early church might be given. But that they did not represent the true genius of early Christianity is evident from later history. New Testament Christianity, as we have previously emphasized, was not ascetic. There was in it a genuine appreciation of the natural goods of life. This was implied in its doctrine of creation. And in later times it manifested itself in an active interest in politics, culture, and economic affairs. The church became a worldly power. It was inevitable that it should become such if it were to fulfill its function in the world. And with this change came a broadening of the Christian ethic. The natural virtues such as patriotism, courage, justice, economic prudence, and love of learning and art were no longer viewed as "splended vices" or as alien to the Christian spirit. They were incorporated in the Christian ethics, not as distinctly Christian virtues, but as factors in that compre-

---

[30] *Apologeticus* xxxviii. xxi.

[31] *On the Duties of Ministers* i. 23.

hensive Christian moral ideal without which both the church and the individual Christian would be unable to fulfill their divinely appointed mission in the world. This mission is not conformity to the world but transformation of it. An ideal good to be achieved in the midst of a resisting environment is the ethical bond of union between ancient Christian dualism and the modern personalistic doctrine of the divine immanence.

PART IV

PRACTICAL APPLICATION

CHAPTER IX

THE INDIVIDUAL

THUS far we have been primarily concerned with the theory of Christian ethics. We have considered its province, its presuppositions, and its moral ideal. Some account has been taken of the history of Christian morality, of the example of Jesus, of the relation of Christian to "natural" morality, and of the distinctive elements in Christian character. But the discussion has for the most part been general and more or less abstract. It has dealt with principles rather than with their application to concrete conditions. To the latter problem we now turn; and we begin with the life of the individual.

Under the ethics of the individual we include not only duties to self but also such duties to others as are involved in their rights as individuals. These duties and rights would exist in a state of social chaos. We are obligated to others as individual human beings, regardless of any social ties that may bind us to them. And these obligations, as well as those to ourselves, may be regarded as belonging to individual, as distinguished from social ethics.

There is, however, no hard and fast distinction between individual and social ethics. No one exists wholly for himself, and no society exists merely for itself as a social group. Duties to self, as well as duties to other men viewed as mere individuals, have to some extent social implications; and duties commonly described as social have more or less significance for the individual. The difference is one of degree, but the difference of degree is in general so clearly marked that the distinction between individual and social ethics has been commonly recognized both in philosophical and theological ethics.

Duties to Self

Attempts, as we have seen, have been made by some philosophical and theological moralists to reduce the moral life to duties to others. Duties to self, it is said, such as eating, drinking and making provision for the future, are natural. They fulfill themselves and have no real ethical quality. Only duties to others require spiritual initiative and are truly moral. But this distinction between self-regarding duties as natural or in a sense automatic, on the one hand, and altruistic duties as alone moral, on the other hand, cannot be consistently maintained. For even elementary physical duties, such as those mentioned, require guidance and self-control. Freedom and responsibility are involved in them as truly as in duties to others. And this is still more true of the higher egoistic duties involved in self-realization. Indeed, one is more directly and completely responsible for himself, for the development of his own character and ability, than he is for anyone else. In this respect duties to self have the primacy over duties to others. If one is to be sacred in the eyes of others, he much be sacred in his own eyes, and this sanctity must condition his obligations to others. Each one must respect the ideal of humanity in himself if he is to respect it in others.

Morality is not exhausted in altruism. The law of good will, as already made clear, must be supplemented by the ideal of humanity before there can be a truly moral life. Ethical responsibility cannot, therefore, be reduced to duties to others. A rational ethics must recognize duties to self.

But there are some theologians, as we have noted, who at this point draw a sharp distinction between rational or philosophical ethics and Christian ethics, and who deny that self-regarding duties have any place in the latter. According to their theory, the Christian ethic is purely an ethic of grace. It allows no place for self-realization. It looks upon everything that is good within us as the gift of God. We do not attain it through any effort of our own. The love of God is the source of it. And as the divine love is spontaneous and unmotivated, so our love must be if it is to be truly Christian. There is in the Christian ethic no place for self-love nor for duties to self. The self has no independent worth and no independent moral initiative. God loves us, not because we are worthy of it, but because he is himself love and his love is unmotivated. He loves us even though we are sinners; and in a similar way, if we are Christians, we must love others. Only such love is Christian love. Self-love is not Christian.

Love, however, which is thus detached from the idea of worth and from the idea of duties to self has ceased to be love in the moral sense of the term. If there is no worth in ourselves or in others, which imposes obligations upon us, it is clear that love in the latter as well as the former case has no moral or rational basis. It was insight into this fact that led Augustine to base both the love of self and the love of others on the presence of God in the human heart. Self-love, as he conceived it, means loving God in ourselves, and the love of others means loving God in them. In other words, it is the divine sanctity of the human soul that imposes the obligation of love upon us, and this obligation applies to ourselves as well as to others.

Theological grounds for rejecting duties to self as nonmoral are, therefore, no more valid than philosophical ones. Neither the doctrine of divine grace nor the law of good will excludes such duties. Rather do they both assume them. Indeed, they are founded upon them, and upon the underlying idea of the sacredness of the individual soul. Without the sacredness of the individual and the duty of guarding it the divine grace would lose its meaning and the law of good will would cease to be a universal moral imperative.

Duties and Rights

There are, then, duties to self as well as duties to others. The latter presuppose the former. In both senses of the term duties imply rights. The duties I owe myself are rights as over against others, and the duties I owe others are their rights as over against me. Rights and duties are thus opposite sides of the moral relation binding two or more persons together. This relation involves both obligations to, and claims upon, others, and is itself rooted in human nature.

As duties to self have been denied by some moralists, so also has it been with natural rights. The individual, it is said, has no such rights in the ethical sense of the term. The only right recognized by nature is might. Men in their natural state are at war with each other. The only law they recognize is the law of the stronger, and this law is obviously devoid of ethical quality. It rests on might, not on right. The natural man has then no rights. Such "rights" as are accorded him have their source in positive law. Society, not nature, creates them. "Apart from society, rights are only a question of power; within society they are what society enforces or permits."[1] The latter view, however, does not differ in principle from the former. It simply substitutes the power of society for that of the individual, and thus is equally fatal to the ethical doctrine of rights. Society, it is true, establishes many rights and determines to a large extent the particular form and measure of rights in general. But the fundamental rights of men are inherent in the moral nature. Society does not create them, but finds them, and has the special task of developing and defending them.

Some take a negative attitude toward the ethical doctrine of natural rights on theological grounds.[2] Rights they say have no place in the Christian ethic of love. From the Christian standpoint life and its most precious possessions are all the gracious gifts of God—they are not rights. We cannot call them

[1] So Hobbes and Spinoza. Cf. Bowne, *Principles of Ethics,* p.215.

[2] Cf. Brunner, *The Divine Imperative,* p. 691.

our own. But if this be true in an absolute sense, there is no moral order. Duties vanish as well as rights. The only way in which the idea of a moral universe can be maintained is by ascribing moral responsibility to God and a limited independence to man. As Creator of the world, God is a responsible Being, and we his creatures have rights over against him as well as duties to him. The failure to see this is due to a one-sided and exaggerated conception of the divine grace, a conception that is excluded by the fact of human freedom. Duties both to self and to others imply rights, and rights imply duties. Without both there could be no self-consistent ethic either Christian or non-Christian.[3]

It is customary to distinguish two fundamental duties to self: the duty of self-preservation and the duty of self-realization. Corresponding to these duties or implied in them are various fundamental rights, such as the right to life and the right to self-defense, the right to freedom, the right to the truth, and the right to property. These different rights and duties we shall now briefly consider. They are the main topics commonly comprised under individual ethics.

Self-Preservation and Self-Realization

By the duty of self-preservation is meant the obligation to take such care of oneself as may be necessary to maintain the proper functioning of body and mind. This functioning has a value in and of itself. But from the Christian standpoint it also serves a higher purpose. The body does not exist for its own sake. It is the "temple of the Holy Spirit."[4] It is a means to a divine end. And so it is with our life as a whole. We are not our own. We have a divine mission. This gives a new sanctity

---

[3] This, however, does not exclude as nonobligatory acts of grace, both human and divine, which the recipients of these favors do not and ought not claim as their rights. Duties and rights are reciprocal, but not so the recognition of the former and the claim of the latter. "The complete and proper fulfillment of the law is to listen to and obey the demands of grace." A. D. Lindsay, *The Two Moralities* (1940), p. 94.

[4] I Cor. 6:19.

to life and invests the duty of self-preservation with a spiritual motive. We are obligated to avoid vice and to practice virtue, not simply because one is injurious and the other conducive to a healthful vigorous life, but because such a life is essential to the performance of our divinely appointed task in the world. There is thus a theistic as well as a naturalistic basis for the obligation to preserve the integrity of one's own being and to maintain it at its full strength and efficiency. The theistic basis, it is obvious, greatly accentuates the obligation. And the obligation is also strengthened by its social importance. But apart from its altruistic and theistic basis the duty of self-preservation has its own independent ground. This ground is found in the intrinsic value of personality. If the self is an end in itself, there is a manifest duty on each one's part to do all that he can to preserve it in the unity and totality of its being.

But preservation is not the only duty we owe ourselves. We are growing and developing beings. There is a goal set before us which can be realized only through deliberate effort, and to realize this goal is the chief task of all high moral endeavor. The goal is in part physical; but it is primarily intellectual, moral, aesthetic, and religious. It is the realization in the individual life of as much as possible of the highest good. Not to seek this human ideal but to treat it as an idle dream and to acquiesce in admitted imperfection is perhaps the chief and most common sin against oneself.

In connection with the duty of self-realization there are four historic problems that may be briefly considered. One has to do with the Christian's "calling." This term has had various meanings, and several stages in its development may be noted.[5] In the New Testament it was used in an almost exclusively religious sense and referred to the divine call of the Christian to eternal salvation.[6] The only exception to this spiritual use of

[5] See essay by Karl Holl on *"Die Geschichte des Wortes Beruf"* in his *Gesammelte Aufsätze zur Kirchengeschichte,* III, 189-219.

[6] Rom. 11:29; Phil. 3:14; II Thess. 1:11; Eph. 1:18; 4:1; II Tim. 1:9; II Pet. 1:10.

the term is in I Cor. 7:20, where it means one's earthly calling or station in life. This use of it by Paul, however, had no appreciable influence in the early church. A divine summons to a supramundane hope was the prevailing idea expressed by the term in early Christianity; and this interpretation of it was based on a charismatic experience, an actual inner calling or *klesis* of the Christian. But this experience became less and less common as the church grew in numbers, and with the establishment of infant baptism tended to disappear altogether as a presupposition of the Christian life. One was now born into the church; he did not enter it as the result of a conscious divine call and a personal decision.

The idea of a Christian "calling," however, was so deeply imbedded in the tradition and faith of the church that it could not be wholly allowed to lapse. In the common religious experience of ecclesiastical Christianity there was little basis for it, but in monastic Christianity it came to life again. The monk had a divine call, a call to perfection, a call to fulfill completely the command of Christ, especially the command to love God. This marked a decisive stage in his experience. It was comparable to the call of Abraham;[7] it was a "conversion," a "second" or "new baptism," and particularly a summons to a special mode of life, which henceforth came to be known in a distinctive sense as a "calling" or "vocation." People engaged in manual or other forms of secular work might be regarded as rendering a divinely appointed service, but they had no "calling" or "vocation" in the proper sense of the term. This was the medieval point of view. Against it there was, it is true, a reaction on the part of some mystics, such as Eckhart and Tauler. These men recognized a divine "call" that comes to men entirely independently of their relation to the monastic orders. They also emphasized the religious value of the common daily tasks and thus introduced into popular speech the idea of

[7] Gen. 12:1 ff.

an "earthly calling." This marked a distinct advance. But a privileged position was still accorded the ascetic and contemplative type of life. And in the ordinary relations of men to each other it was the passive rather than the active virtues that were as a rule most highly commended.

The decisive break with the monastic conception of the Christian's calling came with Luther.[8] He and Calvin completely transformed the meaning and application of the word "calling" or "vocation." Heretofore the German *Beruf* and the Latin *vocatio* had been appropriated by the monastic orders as their peculiar possession. Only monasticism had a *Beruf*. This Luther reversed. It was just monasticism, he affirmed, that had no *Beruf*. The true calling of God was to be realized in the workaday world. This revolutionary change, as we have previously pointed out, was based on the doctrine of the universal priesthood of believers and on the doctrine of the sanctity of the common life. Its moral influence, both immediate and remote, was not all that might have been expected, but as an ideal its importance could hardly be exaggerated.

It has been objected that the Protestant conception of vocation has to a large extent lost its meaning in the modern world because of the declining belief in God, because of the extreme division of labor, because of the complex and fluctuating conditions in our industrial life, and because of the widespread unemployment. That these altered circumstances have seriously affected the popular use and influence of the religious conception of vocation can hardly be questioned.[9] But for the thoughtful Christian believer the conception seems to me to be about as significant as ever. It is not or should not be restricted to one's profession or trade or other line of economic activity. It has a broader meaning. It includes the sum total of one's concrete duties. What these duties are may be somewhat more difficult to determine at present than under simpler

[8] Cf. Max Weber, *The Protestant Ethic and the Spirit of Capitalism*, pp. 79-92.

[9] For a fresh and informing study of the subject see R. L. Calhoun, *God and the Common Life*, pp. 24-72.

social conditions, but the principles that underlie them remain much the same. It is their utility, their value to ourselves and to society, and our ability to perform them, that enable us to decide whether they are really our duties and as such belong to our vocation. And these are questions that each one must answer for himself in the light of the concrete situation that confronts him and in the light of what he believes to be the divine purpose in his own life. The obligation to do so is as real and as urgent today as it ever was. And in this connection the basal thing still to remember is that the true Christian vocation is not to be found in asceticism but in the moralization of the natural life. Not through antagonism to nature but through elevating nature to the moral or spiritual plane can man realize his true self.[10]

In the process of self-realization every one is confronted at times with what is called a "conflict of duties." Love, for instance, seems to require a different course of action from that required by justice or truth. But in such cases it is a mistake to suppose that these abstract principles impose duties upon us regardless of the concrete situation. In every situation calling for a single line of conduct there can be but one duty. What that duty is may not be clear. The general principles of love, justice, and truth may help us in coming to a decision. But they do not themselves impose conflicting duties upon us. There can be no duty in the subjective sense of the term apart from our own moral conviction. In each case we weigh the evidence for ourselves and decide what our duty is. There is, therefore, strictly speaking, no conflict of duties in such instances, but simply conflicting evidence as to what our duty is under the particular circumstances.

Another historic problem related to the subject of self-

---

[10] There is a notable essay on "My Station and Its Duties" by F. H. Bradley in his *Ethical Studies*, pp. 160-206. A. D. Lindsay, *Two Moralities*, utilizes the title of this essay, distinguishing this type of morality from the morality of grace or perfection (Matt. 5:34-42) and discussing their relation to each other in a very clear and convincing manner. Hegel's *Philosophy of Right* is the greatest treatise on the morality of "mv station" from the standpoint of general ethics.

realization is the question as to works of supererogation. Can we do more than duty requires of us? The answer is dependent on one's conception of the standard of duty and of the nature of the divine grace. If we hold to an absolute standard of duty, it is clear that we cannot transcend its requirements. In that case duty embraces the highest demands of the moral nature. If one has done his full duty, he has fulfilled the whole moral law. Nothing beyond it is morally possible. But if we accept a relative standard of duty, a standard fixed by social convention or by the "commandments" of God as distinguished from his "counsels" of perfection, it is obvious that the performance of duty can be transcended. We can exceed the requirements of the moral law and thus acquire excess merit. This is the teaching of the Roman Catholic Church, as commonly understood. But in the acquisition of this merit and of merit in general we are dependent upon the divine grace. The dependence, however, is not absolute. We have a measure of freedom and must co-operate with the divine grace if our acts are to be truly ours as well as meritorious. This applies both to our common duties and to works of supererogation.

Protestants have for the most part rejected the idea of supererogation. Some have done so because they have been strict *monergists* as opposed to *synergists*. They have denied to man any independent power to co-operate with the Divine Spirit. They have made the divine grace the sole agent in his redemption. Man, they have said, is in his present state so completely a sinner that he can of himself do no good thing. He is, therefore, incapable of acquiring any merit whatsoever, to say nothing about supererogatory merit. Other Protestants have been in substantial agreement with the synergism of Catholicism. They have ascribed to man a limited freedom, but they have refused to recognize the Catholic distinction between "commandments" and "counsels" and have laid such emphasis on an absolute moral law for all that no place has been left for works of supererogation. Duty for them has been all-inclusive. It has had no "ceiling." Indeed, so lofty has their conception of the obligatory moral ideal been that in its presence it has seemed to them unfitting to speak of any human acts as "meritorious." Actually they may have been such, and must have been such if morally good. But the feeling has been that in the Christian life with its exalted ideal and its overshadowing sense of the divine grace the standpoint of merit has no place. Roman Catholics have a different feeling at this point. They ground the idea of merit in the divine grace. Grace with them does not exclude merit; rather does it make a human act "meritorious." [11] This difference between Catholicism and Arminian Protestantism no doubt implies a difference of attitude toward "good works." But at bottom the difference seems to me one of words more than of substance. For both sides lay primary stress on the divine grace. The real difference between them has to do with the mode of operation of the divine grace rather than with our dependence upon it. And in the present connection the latter is the important point. It profoundly conditions the Christian conception of self-realization.

Still another problem that has a bearing on the subject of self-realization and that has received considerable attention in the past is the question as to whether there are morally "indifferent" spheres of conduct. Such spheres of conduct were in earlier times spoken of as "adiaphora"; since the time of Schleiermacher the word "permissible" has been more commonly applied to them. Acts have been classed as ethically indifferent or permissible which lay outside of the field of the established moral law, and in some instances acts commonly regarded as evil have been declared to be "permissible" on the ground that the end justifies the means. In Protestant circles it has been argued that certain religious rites or customs are matters of moral indifference, and that this holds true also of certain forms of recreation or pleasure.

Theodor Haering[12] has spoken of this general problem as

[11] Karl Adam, *op. cit.*, p. 182.

[12] *The Ethics of the Christian Life*, p. 236.

"the third master-question of ethics," the other two being the question as to the conflict of duties and the question of supererogation. The reason for attributing such significance to this problem and also to the other two is the fact that they all find their solution in a personal, as distinguished from a legalistic, conception of duty. If duty is in the last analysis an individual affair, and if its performance means conformity to the all-embracing will of God in one's own life, it follows that, as there can be no conflict of duties and no works of supererogation, so there can in the ideal be no free acts that lie below the plane of duty. "Whatsoever ye do, in word or in deed, do all in the name of the Lord Jesus."[13] But while in the ideal or in the abstract this is true, it is obvious that there are many voluntary acts in which the moral element does not come to clear recognition and which it would be pedantic to include within the conscious moral sphere. Attempts to universalize our moral concern so as to include the most trivial acts are, as Westermarck says, "only theoretical fancies without practical bearing, a hollow and flattering tribute to the idol of duty."[14] Still it is important to bear in mind that in the Christian ideal of self-realization life as a whole is embraced. No voluntary phase of it can be regarded as morally indifferent.

The Right to Life and Self-Defense

The duty of self-preservation has as its counterpart the right to life and to self-defense. If I had no right to life, I would be under no obligation to preserve it. Life is both a gift and a possession. It comes to us as such from God and hence to preserve it is both a right and a duty. But what is involved in this right and duty is a question that in certain instances has led to considerable difference of opinion.

Does the right to life involve the right to eternal life? Or ought we be willing "to be damned for the glory of God"? This is a religious rather than a strictly ethical question, and we

[13] Col. 3:17.

[14] *The Origin and Development of the Moral Ideas,* I. 157.

need not here concern ourselves with it. Suffice it to say that the moral character of God would seem clearly to exclude the arbitrary "damnation" of any of his creatures and that his moral purpose in creation would seem to imply eternal life for those who love him. But this eternal destiny we ascribe to divine grace rather than to human right.

The right to life, as commonly understood, applies only to our earthly life. This right is generally conceded, so far as the relation of individual men to each other is concerned. Murder is condemned by the common conscience of mankind. Human life is sacred. No one under normal circumstances may deprive another of it, nor may he deprive himself of it. Suicide, as well as murder, is condemned by the Christian conscience.

But are there any exceptions to this rule? May an incurable invalid, for instance, suffering incessant pain, end his own life by taking a deadly potion, and thus not only terminate his own suffering but relieve others of the burden of caring for him? Or may a physician out of sympathy for such an invalid administer a drug that would end his life? These questions have been answered in the negative on the ground that "the child of God cannot at his own will excuse himself from God's school," and that "the sacredness of life and God's responsibility for it forbid the assumption of any medical lordship over it." [15] But it is by no means clear that such an absolute identification of Divine Providence and of human probation with the order of nature and such an absolute ascription of sanctity to the physical life are involved in the Christian faith. Life is sacred because of its intrinsic worth; and when it has lost its value and means only pain and agony, it is at least doubtful whether its continuance has the sanction of Divine Providence. No doubt the termination of human life at the will of any individual has its social perils and if legally permitted would need to be carefully safeguarded. But its moral justification in certain ex-

[15] Newman Smyth, *Christian Ethics,* pp. 343, 347.

treme cases can hardly be regarded as excluded by the Christian ethic.

The right of self-defense is obviously involved in the right to life. If life is a trust, it is both our duty and right to protect it, and this means self-defense against unjust attack. Such defense, it has been argued, is permissible to us as citizens but not as Christians. As Christians we "must simply endure wrong."[16] Only as representatives of the state may we "resist evil." But such a bifurcation of the Christian's moral life leads to an unnatural dualism and does not ring morally true. It makes the Christian ethic a moral abstraction and deprives the Christian conscience of that inner unity without which it cannot effectively function in the world in which God has placed us. To resist evil and to defend oneself and others against serious injustice is both a Christian and a civil duty. Only by recognizing the moral right of self-defense can the Christian ethic be realistic and self-consistent. This right, however, on the part of the individual is not absolute. It is limited by the claims of society and of the state. Christianity recognizes this in its principle of self-renunciation. The claims of the state upon the individual will be considered in a later chapter.

THE RIGHT TO FREEDOM

As the duty of self-preservation implies the right to life and self-defense, so the duty of self-realization implies quite distinctly the right to freedom. By freedom as here used is meant, of course, not metaphysical freedom, which we discussed in an earlier chapter, but personal freedom.

Without freedom in this sense of the term there could be no adequate self-directed effort toward the attainment of the divinely appointed goal of one's life. Subjection to the will of another would mean the crippling and misdirection of one's vital energy. Only through the free relation of men to each other can the normal development of human life take place. But this freedom is not and cannot be absolute. It is

[16] Brunner, *The Divine Imperative,* p. 691.

limited by the equal rights of others and presupposes essentially the same degree of development on the part of those who share in it. Where such equality exists, freedom is commonly recognized as the moral ideal. Reactions may take place against it in the interest of some pagan theory of the superman or of racial superiority, but they are merely passing episodes in human history. Freedom is implicit in the Christian ethic and in all high moral endeavor and is certain to remain the ideal of human society.[17]

In the exercise of freedom, however, there are two important limitations, implied in what has just been said. One is in the case of children and undeveloped peoples or races. Children require restraint and discipline for their proper training. They need to have their wills to some degree subjected to the wills of their superiors. Only thus can they be taught self-control and be prepared for the responsibilities of mature life. In a similar way undeveloped tribes and races may to their own advantage and that of the world be kept in tutelage by more highly civilized peoples. But this diminution of freedom must be limited both in time and degree. Permanent slavery or absolute subjection on the part of an individual or nation has no place in a truly ethical system.[18]

The other limitation of freedom referred to it that imposed upon those whose conduct is seriously detrimental to the community. Such people have no right to freedom. Freedom is a right accorded by ethics to the moral, not the immoral, person. In so far as people are immoral they are justly subject to restraint by the community.

But it is often difficult to draw the line between the rights of the individual and those of the community. The New Testament contains no infallible rule by which we may decide when the claims of one should yield to those of the other. There is

---

[17] Cf. E. S. Brightman, *The Spiritual Life* (1942), chap vi. This book deserves to rank with Bowne's *Immanence of God* as a classic in its particular field.

[18] On the freedom of nations or peoples see W. E. Hocking, *The Spirit of World Politics,* pp. 3-39, 196-224, 500-519.

food for reflection in a statement by Father Tyrrell. "It was," he said, "a mere accident of his times and circumstances that Christ died at the hands of authority in the cause of reason and liberty. In other conditions he would have died at the hands of liberty in the cause of authority and tradition." [19]

The Right to the Truth

The right to the truth is a right that may be claimed in the interest both of self-preservation and self-realization. A falsehood might easily be injurious and even fatal to the physical life of another, and still more so might it be detrimental to his reputation and to his spiritual development. Mutual confidence constitutes the very essence of our social life. Without it society and human life would disintegrate. Truthfulness, therefore, on which confidence is based, is commonly regarded as a virtue of fundamental importance. Both personal character and social welfare are to a pre-eminent degree dependent upon it. The duty of truthfulness is thus firmly grounded in the moral and social nature of mankind.

But while this is true, it is also true that the right to truth and the duty of truthfulness presuppose normal human relations. Where these are lacking, adherence to the truth may cease to be absolutely obligatory. In time of war, for instance, the enemy has no right to the truth. If by deceiving him we could save our own troops from defeat, we would feel justified in doing so. We would also at any time take a similar attitude toward a man who was seeking information in order to make an evil use of it. He has no right to the truth and, if necessary, might justly be deceived. We also feel no absolute obligation to tell the truth to a person who is seriously ill if doing so would imperil or lessen his chances of recovery. There are also many private matters in every person's life which he is at liberty to keep secret. So far as they are concerned, no outsider has a right to the truth. They are none of his business. There

[19] *Through Scylla and Charybdis,* pp. 41 f.

are thus generally recognized limitations to the duty of truthfulness and the right to the truth.

But these limitations arise for the most part in abnormal or unusual circumstances, and there is obvious peril in emphasizing them unduly. The tendency toward deceit in human nature is too strong to need encouragement. Some of our greatest theologians and philosophers, consequently, such as Augustine, Calvin, Kant, and Fichte, have insisted on the absoluteness of the duty to tell the truth. They would allow no exceptions, regardless of the evil consequences that might in certain instances result. This attitude no doubt may for a time serve as a moral tonic. But it subordinates the spirit to the letter of the law. It puts formal rightness above material rightness. It makes obedience to a rule more important than the achievement of a personal good. In the last analysis the good to be attained must decide what is right. The right to the truth must not contradict the law of love.

The Right to Property

The right to property is another fundamental right involved in the duties of self-preservation and self-realization. This right, so far as it relates to the individual, has at various times been called in question. Private property has been rejected as having no place in the law of nature or in original human society. This was the teaching of many of the Church Fathers, such as Tertullian, Irenaeus, Cyprian, and Chrysostom; and it has been a common doctrine among modern socialists. Early Christian theologians attributed the institution of private property to the effects of the Fall, and Marxian socialists have seen in it both the cause and effect of the long class struggle that followed the dissolution of the primitive communistic social order. But these extreme theorists have not in practice meant to eliminate all private property. Doing so would make both self-preservation and self-realization to a large degree insecure, if not impossible. In order to live we need some property, such as food, clothing, and shelter, that we can call our own, and in order to fulfill a worthy mission in life we need considerable more in the way of private possessions. How much we actually need or ought to have is a question on which people differ widely. But some private property is generally assumed to be a condition of human life. Communists do not seek to eliminate it altogether. What they aim to do is to introduce such limitations of it as are necessary to bring about a much larger degree of economic equality than at present prevails.

The right to property grows out of the fact that the means of existence are limited. If they were as common and as free to all as air and light, they would not be subject to ownership. There would be no property in them. What creates property is the fact that the ordinary means of existence are not the free gifts of nature. We have to labor and struggle for them, and since we thus acquire them we claim them as our own. But our ownership is not absolute. We do not create the raw materials we use; we find them. And hence society claims a part right in the products of our labor. It lays down the conditions and limits under which property may be acquired. But the principle of individual ownership it does not completely abrogate. To do so would be ruinous to society as well as to the individual. For the life of the social group as well as that of the individual is dependent on the possession of property. Without it civilization would be impossible.

CHAPTER X

THE FAMILY

FROM the ethics of the individual we now pass to social ethics. And here we begin with the ethics of the family.

First, however, a word about social ethics in general or what is called "the orders of creation." The latter expression has a religious connotation that the former lacks. It implies a divine creative source of the fundamental institutions and modes of activity that go to make up the social order. It is, therefore, a term that belongs to Christian, as distinguished from general, ethics. The term social ethics is religiously neutral. The corresponding religious term, used especially in England and America, is the "social gospel."[1] This term denotes a religious approach to social ethics, as does the term "orders of creation," used more commonly in Germany. But there is this significant difference. When we speak of the orders of creation, we have in mind chiefly the fixity of the social order. It is a divinely established order to which we must submit and to which we must adjust ourselves. When, however, we speak of the social gospel, we think primarily of the plasticity of the social order. It is an imperfect order subject to change and one which it is our duty to seek to transform into greater conformity to the Christian ideal. In other words, the "social gospel" is an activistic conception, while the "orders of creation" suggests a quietistic point of view. But both have to do with the social framework of the moral life, and hence in Christian ethics may be used as synonyms of social as distinguished from individual ethics.[2]

Social ethics may naturally be treated under five main heads

---

[1] For a history of the movement represented by this term in America see C. H. Hopkins, *The Rise of the Social Gospel in American Protestantism, 1865-1915.*

[2] Cf. Brightman, *The Spiritual Life,* pp. 69-102.

or divisions: the family, the state, the church, culture, and the economic order. These divisions represent fundamental distinctions in the structure of society and may be called orders of creation. Each of these orders is variable in its historical form, but in its essential nature is a permanent and constituent element in human community life and embodies a definite mode of union among men. It is this definiteness, distinctiveness, and necessity of a social institution or mode of social activity that constitute it an order of creation and that form the basis of the above divisions of social ethics.

Ethical Significance

Of the various orders of creation the family is generally conceded to be morally the most fundamental and the most significant. It owes its existence to the conditions under which human life begins and develops. There are analogous groupings of parents and offspring among some of the lower animals, but they are of comparatively brief duration and have no other aim than the preservation of the species. What gives distinctiveness to the human family is its relative permanence and its ethical character. These two go together. The long period of infancy and of physical and mental development gives rise to a profound moral relationship within the family that would hardly otherwise be possible. And this moral bond in turn transforms the long period of necessary dependence of children on parents into a life-long relationship. What thus gives permanence to the human family is not simply the peculiar physical conditions under which it arises but the ethical union which is cemented between its members. Indeed, it is the latter that alone makes the family relationship truly human. The human family is primarily a moral institution, though it has a physical foundation.

There has been considerable difference of opinion among modern investigators as to the historical origin of the family. Some have argued in favor of an original promiscuity and relegated the rise of the family to a comparatively late date. This theory is less commonly held now than it was a generation or two ago.[3] But whether true or false, it does not necessarily affect the rational status of the family. The worth of a developing institution is dependent on its outcome, not on what it came out of. It is the family of today that constitutes the basis of our estimate of its racial and ethical significance, not the family of primitive mankind or its possible precursor.

In evaluating the family we may, then, disregard the various questions as to its origin and historical development. One phase of its history, however, we need to consider. This is the influence of Christianity. It has been argued that this influence has in several respects been injurious. Christianity, it is said, has during a large part of its history ranked celibacy above marriage and thus made family life "at its best only a second best." This view finds some support in the example and teaching of both Jesus and Paul,[4] and in the early church was held in a pronounced form. It was a presupposition of the monastic movement, as commonly understood, and was explicitly affirmed at the Council of Trent in 1563. Canon X in the section dealing with the sacrament of matrimony reads thus: "If any one saith, that the marriage state is to be placed above the state of virginity, or of celibacy, and that it is not better and more blessed to remain in virginity or in celibacy than to be united in matrimony: let him be anathema."[5] This canon was directed against the teaching of Protestantism, and probably still represents the official and dominant attitude in the Roman Catholic Church, though, as we have seen, there is at present a tendency to explain it away.[6]

Protestant Christianity repudiated the ascetic doctrine of the superiority of the celibate to the married state and thus incorporated marriage in the full Christian ideal. But there

---

[3] Edward Westermarck, *The History of Human Marriage* (1891) has been argely responsible for this change.

[4] Mark 12:25; Matt. 1912; I Cor. 7:1, 2, 7, 8.

[5] Philip Schaff, *Creeds of Christendom,* II, 197.

[6] Cf. Karl Adam, *op. cit.,* pp. 203-7.

nevertheless lingered in Protestant circles more or less of the feeling that "there is something sensually base in sex-intercourse." There was no definite recognition in Protestant ethics of "an intrinsic value in sex experience." Marriage was regarded as instituted for "these two ends, either to beget offspring or as a remedy for incontinence."[7] So, despite the theoretical teaching of early Protestantism, the marriage relation was not wholly emancipated from the influence of the dualism and asceticism of the ancient and medieval church. Sex relations were not fully moralized and treated as having value in themselves. A moral shadow still rested upon them and hence upon the marriage or family relationship.

A further unfavorable influence attributed to Christianity is the lowered status of married women. The common view, it is conceded, is the reverse of this. It is quite generally held that woman owes her present high position to Christian teaching. But this, we are told, is a mistake. Christianity inherited and perpetuated the Hebrew conception of woman, which was based on the story of Eve's part in the Fall and was distinctly lower than that current in Rome in the first century. Westermarck, for instance, after reviewing the history of woman's status in Christendom declares that the personal independence enjoyed by the married woman under the later Roman law was lost through the influence of Christianity on European legislation and that it has been regained only after the lapse of nearly two thousand years, and then "not by the aid of the churches, but despite their opposition."[8]

Attention is also directed to certain sayings of Jesus which, it is said, imply a depreciation of family relationships. According to Mark 3:31-34, he took an inconsiderate attitude toward the members of his own family. In other instances he expressed a disregard for family obligations in general that seems to us harsh and even fanatical. Not only were his disciples in the

---

[7] See A. G. Widgery, *Christian Ethics in History and Modern Life,* pp. 218-23.

[8] *Christianity and Morals,* pp. 342 f.

interest of the Kingdom of God to forego the courtesy of a farewell to relatives and such an act of filial piety as the burial of one's father;[9] not only were they to love the members of their own household less than himself;[10] they were to hate father and mother, wife and children, and brothers and sisters.[11] Such utterances as these, it is urged, have at times had an unwholesome effect on family life.

But whatever truth there may be in the foregoing adverse considerations, there can be little doubt that on the whole Christianity has exerted an elevating influence on the family. So far as the above criticisms of its influence are concerned, it may be noted that they do not take account of the total Christian attitude toward the family. They fail to point out that the ascetic depreciation of the family in the Catholic Church or churches was from the beginning to a large extent offset by the conception of marriage as a sacrament. If marriage has divine sanction, there would seem to be no valid reason for regarding sexual intercourse as defiling. They also fail to point out that married life is in danger of becoming sensual, and family life narrow and selfish. There is such a thing as chastity in the married state. Sexual excesses are to be avoided. It was this sound ethical judgment that in the past lay back of, and to some extent accounted for, the Protestant feeling, usually unexpressed, that a certain baseness attaches to sex intercourse. It is also obvious that family relations may at times so completely absorb a person's interest as to blind him to the broader and higher obligations of life, to those imposed upon him by the Kingdom of God. Such stern words as those of Jesus about hating father and mother may, therefore, under certain conditions be necessary, and that without any reflection on the essential sanctity of the family.

The further charge that Christianity had an unwholesome influence on the family by lowering the legal status of married

[9] Matt. 8:21 f.; Luke 9: 59-62.
[10] Matt. 10:-37.
[11] Luke 14:26.

women may have some historical basis. But their reduced legal rights were certainly more than offset by the New Testament teaching with reference to the religious equality of "male and female" [12] and the duty of husbands to love their wives as Christ loved the church.[13] It is the general Christian conception of womanhood and motherhood that has had most influence on the family; and that this influence, in view of its religious and ethical basis, has been of a deepening and enriching character can hardly be questioned.

What is true of the married woman is also true of the family as a whole. It is the general Christian conception of the family, not incidental imperfections in its realization, that gives the key to the real influence that Christianity has had on the family. What this influence has been cannot be determined by a mere collection of external data. The inquiry must also take account of the transcendental element in the Christian faith—the faith in God and the Kingdom of God. According to this faith God is a Father who seeks to make all men sons to himself and brothers to each other. This means that the Kingdom of God is the family of God and that every family on earth should in its spirit be a part of the divine family.[14] This is the Christian ideal, an ideal that cannot be surpassed; and it is this ideal that has constituted Christianity's chief contribution to the family. It has not only put a divine sanction on the family as an institution but inspired it with a moral goal than which no higher can be conceived.

The family has always been the great moral school of mankind, and its function in this respect has to a marked degree been augmented under Christian influence. It is in the family that we learn the first and best lessons in obedience, reverence, truthfulness, fidelity, patience, self-control, unselfish devotion, purity, love, and all those virtues that go to make up Christian character. There it is that the sacredness of personality first

[12] Gal. 3:28.
[13] Eph. 5:25-33.
[14] Eph. 3:14 f.

dawns upon us, and we experience there as nowhere else the richness of personal communion. The family is the great training school of the moral life. This is true for parents as well as for children. Without the family, if that were possible, humanity would suffer an irreparable moral loss. The family has an ethical significance beyond that of any other institution.

The Moral Validity of Marriage

It is through marriage that the family is created. By marriage we mean a union of the sexes sanctioned by custom or law. In a normal marriage there are three essential elements: "the gratification of the sexual impulse, the relation of the husband and wife apart from it, and procreation."[15] These three factors, emphasized in different degrees by different peoples and persons, have produced the family and given to it what may be called its natural values. But it is not these physical and psychological values of marriage nor its complex and varied history with which we are here concerned. We here accept the legitimacy of the married relation without inquiring into its historical development and merely raise the question as to the nature or ground of its moral validity. Is the marriage bond dependent for its moral validity on some objective rite or ceremony? Or if not, on what is it dependent?

In answering this question it is important to distinguish between moral validity, on the one hand, and legal or ecclesiastical validity, on the other hand. Legal validity and ecclesiastical validity obviously require an objective rite or ceremony of some kind as evidence that the marriage has been consummated in harmony with civil or ecclesiastical law. But the situation is quite different when it comes to moral validity. Here everything depends on the couple concerned, on their free choice and action. "No law can make a forced marriage valid; and

---

[15] E. Westermarck, *The Future of Marriage in Western Civilization*, p. 21. These and other factors in the marriage relation are discussed in a popular, frank, and discriminating manner by E. R. Groves, *Christianity and the Family* (1942).

no law can make a voluntary marriage morally invalid."[16] It is the free will of those immediately involved that alone gives moral character to a marriage. But this does not mean that they may do as they please in the case. Society has a stake in every marriage, and hence it has the right to make rules or laws to which marriage must conform. This makes necessary some sort of marriage ceremony conducted by a recognized representative of organized society. This representative may be a civil officer, or a priest or minister in some religious body. In the one case marriage may be thought of as a civil contract, and in the other as a religious sacrament. But both kinds of ceremony serve in one respect a common purpose. They give notice to society that the marriage has taken place in conformity with the laws of the state. This is their primary function. Neither ceremony is essential to the moral validity of the marriage. The moral validity depends solely on the mutual pledging of faith by the couple. This pledging may form a part of the marriage ceremony, but it has moral value only in so far as it is expressive of their free and sincere attitude one toward the other. Their free choice of each other, and it alone, gives moral validity to their marriage.

The religious ceremony has this significance over and above the civil right, that it relates the marriage to the divine order and puts upon it a divine sanction. Whether marriage be called a sacrament or not does not matter much. But it is a matter of great significance to invest the marriage relation with all the sacredness that grows out of profound religious belief. It is at this point that Christianity has rendered its greatest service to the family. It has idealized the physical relation of the sexes, has emphasized the moral obligations of husband and wife to each other, and has put back of these obligations a divine imperative that has given to them a binding power that they would not otherwise have had. The religious marriage ceremony is, therefore, not a matter of indifference. But in order to guard

[16] Bowne, *Principles of Ethics,* p. 236.

against ecclesiastical tyranny it has at times been necessary to remind the church that a civil marriage serves the purpose of society about as well. And in order to save the marriage bond from the appearance of being an arbitrary social or ecclesiastical imposition, it is well to emphasize the fact that its moral validity is dependent wholly on the free choice of the contracting parties.

Monogamy

In the historical development of marriage and the family the tendency has on the whole been toward a strict monogamy. The advent of Christianity marked an epoch in this development. Jesus' teaching on the subject was explicit: "From the beginning of the creation, Male and female made he them. For this cause shall a man leave his father and mother, and shall cleave to his wife; and the two shall become one flesh; so that they are no more two, but one."[17] Statements equally explicit may, it is true, be found in ancient extra-Christian sources, as for instance among the Stoics, but it was only through Christianity that the strict monogamistic demand gained general recognition. This does not mean that even in Christendom it was recognized as universally binding either legally or ethically. Exceptions were in many instances allowed. But the tendency was more and more to regard strict monogamy as the moral ideal. So much so was this the case during the past century that the textbooks on ethics during this period hardly regarded monogamy as a "problem." Its general acceptance was taken for granted.

But more recently there has been a rather widespread revolt against the strict monogamistic standard. This revolt has been both theoretical and practical. The reasons for it are varied. Four or five may be mentioned, such as the economic and intellectual emancipation of women, the numerical surplus of women in Europe following the first World War, the invention of modern contraceptives, the housing conditions in our large

[17] Mark 10:6, 7.

cities, and the accentuated individualism of our time. These and other factors have tended to weaken the sense of obligation to the monogamistic ideal, and to encourage nonconformity to it. The result is that many feel that the Christian ideal of marriage is facing a crisis such as it has not faced before, and that it calls for a new defense.[18]

For this feeling there is some justification. Certainly in view of current opinion and practice we can no longer treat the monogamistic ideal as sacrosanct and beyond criticism. Some defense of it is needed. And this defense has not been lacking.

Anthropology and history have on the whole given their support to monogamy. Some theorists have argued in favor of an original promiscuity of sex communism or "group marriage," and others in favor of an original polygyny or polyandry. Even if one or the other of these theories were true, it would not follow that present-day monogamy is a departure from what might be called the natural norm of sex relations and that it should be discarded. But scholarly opinion has veered away from these group theories and now favors the view that monogamy has been the rule in human history as a whole, in the most primitive as well as the later stages of human development. Indeed, it is maintained by representative anthropologists not only that monogamy has been the general rule but that it is the universal "pattern and prototype of human marriage," that there are no "rival forms of marriage," that "monogamy is, has been and will remain the only true type of marriage." "Polyandry and polygyny are compound marriages, ... each of them constituted upon the pattern of a monogamous marriage." True marriage "requires essentially two people, and two people only." [19]

Monogamy, it is true, in the strict and exclusive sense of the term, a monogamy that bans bigamy and polygamy as criminal and sacrilegious, has not been common until comparatively re-

[18] Brunner, *The Divine Imperative,* pp. 340 f.

[19] B. Malinowski in *Encyclopedia Britannica,* 14th Ed., XIV, 950.

cent times, and during this period it has been largely confined to our modern Western culture. Polygamy was recognized as legal by the medieval church, and occasionally here and there it received such recognition both by church and state as late as the middle of the seventeenth century.[20] Concubinage and other sexual irregularities have also often coexisted with the institution of marriage. Demosthenes, for instance, is credited with saying, "We keep mistresses for our pleasures, concubines for constant attendance, and wives to bear us legitimate children and to be our faithful housekeepers." [21] But, despite such extramarital sex relations and other departures from strict monogamy that have been permitted by law and custom, it is still true that monogamy has been almost universally recognized as the standard form of marriage and of sex relationship. Neither anthropology nor history affords any support to the view that men and women are polygamous by nature to such an extent as to threaten the present monogamous type of marriage.

Another strong argument in support of monogamy is the numerical equality of the sexes. This equality is obviously not the result of human design. It belongs to the order of nature. War, it is true, has at times upset to some extent this numerical balance. So many men have been killed in battle that there has been a surplus of women. But this disparity seems to be over come by "an inexplicable natural tendency." The tendency, following the loss of a large number of men in war, has been for the balance to be restored by an "unusual surplus of boy-babies." [22] This was quite marked during the period following the Napoleonic wars. It has also been observed since the first World War.[23] But, apart from this interesting tendency, the remarkable numerical balance between the sexes, which has been maintained through the milleniums of human history,

---

[20] See Westermarck, *The History of Human Marriage,* III, pp. 50 f.

[21] Quoted by Westermarck, *Christianity and Morals,* pp. 363 f.

[22] Alexander von Oettingen, *Die Moralstatistik* (1868), pp. 337-52.

[23] *Enc. Brit.,* 14th ed. XX, 419. Article on "Sex-Ratio at Birth and Death," by S. De Jastrzebski.

certainly points to monogamy as the normal mode of union between them.

A third consideration in favor of monogamy is drawn from the subjective realm and is based on the exclusiveness of the love relation. This relation in its sexual form is limited to two and only in monogamy can receive its true expression. If a third person is introduced into the marital relation, the whole is vitiated. True marital love excludes the thought of being shared with more than one of the opposite sex. But while under normal circumstances this romantic contention may be true, it is important to distinguish between emotional and ethical love. Love as an emotion is variable, and in this sense it is quite possible that one might at the same time love more than one person of the other sex, or at least that love might shift from one to another. To base marriage on love of this kind is, as Brunner says, "to build on the sand."[24] But it is different with ethical love. Here the emotional element is not lacking, but it is based on something deeper, on fidelity. There is here a recognition of monogamy as a divine order, an order realized in one's own marriage and carrying with it a divinely imposed obligation, an obligation to mutual faithfulness, whose fulfillment, we believe, will ultimately yield the richest type of personal experience despite the shifting sands of emotion. It is in this moral and religious form of subjectivism that the most abiding basis of monogamy is to be found. The objective considerations have their value, but it is only in the higher spiritual experiences of the race that a strict monogamy can be adequately grounded.

Divorce

In Jesus' recorded teaching concerning marriage there are two cardinal points. One we have just considered. Marriage should be monogamous. The other is that it should be permanent. "What . . . . God hath joined together, let not man

[24] *Op. cit.*, p. 435.

put asunder."[25] That this is the ideal would generally be admitted. It is implied in monogamy, in the very nature of love as distinguished from passion. Love would not be true or ethical love if it did not involve the idea of an abiding loyalty. Nor could the moral ends of the family be attained without the permanence of the marriage bond. Marriage, to fulfill its true mission, must be lifelong.

But such a lifelong union presupposes favorable conditions. Where these conditions do not prevail—and they often do not—it is quite possible that the marriage bond would better be dissolved. This is the way the non-Christian world has generally viewed the matter, and hence it has made divorce relatively easy. It was so in the pagan Roman Empire. Christianity however, "revolutionized European legislation" on the subject.[26] The New Testament forbade divorce but allowed two exceptions. According to Matthew 5:32 and 19:9, fornication was a ground for one exception, and according to I Cor. 7:15, desertion by an unbelieving wife or husband was apparently regarded by Paul as a sufficient ground for another. But the early Christian attitude in general was hostile to divorce; and later, largely as a result of Augustine's influence, the church denied the dissolubility of any valid and consummated Christian marriage. This position was dogmatically affirmed by the Council of Trent,[27] and during the past century was reaffirmed by Pius IX and Leo XIII. The chief reasons offered were these: that a consummated Christian marriage is a sacrament, and that it represents the union between Christ and the church. The latter union is indissoluble, and a sacrament is permanently valid; therefore, Christian marriage must be such also. But while Roman Catholic doctrine thus seemed to close the door completely to divorce, legal devices for escaping this conclusion became in the course of time, as Lord Bryce said, "so numerous and so intricate that it was easy, given a sufficient motive,

[25] Mark 10:9.
[26] Westermarck, *op. cit.*, p. 344.
[27] P. Schaff, *op. cit.*, II, 196.

whether political or pecuniary, to discover some ground for declaring almost any marriage invalid."[28]

The Reformation restored the biblical teaching with reference to fornication as a ground for divorce. And in Continental Europe various other grounds were legally recognized, such as desertion, cruelty, conviction of a crime, sexual impotence, insanity, and certain diseases. In England the law remained stricter and allowed divorce only on sexual grounds. In the United States the divorce laws have varied in the different states from great laxity to extreme strictness. It is said that South Carolina "is the only Protestant community in the world which nowadays holds marriage indissoluble."[29]

The moral validity of marriage, as we have seen, is dependent exclusively on the free choice of the couple concerned. From this it might be concluded that mutual consent should be a sufficient ground for the dissolution of a marriage. And if the pair were the only ones concerned, this conclusion might be warranted. But society has as great an interest in the permanence of a marriage as in its consummation, And as it regulates the latter, so it seeks to protect the former. It makes laws governing divorce and at times forbidding it altogether. That it has the right to do this can hardly be questioned. But what measure of legal restraint should be placed upon divorce is a question that can be settled only by experience. What the law should aim at is "a maximum of social health and decency," and experience would seem to indicate clearly that this cannot be obtained by an absolute prohibition of divorce. When the union of husband and wife has lost its moral purpose and become revolting to both of them, there is no good reason why they should be compelled to live together. The result would be evil rather than good.

This, however, does not affect the absoluteness of the Christian ideal with respect to the permanence of marriage. It is

---

[28] *Studies in History and Jurisprudence,* II, 826.

[29] Westermarck, *The Future of Marriage in Western Civilization,* p. 204.

probable that the words "except for fornication" in Matthew 5:32 and 19:9 were added to the text later so as to make it conform with later practice in the church, and that Jesus himself allowed for no exception to his condemnation of divorce. But if that be true, it would mean that he was speaking not as a lawgiver, but rather as an upholder of the moral ideal.

Birth Control

Another problem in connection with marriage that has in recent years attracted considerable attention and been the subject of lively debate is that of birth control. There are here two main questions at issue. First, is procreation the only legitimate and sufficient purpose of sexual intercourse? And second, is it permissible to employ artificial means to prevent conception? If one answers the first question in the affirmative, he is likely to answer the second in the negative. And conversely, if he answers the first question in the negative, he is likely to answer the second in the affirmative. Throughout most of its history the church has inclined to the ascetic view that the sex life has no intrinsic worth, that in and of itself it is a base and unseemly thing and that its sole legitimate function is the perpetuation of the race. When, therefore, modernists began to advocate birth control, there was a widespread revulsion against it. The Roman Catholic Church officially repudiated it,[30] and Protestants were quite generally prejudiced against it. Aside from this spontaneous aversion to it, based on traditional asceticism, it was argued that the use of contraceptives by married people would have a demoralizing effect on unmarried young people, would limit unduly the size of families, and would have an injurious effect on those who used them. But, despite such arguments as these and the traditional prejudice against the newer view of the sex life, the latter has rapidly gained currency in the Protestant world. This change is one of the most important in the history of the Christian conception of marriage.

---

[30] Pope Pius XI, *Encyclical Letter on Christian Marriage,* 1930.

In support of the change there are three general considerations that may be urged. For one thing it may be pointed out that the dualistic type of thought, on which the older depreciation of the sex life was based, has in modern times been supplanted by the doctrine of the divine immanence. God is present in the natural order as well as in miracles. He has created men, male and female, and established their relation to each other. This relation has no stigma attached to it. Nor does it exist simply for procreation. If it did, one would hardly expect that the need of sex expression would be as relatively permanent as it is. The nonperiodic character of passion suggests that sexual intercourse not only does have the purpose of procreation but was itself designed by the Creator to be a means by which married people express their love for one another. At any rate there is no reason why this should not be so. The sense of shame associated with the sex organs does not point to any inherent baseness in them but is more likely due to a primitive sense of sacred mystery suggested by their creative function. It is these two things, the sense of shame and the permanence of the sex impulse that, according to von Hartmann, are "the earliest foundations upon which is based the fact that the sex relations of human beings are in a higher sphere than those of the animals."[31]

Another point worthy of note is that there is nothing in the use of contraceptives that is inconsistent with a sincere faith in Divine Providence. It is a serious mistake to suppose that it is a religious duty to allow nature to have its way in the sex life. This attitude of mind reminds one of the good people in the eighteenth century who condemned vaccination as an attempt to thwart the divine will, the assumption being that small pox is a divine visitation and that no artificial means ought, therefore, be employed to prevent it. The truth, of course, is that the natural order is given us, not as an absolute finality, but as something to be guided and controlled. And in the case

[31] Quoted by Brunner, *op. cit.*, p. 649.

of birth control the real question at issue is that between rational control and resort to chance. The question of Divine Providence is not involved in it. Indeed, if anything, providential guidance would seem more probable through rational control than through the operation of chance. And the fact is that there is nothing new about birth control except the name and some of the methods employed. The practice itself in one form or another has come down from time immemorial. Though condemned in principle by Augustine and other church leaders it was never completely suppressed, even in Christian families.

The third consideration in support of the modern Christian view of the sex life is more practical in nature. It has to do with the changed conditions under which we at present live. Some of these conditions obviously make smaller families desirable, if not necessary. For instance, the limited quarters available in our large cities and the high cost of living preclude such large families as were common a century or so ago. Accommodation to the spatial and financial limitations of city life is necessary if the standard of living is to be maintained, to say nothing about its being improved.

Then, it is a significant fact that as a result of better medical attention, infant mortality has been greatly reduced. The mortality rate used to be so large that on the average only one-third of the children survived. Merely to preserve the race each mother, consequently needed to bear six children. At present it is said that three births by each mother are enough for the purpose. Under the circumstances the population would increase with undue rapidity if some limitation were not placed on the natural fertility of the race.

Again, there is a revolt on the part of women against the older conception of their place in the world which made of them hardly more than "breeding machines." They recognize that their primary obligation is that of motherhood, but they want it to be a "responsible motherhood"—a motherhood to which they have given their consent, not a motherhood due to impulse and to chance. And this probably means birth control in some form. The higher estimate of womanhood has thus combined with the marked decrease in infant mortality and the altered economic conditions to bring about an important change in the Christian view of marital sex experience.

CHAPTER XI

THE STATE AND WAR

NEXT to the family comes the state as a primal factor in the structure of human society. The state as well as the family is implicit in the earliest forms of human life. As the family provides for the propagation of the race, so the state provides for its security against internal and external foes. Without both organized society would disintegrate. Together they constitute for us a kind of external fatality. We do not choose them; we are born into them. We do not create them; we find them. They form the necessary framework of our human life. We may, and rightly, seek to improve them. At times we may in our folly revolt violently against them and seek to destroy them. But the revolt will be of no avail. Society cannot dispense with either the family or the state. Both are orders of creation.

As some critics of the family have argued in favor of an original sexual promiscuity and represented the family as a later human device, so some critics of the state have contended that it had no place in original humanity but was a later artificial product. The assumption underlying both of these theories is that what is "natural" in its origin has a higher degree of authority than any institution that owes its rise to deliberate human initiative. If it can, therefore, be shown that the family and the state are not original and "natural" phases of human life but later artificial developments, it is quite possible that they were both "human" misadventures, experiments that have failed to justify themselves and that we are warranted in discarding. For what man has made, he can also unmake.

ORIGIN OF THE STATE

A fundamental question that has consequently arisen with

reference to the state has had to do with its origin. Was it a natural growth or an artificial creation? This quetsion was first brought to a sharp issue by Thomas Hobbes (1588-1679) in his famous work *Leviathan*. According to Hobbes, the state was based on a social contract. This contract, as commonly understood, was an historical event, and hence the state was obviously an artificial product. But this was probably not Hobbes' own view. With him the social contract was a myth or symbol by means of which he sought to bring out "those states of mind which no more at the beginning than at all times give the state its firm seat in the saddle of human nature."[1] His theory, in other words, was psychological rather than historical and as such would be consistent with either the artificiality or naturalness of the state. Whether an institution is natural or artificial depends on the degree of distinctness with which its purpose emerges in consciousness at the time of its origin. If its purpose is clearly conceived and deliberately carried out, the institution may be classed as "artificial." If, on the other hand, it comes into being as the result of dispositions operating more or less automatically, it may be said to be "natural."

In the light of this distinction it would seem clear that the state is both natural and artificial. There must have been more or less conscious and deliberate purpose in its formation, even though it did not have its source in a contract. But back of this purpose there were involuntary social and political needs that sought satisfaction and without which there would have been no corresponding purposive action. This is true also of the family. "Marriage is a matter of will," but "the disposition to marry is not."[2] What makes the family a natural institution is "a durable instinctive foundation." The same may be said of the state. It has its rootage in our instinctive human nature. Man, as Aristotle put it, is "a political animal." There are in him state-forming dispositions that are deeper than volition.

---

[1] W. E. Hocking, *Man and the State,* p. 143. This very able work is worthy of careful study.

[2] *Ibid.,* p. 141.

It may then be said that the state has its ultimate foundation in human nature rather than in the human will and hence may be regarded as a natural growth and from the religious point of view as an order of creation.

The psychological needs that enter into the foundation and structure of the state are numerous. But there are two in particular that make the state a practical necessity. One of these is the need of fellowship or community. The need is instinctive. Men are by disposition gregarious. Sociability is native to them. Men are born to live together, and apart from this togetherness would not be truly human. The social instinct thus represents a compelling need. The need is met to some extent by the family; but a broader and more complete satisfaction is instinctively sought, and this can be attained only through an ever-widening human circle until the state is reached. The state is the broadest expression of full community life, apart from humanity itself, and in this respect is necessary to a complete satisfaction of human sociability.

The other fundamental need met by the state is that of right or justice in the relation of men to each other. Without justice there can be neither security nor peace or co-operation. To establish justice is, therefore, of primary importance in human life, and to do so is the distinctive function of the state in so far as the use of force is necessary. Under special circumstances individuals and smaller social groups may resort to physical measures in resisting unjust aggression and be justified in so doing. But for the most part the state reserves this right to itself. Its very existence is dependent upon the use of force or the threat of it. Without the power to enforce its will the state would disintegrate. It would be unable to administer justice and to defend itself against its foes, internal and external. If it did not employ force, others would take the law into their own hands. In order to avoid this necessity, the state must itself have the right and power of coercion. It is the forcible resistance of the state to evil that alone makes possible a limited degree of nonresistance to it among individuals.

Essential Nature of the State

Power thus belongs to the very essence of the state. But the further question now arises as to whether it is pure, unalloyed power that constitutes its nature or whether it is power based on the need of justice or employed with a moral purpose. The former view has been and is held by able political theorists and by some theologians. It is usually expressed in the simple formula that "the state is power." Machiavelli (1469-1527) was the first to formulate this doctrine distinctly. He subordinated morality wholly to the state's quest of power. Power with him was ultimate. It needed no moral justification. Heinrich von Treitschke (1834-96) accepted enthusiastically Machiavelli's dictum that the state is power, and became the most brilliant and influential exponent of it in Germany; but he regarded the state as having a moral function and as being "in itself an ethical force and a high moral good." He distinguished, however, between the morality of the individual and that of the state, and declared it "preposterous" for a citizen to claim the right to withhold his support from the state if it declared a war which he believed unjust. "My country, right or wrong," was his avowed position. To uphold the fatherland was with him an unconditional moral duty. Obedience to the state took precedence over the dictates of the individual conscience.[3]

This conception of the power of the state has been accepted by some theologians, though with a different moral appraisal of it. Emil Brunner, for instance, says that "the fundamental character of the state is not right, but might," and that "it belongs to the essence of the state that it should have the power to compel obedience."[4] Compulsion, however, is in itself contrary to love; it is sinful, "demonic." Yet without this demonic, violent power of compulsion the state could not

[3] *Politics,* I, 104-6. For an exposition of this theory of the state and related social theories as embodied in Fascism, Nazism, and Communism, see J. A. Leighton, *Social Philosophies in Conflict* (1937). These theories are here contrasted at length with liberal democracy.

[4] *The Divine Imperative,* pp. 446, 445 (Ger. ed., pp. 433, 431).

come into existence nor could it fulfill its divinely appointed purpose in and for society. It is, therefore, a necessity—not, however, a "lofty necessity of nature," as Treitschke affirmed, but a "necessary evil." It is a "product of collective sin," a consequence of original sin, which we as Christians must accept as "both an act of discipline and an act of repentance."

In this theory of the state as primarily and essentially power there is obvious peril, whether viewed from a purely political or theological standpoint. There is danger that the theory may be used as a justification of unwarranted aggression or as a ground for social and political pessimism. To both of these uses it has been and is being put. Furthermore, it tends to blind the human conscience to important moral differences. No matter how much more guilty one of two warring nations manifestly is than the other, it is said that both are by their very nature selfish and as aggressive as they dare be. There is no real moral difference between them, and the only proper attitude, therefore, for an outsider to take is that of moral neutrality. Every state in its essence is a nonmoral exercise of power. Its only crime is weakness; and hence there is, as Treitschke said, an "undeniably ridiculous element in the existence of a small state." [5] No state has any rights beyond its own power to protect itself.

Over against this pessimistic and so-called realistic conception of the state, which subordinates justice to power, is a more optimistic and ethical view. According to this view, the state had one of its chief roots in the need of justice, a need which could be met only by the possession of sovereign power. But the power came second, not first. It was not power that created right but rather right that created power. In other words, the power of the state is instrumental. It did not owe its origin to an independent instinct of self-aggression, as would seem to be implied in Treitschke's theory of an original "state-building instinct." It had its source rather in the need of a just and secure social

[5] *Politics*, I, 34.

order, an order that can be realized only through the exercise of sovereign power. That such power, embodied in the state, has often been employed in an arbitrary and unprincipled manner is evident from human history. But it does not follow that such an unethical use of power is inherent in the nature of the state, and still less does it follow that coercion by the state is a negation of love and that the power of the state is necessarily more or less "demonic." Good and evil are mixed in the state as in the individual. The ethics of the state differs, it is true, in some respects from that of the individual,[6] but the difference is not such as to warrant ascribing demoniacal possession to one and not to the other. It is misleading to speak of "moral man" and "immoral society."[7] Society or the state is the collective will, and as such there is no reason why it as well as the individual, should not be capable of being moralized. Even as it is, the state is obviously a moral agent. It is both a providence and a stern judge.

The point at which the criticism of the state is chiefly leveled is its sovereignty, a sovereignty supported by its exclusive right to use physical force in bringing about obedience to its will. This whole conception of state authority has been rejected by philosophical anarchists such as Bakunin, Tolstoi, and Kropotkin. These men repudiated the state altogether, condemning it as an organ of oppression. But their idea of a stateless humanity is obviously so incapable of realization under existing conditions that it has had comparatively little influence. Instead of advocating the destruction of the state, the tendency among its critics in recent years has, consequently, been to advocate a limitation of its power. The political pluralists, for instance, have argued that the state should renounce its claim to exclusive and absolute sovereignty, and should share its authority with the churches, labor unions, and other associations or societies. In so far as this contention is directed against the current deification of the

[6] Cf. the chapter on "The Ethical Queerness of States" in W. E. Hocking, *The Spirit of World Politics,* pp. 482-91.

[7] Note Niebuhr, *Moral Man and Immoral Society.*

state—against the view that the state is virtually omnipotent, that it is above criticism, above moral obligation, beyond good and evil—it represents a needed emphasis. The state, as a matter of fact, is not the sole authority in human society. The various religions, labor, cultural, economic, and other social groups all exercise authority in one way or another. In every nation there are numerous authorities. But this, it should be noted by way of response to the more radical political pluralists, is not inconsistent with the recognition of the state as the supreme authority. Indeed, the existence of a supreme authority is necessary to maintain a proper balance among the less inclusive groups. These groups represent for the most part special interests, and it is highly important that no one of them, such as the economic, should gain an undue ascendancy. To prevent this and thus insure a just social order, there is need of a sovereign state endowed with the exclusive right to employ physical force.

Sovereignty, however, it should be borne in mind, does not mean absolute and unlimited power. It implies the rule of reason and conscience. It implies recognition of the normal interests and rights of men and the duty of the state to protect these rights and interests. Instead of seeking to suppress or absorb them, the truly sovereign state will rather encourage their independent development in so far as they minister to the physical and spiritual welfare of the people. Its own supreme authority will co-operate with the lesser authorities embodied in every normal and progressive human society. Indeed, this is its essential function, "to hinder hindrances to the good life" and thus "provide a framework within which men shall have room themselves to lead the good life."[8]

Penal Law

Treitschke declares that the chief tasks of the state are war and the administration of justice; and in past history there is much to confirm this statement. In any case these two activities

[8] A. D. Lindsay, *The Essentials of Democracy*, pp. 77 f.; *Christianity and Economics*, p. 33.

of the state are the ones that have the most direct bearing on ethics and especially Christian ethics. We have just considered the administration of justice in general, but have said nothing in particular about penal justice or the penal law. This calls for brief consideration, after which we shall take up the more pressing problem of war.

That a bad man should be treated differently from a good man and that in some way or other he should be punished for his evildoing is a profound moral conviction. It is this conviction that lies at the basis of the penal law. In it penalties are imposed on persons who are guilty of acts forbidden by the state. The imposition of these penalties is commonly regarded as having two moral grounds. One is demerit. But just how to define merit and demerit is not altogether clear. Perhaps we may say with Bowne that merit is "the desert of moral approval, and the right to be treated accordingly," and that demerit is "the desert of moral disapproval and its appropriate treatment."[9] These definitions are as satisfactory as any I know, but they do not take us much beyond the general idea that good deeds should be rewarded and evil deeds punished. The only advantage they have is that they make explicit the idea of desert, and this in the case of demerit is about synonymous with guilt. Guilt implies freedom, responsibility, and merited punishment, and thus constitutes a moral basis for the penal law.

The other moral basis is the right of self-defense on the part both of individuals and of society. This right is grounded in the sacredness of the moral personality. Without the security of the individual and the social order there could be no proper development of the moral life. Under such conditions, if they were possible, there would be a reversion to Hobbes's "war of all against all." The only way to avoid such an anarchic state is to resist and punish evildoers. This is the obvious lesson of human history, and it is implied in biblical teaching as a whole.

[9] *Principles of Ethics*, p. 171.

Absolute nonresistance to evil would mean the disintegration not only of society but of the moral personality itself.

The question has been raised as to whether wrongdoing should not be regarded as a disease rather than as a crime. In some cases, and probably more frequently than is commonly supposed, it is the former. But to universalize this view would be to deny freedom altogether and undermine moral responsibility. It would logically make the cure of wrongdoing a matter of hygiene and medicine rather than the concern of religion and of moral education and discipline. It would lead to physicians' taking the place of preachers and judges and to the substitution of hospitals for prisons. These changes have been proposed, but the proposals have never gotten beyond the theoretical stage. In practice the common conscience has prevailed. There has been no serious question as to the freedom and responsibility of evildoers in general, and this will probably continue to be the case indefinitely despite the theories of both naturalistic and theological determinists.

Penal law, however, has often been administered in an inhumane and brutal manner. Persons sent to prison have often been treated as though they had lost all human rights. This inhumanity has no doubt been due in a considerable degree to the general cruelty and evil passions of the time. But imperfect conceptions of punishment and of crime have also had something to do with it.

Punishment is morally permissible only where there is guilt. But it has not infrequently been justified on other grounds. Caiaphas, for instance, said "it was expedient that one man should die for the people,"[10] or, in other words, that in the case of Jesus public expediency was a sufficient reason for his execution. And in our day innocent hostages are being shot in order to terrorize defeated peoples into submission and to serve the interests of the conquerors. It has also been held that a person may be punished for his own improvement as well as

[10] John 18:14.

for the public good. But all such theories and practices are unethical. The only moral justification of punishment is its essential justice. Punishment implies "retribution on the part of the punisher and expiation on the part of the punished." Where these are lacking and there is no underlying idea of guilt and its desert, it sinks to a nonmoral level.

But recognition of guilt as the basal element in punishment does not decide who the punisher should be nor the extent and method of the punishment. In primitive societies punishment was left largely in the hands of individuals, but with the growth of civilization the tendency has been more and more for the state to reserve this function to itself. Individuals may defend themselves and others against attack, but in general the right and obligation to punish offenders rest with the government. This has many advantages. It eliminates passion, revenge, and resulting feuds. It assures objective and impersonal justice. It makes punishment certain because of the power of the state. But while punishment by society instead of by individuals has these practical advantages, there is nothing in the nature of punishment or guilt that requires it, nor is there anything in the principle of retribution that determines the kind and degree of punishment for any particular crime or offense. The ancient law of retaliation contained such a standard, but this standard was sub-Christian. And not only was it sub-Christian; its application in many cases was submoral, indeed immoral, as unjust and evil as the crime itself.

Our present penal law lays down specific penalties for specific offenses. But in doing so it is guided by practical experience rather than by an abstract standard of justice. Its aim is not to satisfy the absolute demands of the principles of expiation and retribution but rather to reform the criminal, to protect society, and "to make the criminal industry unprofitable." [11] The latter is a standard that we can gauge and apply with a fair degree of accuracy. But the measurement of a person's guilt lies beyond

[11] Bowne, *op. cit.*, p. 275.

us. So many unknown factors enter into and condition his conduct that we are unable to determine the precise extent of his responsibility for any crime he may have committed. This must be left to God. Sociology has, however, made it clear that the individual is much more dependent on his social environment than was previously believed to be the case. His misdoings may in many instances be traced to the evil surroundings in which he was brought up. Society thus shares in his guilt. The increasing recognition of this fact has profoundly influenced modern penology and has led to a much more humane treatment of the inmates of our prisons than was customary in the past The difference between them and people in general, it is now seen, is not so radical, nor is the legitimate function of punishment such, as to justify the extreme disciplinary and punitive measures formerly resorted to. Persons in prison have rights and possibilities of improvement; and, next to the protection of society, these are the primary things to be taken into account in their prison life. This is becoming more and more the conviction of the common as well as the Christian conscience.

With respect to capital punishment opinion is divided. The sanctity of human life is a deep-seated Christian and human sentiment. If left to itself, this sentiment would save the lives of all men, murderers as well as others. But here a conflict arises. To save the lives of murderers might imperil the lives of innocent people. In this situation a choice must be made; and the choice, as a rule, is not a difficult one. If capital punishment is necessary to restrain homicide effectively, it should be retained. But if not, there is no moral justification of it. The question at issue is, therefore, one of fact; and experience alone can give the answer.

War and the Christian Ideal

In principle war is akin to the execution of the penal law. Both are in their ideals concerned with the defense of the state and with the establishment of justice. Both also employ force in order to achieve their ends, and in this and other respects have seemed to be out of accord with the Christian ethic. Both were condemned in the early church, but they could not be eliminated; and when this became clear efforts were made in subsequent centuries to humanize and Christianize them as much as possible. War has resisted these efforts more effectually than the penal law and today is the most serious moral problem confronting the church. "War," says Westermarck, "is a rock on which Christian principles have suffered the most miserable shipwreck." [12]

So it seems on the surface. But Christian thought on the subject is far more complex than the statement by Westermarck would suggest. Indeed, so divided is Christian opinion with reference to war that it is only in a very limited sense that we can speak of a Christian attitude toward it. The one point on which all representative Christian thinkers seem agreed is this; that the perfect relation of moral beings to each other is that of peace, and that all war, in heaven or elsewhere, is a breach of the Christian moral ideal. The Christian ideal is not only that every person and every group of persons respect the rights of every other person and group of persons but that all have a positive attitude of good will toward each other. It is also an ideal that assumes a sufficient degree of intelligence on the part of all persons to prevent their being led into conflict with each other through ignorance. Where these conditions prevail, war would seem to be impossible. The law of love combined with adequate intelligence would seem to exclude it. For war is the attempt of one group to impose its will upon another and resisting group by violence, and this could hardly be conceived as taking place where there is universal and intelligent good will.

There are some, it is true, who profess themselves Christians, as Treitschke did, but who glorify war as the nurse of heroism and other manly virtues, who speak of its "sacredness" and describe it as a "part of the divinely appointed order," who look upon it as the sphere in which the "grandeur of history lies"

[12] *Christianity and Morals,* p. 236.

and in which "we can most clearly trace the triumph of human reason," and who condemn the ideal of perpetual peace as "not only impossible, but immoral as well." [13] But it could hardly be said that anyone holding such views as these is a representative Christian thinker. He may profess acceptance of the Christian ethic of love, but there is no way of harmonizing it with his ethic of power and war. War has no place in the abstract or absolute Christian moral ideal. Treitschke himself at times virtually admits this by grounding the perpetuity of war in "human sins and passions" and by representing war as "the one remedy for an *ailing* nation." [14]

We may then say that Christians are agreed in excluding war from the moral ideal. But this is about the only important point with respect to war on which they are agreed. They differ as to the possibility of realizing on earth the ideal of a warless world. They differ as to whether there ever was or can be such a thing as a "just" war in the ethical sense of the term. They differ also in their views of the method or methods to be employed in promoting universal peace. Each of these points of difference will be considered briefly.

Is War Inevitable?

We begin with the question as to the inevitability of war. There are many who on naturalistic and empirical grounds answer this question in the affirmative. They lay stress on the experience of the past and the present, on the native pugnacity of the human species, on the struggle for existence made necessary by the conditions of human life, on the conflicting interests of different nations and races, on the growth of population, on the pride and ambition of the more powerful states, and on the forward and upward surge of human life as a whole. Much is also said about the nature of the state, its sovereignty, and "its incompatibility with any power over it." The very fact of

[13] *Politics,* I, 29, 21; II, 598-99.

[14] *Ibid.,* I, 66; II, 599.

such incompatibility, it is argued, makes war inevitable, for it excludes the idea of any authority beyond that represented by its own strength. "The arbitrament of force is the logical outcome of the nature of the state. The mere fact of the existence of many states involves the necessity of war." It is, furthermore, asserted that a long period of peace causes nations to degenerate. This is contrary to the divine plan. Hence "God will see to it that war shall return again, a terrible medicine for mankind diseased." [15]

The conception of war as inevitable and as salutary under certain conditions is held by many conservative theologians. But they do not look upon it as having a place in the ideal order. They regard it as necessary but as a necessary evil. Its necessity is due to the fall of man, which, however conceived, resulted in the descent of the world from a pure to an impure, from a higher to a lower, from a primal to a secondary, order of being. This secondary world order, in which we live, is dominated by the tragic law that life can grow only through the destruction of life. The order is itself evil. It belongs to a fallen, a sinful, world. But it is nevertheless a divine order. God established it as a consequence of, or penalty for, human sin. Hence its tragic law of life through death is also his law. This law makes war necessary, and consequently we must look upon war as having a place in the divine plan. "All organic life," says Karl Heim, one of Germany's most devout and most distinguished theologians, "stands in this temporal order under the tragic law that life cannot unfold itself except by slaying life; war is, therefore, not the offspring of individual sin, but a divine order of life, whose necessity is grounded in a primal fall, an over-individual and collective sin." [16]

This line of argument, however, is far from convincing. The idea of a primal fall, on which it is based, is itself unhistorical; and the notion of an original superindividual and collective sin

[15] *Ibid.*, II, 599; I, 69.

[16] *Glaube und Leben*, p. 265.

has no warrant either in faith or reason. Furthermore, it is a far cry from the animal struggle for existence to the necessity and moral justification of war as a permanent phase of human life. Sacrifice is no doubt a universal law of life. It applies to life in its highest as well as its lowest forms. "Greater love hath no man than this, that a man lay down his life for his friends." "Except a grain of wheat fall into the earth and die, it abideth by itself alone; but if it die, it beareth much fruit."[17] Sacrificial love does enlarge and enrich human life. But surely this fact does not justify selfish aggression on the part of either an individual or a nation. Rather does it imply a condemnation of such aggression. The life that grows and expands through self-sacrifice is one thing, and the life that expresses itself in brutal self-assertion is certainly a very different thing. The latter type of life cannot be justified by the same law as that which obtains in the former.

Civilization consists largely in the restraints imposed upon the native aggressiveness and pugnacity of men. Only by disciplining and moralizing the impulses and ambitions of individuals and nations can there be true progress. This process of education, no doubt, has limits. But there is no valid ground for believing that man is so completely enchained by his animal inheritance or so totally corrupted by a primal fall of the race that he is doomed in his organized political life to be a beast of prey so long as time shall last. There is nothing in the nature of men or in the nature of the state that necessarily excludes the possibility of a warless world. The problem of war does not differ in kind from other great social and political problems with which the human mind has dealt successfully. It is, to be sure, a more difficult problem, a problem of greater magnitude. But this does not mean that it is insoluble. It simply means that longer time, greater wisdom, more determined effort, and more favorable circumstances will be needed for its solution. When this end will be achieved, no one knows. But there is no in-

---

[17] John 15:13; 12:24.

herent reason why the hope of it should be abandoned. As victory has been won over private feuds and slavery, so it is quite possible that victory will eventually be won over war also. Its elimination would seem to be the great natural, culminating stage in the long struggle that the race has been carrying on against the use of brute force. At any rate there is no adequate ground for dogmatically denying the possibility of humanity's ever attaining this goal.

Can There Be a Just War?

By a "just" war is meant a war in which one side is morally justified in its resort to arms. Many and probably most wars have been due to evil motives on both sides. But in some wars the evil motives, the aggression and injustice, have apparently been largely confined to one side. The other side has fought in self-defense or from some other worthy motive, and hence from its point of view these wars have been just or righteous wars. This distinction between just and unjust wars has been generally accepted throughout most of the church's history.[18] But dissent from it has been expressed by some of the smaller Christian groups such as the Lollards, Anabaptists, and Quakers; and in more recent times this dissent has become common in the larger churches. There are many pacifists who condemn all wars as evil, no matter how they may have arisen, no matter whether they be defensive or offensive. No war is morally justifiable. This view is called absolute pacifism. Its rapid spread between the first and second World Wars made the question as to the possibility of a just war a vital one in the churches of Great Britain and America.

There are three main bases of absolute pacifism. One is the religious principle of nonresistance, the second is the religious principle of the sacredness of human life, and the third is the

---

[18] Augustine, Thomas Aquinas, and Luther held firmly to the possibility and actuality of "just" wars. Cf. T. S. K. Scott-Craig, *Christian Attitudes to War and Peace,* pp. 50-111, 150 ff.; Umphrey Lee. *The Historic Church and Modern Pacifism,* pp. 69 ff., 126 ff.

futility of war. Of these the first has figured most prominently in the pacifistic debate, and we shall concern ourselves chiefly with it. But before taking it up a few comments may be made on the other two.

The Christian and human aversion to the shedding of blood is deep-seated. The commandment not to kill is a basal moral law. Murder is a capital crime. It is not, therefore, strange that some should look upon all war with horror as mass murder and butchery. Many wars, indeed, have been such, and from a strictly individualistic standpoint all wars seem such. Innocent men are ruthlessly slain. But war is not an affair between individuals; it is an affair of state. And few have carried the idea of the sanctity of human life so far as to deny to the state the moral right to take the life of a murderer. The very fact that we speak of murder as a "capital" crime implies the contrary. Murder is, and justly so, a crime punishable with death if the public welfare requires it. This principle also applies to foreign foes who are seeking to destroy the state and the lives of its citizens. These foes, so long as they persist in their violent attacks, have in the eyes of the state the same status as that of murderers. They have forfeited their right to life, no matter how innocent of evil purpose they may be as individuals.

The charge of futility against war has much to support it. Wars often breed wars instead of ending them. They often cause such great misery, suffering, and other evils as completely to offset any benefits derived from them. But to pass from these undeniable facts to a denial that there has ever been such a thing as a beneficial war, is, as Bowne says, to fall into "falsehood and folly." Some wars have been "among the most beneficent events of human history."[19] This does not necessarily mean that there will continue to be such wars in the future, but it does mean that the standard of utility or futility as applied to war is an uncertain one. There is nothing at present

[19] *Op. cit.*, p. 300.

so objectively certain about the absence of value in war as to warrant its absolute and unconditional renunciation.

The chief theoretical ground of absolute pacifism is the principle of nonresistance as expressed in the Sermon on the Mount. "I say unto you," said Jesus, "Resist not him that is evil: but whosoever smiteth thee on thy right cheek, turn to him the other also. And if any man would go to the law with thee, and take away thy coat, let him have thy cloak also. . . . . Ye have heard that it was said, Thou shalt love thy neighbor, and hate thine enemy: but I say unto you, Love your enemies, and pray for them that persecute you."[20] Such utterances as these, it is insisted, absolutely and unequivocally exclude all war, the so-called "just" war as well as other wars. They condemn all resort to force both on the part of individuals and on the part of the state. They lay down the principle of sacrificial love as the one supreme and comprehensive law of social interaction.

But if this interpretation of Jesus' teaching with respect to nonresistance be correct, certain very serious consequences follow. For one thing, the right of self-defense is negated. And this means either that there are no duties to self, no duty of self-preservation, and no duty of self-realization, or that we are to leave their fulfillment to other agents, divine or human. In either case a fundamental moral right and duty is renounced. We may, it is true, interpret nonresistance as meaning simply that in defending ourselves we are as a rule to employ moral rather than physical means, leaving the use of force to the state. This is, as a matter of fact, the sense in which Jesus' words on the subject are commonly understood. They are treated as a prohibition of passion and violence in dealing with our enemies, and not as a complete rejection of the right and duty of self-defense. The use of force even by the individual, it is assumed, is permissible when no other means of self-defense are available.

Another serious consequence of the absolutistic doctrine of

[20] Matt. 5:39-40, 43-44.

nonresistance is that it excludes the right and duty of rendering physical assistance to the weak who are being unjustly and violently attacked. Jesus himself says nothing about this. He did not forbid resistance to evil done to others. And one wonders what the Good Samaritan would have done if he had come upon the scene a little earlier, just as the attack was being made upon the man who was going down from Jerusalem to Jericho. We are fairly certain what the priest and the Levite would have done under those circumstances. They would not have passed by on the other side; they would have made a wide and safe detour. But as for the Good Samaritan, it would seem probable that he would have assisted the traveler in beating off the robbers' attack if there were any prospect of success in doing so. Certainly the Christian spirit of justice and love would have prompted such action. For there is permanent truth in the classical maxim that one who does not defend another from injury is as much at fault as he who commits the injury. Where the welfare of others is involved, resistance to evil is a duty. "If we do not struggle," said Plotinus, "evil men will triumph." [21]

A still more serious consequence of a literal interpretation of Jesus' teaching concerning nonresistance is its bearing on the state. The state, as we have seen, is based on force. Its primary purpose is to defend itself and its citizens from unjust attack. This is the function of the army and the police. Without such use of force the state would disintegrate and there would be anarchy.

The attempt is often made to draw a fundamental moral distinction between an army and a police force. But in theory there is no essential difference. One seeks to defend the state and its citizens against internal enemies, and the other has for the most part the task of defending them against external enemies. The methods of the army are usually and necessarily more violent than those of the police. But it is force that is employed in both cases, and where violent resistance is encountered the

---

[21] Quoted by R. Eucken, *The Truth of Religion*, p. 394.

extreme penalty may be exacted by the policeman as well as by the soldier. Both the army and the police department rest on the same ethical principle, the principle of resisting evil by force, and, if necessary, by violence. If such resistance is unchristian in one case, it is unchristian in the other. If we condemn war because of its use of force, we must, if we are consistent, condemn the police department for the same reason. If, on the other hand, we believe that force may legitimately be used by the police, we must, if we are consistent, admit that it may be legitimately used also by the army. In theory there is no way of distinguishing so sharply between the police force and the army that one is justified in accepting the moral legitimacy of the former and denying completely the moral legitimacy of the latter. It is, indeed, under existing conditions the army and the navy that alone make possible the milder and more humane use of force represented by the police department. Back of every policeman stands the more powerful figure of the soldier.

The whole question as to whether war is under any circumstances morally justifiable, is, therefore, dependent for its answer on one's attitude toward the state. If the existence of the state is necessary to avoid anarchy and if it is, consequently, the duty of the state to defend itself against enemies from within and from without, it is obvious that a just war not only is conceivable but has actually often taken place. Only on the assumption that the existence of the state is unnecessary and that the use of force is morally wrong could the contrary be maintained. With human nature such as it is, we must choose between social chaos and the right to resist evil. Jesus' principle of nonresistance, if taken literally and applied both to the individual and to the state, would be an anarchistic doctrine.

But that Jesus did not intend such an interpretation and application of his saying concerning nonresistance is evident from his life and teaching as a whole. He did not condemn the state as such; he did not advocate its overthrow. He lived in harmony with its laws and rendered unto Caesar what was

Caesar's. In so doing he set the standard for his own disciples and also for the church as a whole. In its attitude toward the state, the church has for the most part taken its cue from Romans 13:1-3 and I Peter 2:13-14 rather than from Matthew 5:39-40. It has accepted the doctrine that "the powers that be are ordained of God" or, in other words, that the state with its necessary use of force is a divinely established institution. Such a view of the state clearly carries with it the possibility of a righteous war. Indeed, anyone who believes in the state and understands what this means must also believe that under certain circumstances war is morally justifiable.

Methods of Promoting Peace

But while there may be and have been just wars in the sense in which we have defined the term, war, we have argued, is not to be regarded as a permanent and inevitable phase of human life. No matter how necessary and how beneficial in their results some wars may have been, war in general is a great evil, one of the worst scourges of mankind. One may view it as a divine punishment and thus fit it into the divine providence as one would a pestilence. But this would not make any less desirable, or obligatory, its elimination from human life. One may also believe its complete elimination impossible and yet believe firmly in the possibility and duty of limiting its frequency and its geographical extent. The movement in favor of peace is, therefore, not dependent on one's theory with reference to the possible total eradication of war. People may disagree on this point and yet be agreed on the importance of promoting peace, so far as possible, among the nations of the world. In this respect virtually all Christians may be classed as pacifists. And beyond the limits of the church the movement in favor of such a limited pacifism has been gaining rapidly since the first World War.

The reasons for the growth of this movement are various. The most influential has no doubt been the experience of the evils of war during the past thirty years. But there are also more permanent reasons. One is the fact that war has now become a totalitarian enterprise and as such has become a graver evil than it was in earlier times when it was confined largely to professional soldiers. It now dislocates the normal activities of the whole nation and destroys the lives of civilians as well as of those in the armed forces. Another fact that has made war more objectionable is that it has become more highly mechanized. This has deprived it of much of the glory that formerly attached to it through the victories won by soldiers in personal combat. It has also made war more destructive of life and property and more of a menace to civilization. Then too, the modern democratic process in government with its appeal to reason rather than force has tended to bring out more clearly the irrationality of war as a method of settling international disputes. These and other factors have in recent years given a new impetus to the peace movement and awakened the hope that now at last we may be approaching a decisive turning point in the long history of war.

So far as the methods of promoting peace are concerned, we may distinguish between the absolutistic method and political or practical methods. The absolutistic method has already been considered. It consists in renouncing or "outlawing" war altogether as evil and refusing to have anything to do with it. The hope is in this way to arouse sufficient antiwar sentiment to make it inadvisable for any government to declare war. So strong was this movement in England a few years ago that Canon Raven in 1938 declared it probable that in the event of another European war "a pacifist secession from all churches would take place on a large scale and that the seceders would constitute a sect of their own." [22] This has not taken place. The grim reality of war has proven too strong for peacetime pacifism of even the most radical type. But this does not mean that such pacifism has no value. It tends to arouse people out of their

[22] *War and the Christian*, pp. 58 f.; 169.

lethargic acceptance of war as a necessary evil; it asserts the rights of the individual conscience; and it directs attention to the moral peril involved in the increasing authority of the state. Its program, however, is too much of the abstract perfectionist type, too narrow, too limited in its appeal, too superficial in its intellectual and theoretical grounding to exert a wide influence and to make a major contribution to the solution of the war problem.

Of the political or practical methods of preventing war, three of a general and long-range character may be mentioned. One is the removal of the economic causes of war by giving all nations access to the raw materials of the world. This is obviously not an easy thing to do. But with good will and a realization of the gravity of the present world situation much could be accomplished in this direction through the ordinary diplomatic channels and especially through an ecumenical economic conference. A second and still more difficult method of assuring peace is to overthrow the nationalistic obstacles to it, the obstacles that have grown up out of the modern deification of the state and the ascription to it of a kind of omnipotent and unconditional sovereignty. So conceived the state knows no supreme law except that of its own self-interest. Aggression is, therefore, justified if the welfare of the nation calls for it. Such a doctrine, when held by a powerful nation, is a constant threat to the peace of the world. Somehow it must be overcome. The current religious nationalism, like the idolatries of the past, must be destroyed; and in place of the deified state a more inclusive ideal must be set up, an ideal which implies the possibility of universal friendship and co-operation among the nations of the world. This is a stupendous task, and progress toward its realization will necessarily be slow. It is here that spiritual religion will make its chief contribution to the cause of peace.

But to this moral and religious offensive against a belligerent nationalism, another must be added. This third method of promoting peace consists in a sustained effort to establish a real world court and a real league of nations—a court and a league that will have authority to enforce their decisions. Only some such supernational organization, supported by adequate military power, will be able to prevent war or suppress it if it should break out. Such an organization would, of course, mean a limitation of the sovereignty of individual states, an abandonment of isolationism, and the creation of a new sense of international responsibility.[23]

These three methods of dealing with the problem of war may to some seem too general, too complex or vague, too prosaic, and too slow to arouse enthusiasm and a crusading spirit. But they or similar methods are the only ones that are likely to command the intellectual and moral respect of peace-loving people in general and thus have a universal appeal. They are the only ones that give promise of ultimate success; and even in their case success cannot be assured unless they are supported by a favoring Providence and by the logic of unforeseeable events. It is the record that war has made, is making, and will continue to make that will eventually seal its fate. War will ultimately destroy itself.

---

[23] Cf. J. F. Dulles, *War, Peace and Change* (1939), an able and informing book.

CHAPTER XII

THE CHURCH AND CULTURE

THE church and culture are here classed together as a matter of convenience and not because of any desire to merge one in the other or subordinate one to the other. They are distinct phases of community life and will be so treated. A separate chapter might have been devoted to the study of culture. But this hardly seemed necessary in the present volume. A brief general discussion of the subject will here suffice; and this may conveniently be appended to our more extended discussion of the church.

THE NATURE OF THE CHURCH

The church is less obviously entitled to be called an order of creation than the family or the state. The latter are inherent in the structure of society. Human life in its organized form would hardly be possible without them. They are responses to universal and compelling needs, and their necessity is generally recognized. This is less true of the church. But there are nevertheless two respects in which it may properly be viewed as an order of creation. We may interpret it in a broad sense as meaning organized religion in general. And if we do so, it is clear that there is no good reason why it should not be regarded as occupying a position parallel to that of the state. Both owe their origin to fundamental human needs, an inner need of the soul in one case and the need of external security in the other. If, therefore, the latter need points to a divine purpose in the state and stamps it as an order of creation, the former need would seem plainly to have a similar significance for the church. For organized religion has been almost as universal as civil government.

On the other hand, we may take the common conception of

the church as a limited institution which had its origin at a definite period of human history. As such we may agree with Troeltsch that its creation was the "real great sociological achievement" of Christianity,[1] and we may accept Harnack's statement that in its Catholic form alone it became "the greatest religious and political creation known to history."[2] Yet we might look upon it, as many do, as an institution that has done more harm than good or that has outlived its usefulness. But such a view would hardly be consistent with a thoroughgoing immanental theism. The theist, not to say the Christian, must see in the church something more than an historical accident. For him it is a divine creation. Though still limited in extent it is potentially universal and thus represents an essential and permanent order in human life. We may, then, think of the church as an order of creation in a twofold sense; in the sense that it meets the common human need which underlies organized religion in general, and also in the sense that it is the product of a unique divine creative activity.

To define the church, however, as an order of creation in either or both of these senses does not determine its ethical nature or function. In taking up the latter question we are confronted with two divergent views that have been rather sharply opposed to each other in Christian and especially Protestant ethics. According to one, the church is primarily a channel of the divine forgiving grace. Its members, through the preaching of the Word and the administration of the sacraments, receive the divine forgiveness. They do not in the strict sense of the term do anything to merit it.

Indeed, they are unable to acquire any real merit before God. Everything in their relation to him is of grace. He forgives men. It is this that qualifies them to be true members of his church. Their forgiveness, it is true, has or ought to have a transforming effect on their character. But the emphasis falls, not on their moral transformation, but on the fact of their

[1] *The Social Teaching of the Christian Churches,* I, 163.

[2] Quoted by K. Adam, *op. cit.,* p. 12.

forgiveness. They are saved *in* their sins rather than *from* their sins. Though saved, they are still sinners. It is not, then, their holiness of character and the consequent holiness of the church that is the fundamentally important thing; it is rather the fact that they are recipients of the divine grace and that the church is the medium of this grace. What, therefore, constitutes the true function of the church is its proclamation of the divine forgiveness through faith, not its attempted realization of the moral ideal. The latter is in any case secondary. It is not the chief standard by which the church is to be judged.

Opposed to the foregoing conception of the church is the view that saving faith is not a mere passive receptivity, that it includes a hungering and thirsting after righteousness, and that the true church is composed of people who not only are saved *in* their sins but are also earnestly seeking to be saved *from* their sins. Holiness, in other words, is inherent in the life and faith of the church. The church is not simply a sign of individual election or a presage of a future heavenly world. It is a regenerated body of believers and, as such, a symbol and pledge of a redeemed and perfected human society. It is "the highest expression of the meaning of goodness and at the same time the supreme organ for the achievement of goodness in the world." [3]

Thus viewed, the church is in its essential nature an ethical institution as well as a worshiping community. It does not exist for its own sake, for the maintenance of its own sanctity. It is not an independent entity, an end in itself. Its high task is not to "*be* the church" in an isolationist sense. It has an ethical and spiritual mission. It is an agent of the Divine Spirit. It has an instrumental function. It exists as the bearer of the Christian moral ideal and as the medium through which this ideal is to be realized. Only from this instrumental standpoint can we understand aright its nature. The church is in its essence constituted by its moral and spiritual function, not

[3] J. A. Mackay, *A Preface to Christian Theology*, p. 159.

by its miraculous origin nor by its possession of a mystical sacramental grace. The true grace of God manifests itself in holiness of life, in faith and love. This applies to the church as well as the individual. The sanctity of the church is personal, not mystical or abstractly metaphysical. It is a conscious possession; and in acquiring it the church is creative as well as receptive. It has the task of bringing in the Kingdom of God as well as the high privilege of receiving it. And bringing in the Kingdom must be understood in an objective as well as a subjective sense. There was, as Bishop McConnell has said, a tendency in the Wesleyan revival "so to emphasize inner virtues as to neglect outer conditions";[4] and this tendency has been more or less characteristic of the church throughout most of its history. "Overcoming the world" has been interpreted too exclusively as an inner experience. It also calls for outer change. The world both without and within us must be overcome. This double task belongs to the ethical mission of the church.

The Unity of the Church

In the ideal and general sense in which we are using the term, the church is one. As there is "one Lord, one faith, one baptism, one God and Father of all, who is over all, and through all, and in all,"[5] so there is or ought to be one church. This has been a strong conviction from the beginning of Christian history. The church in its ideal recognizes no barriers of race, of nationality, or of geography. It is a universal institution. In this respect it transcends the state and all other human organizations. It claims all mankind as its parish. And this universality implies unity. The unity may be conceived of as organizational, or as spiritual, or as both. Roman Catholics have laid stress on the organization as a necessary factor in Christian or church unity, while Protestants have put the emphasis on the unity of the spirit. The latter standpoint implies a distinction between the "visible" and the "invisible" church.

[4] *Human Needs and World Christianity,* p. 96.

[5] Eph. 4:5.

The "invisible" church is the one truly catholic church. It exists in and through the "visible" church or churches but is identical with none of them. It is the church viewed as an ideal spiritual fellowship and as such is an object of faith rather than an historical institution. But there is also a sense in which the unity of the church may from the Protestant standpoint be regarded as an empirical fact. Despite the many divisions and conflicts within the church there is a general conviction that the word Christian has a definite and distinctive meaning and that religious organizations which bear this name have something important in common. They have a community of faith that sets them apart from the rest of mankind. And the recognition of this community is itself a bond of union among them, constituting them in a sense one church. In other words, the sense of unity and universality is implicit in the Christian faith.

It is no doubt true that the average Christian in speaking of the church usually has in mind the local rather than the universal church. It is the local church that gives concreteness and immediate spiritual content to the idea of the church. But a church that is purely local would not be a church in the full Christian sense of the term. The local church derives its Christian character from its relation to the church universal. It is the consciousness of being a part of a larger whole that gives depth and richness to the faith and fellowship of the local church. The broader fellowship of the entire Christian church is thus a creative factor in the life and faith of the local units, of which it is necessarily composed. The church, to be truly Christian, must be one as well as many. This ideal of unity has been generally accepted throughout the history of the church. It is the goal toward which the spirit of love and the community of faith have naturally pointed, and in one way or another the church or churches have on the whole striven for it.[6]

---

[6] For a comprehensive historical treatment of the subject see Gaius Jackson Slosser, *Christian Unity: Its History and Challenge in All Communions in All Lands* (1929).

The schismatic spirit has been condemned, and rightly. The feeling has been that it is an ugly thing for a group of Christians to separate themselves from their brethren on the ground of their own superior righteousness. Such an attitude runs counter to the spirit of love and of humility. But while in the abstract this may be true, it is evident that the established church has at times become so corrupt that schisms seemed necessary in order to restore a purer type of Christainity. In these instances the schisms were probably justified. Purity of faith is more important than unity of organization. And in many other instances less serious reasons may have justified separation from a church or divisions of it. A schism, while a violation of the ideal of church unity, may nevertheless be the lesser of two evils.

Schisms, however, that may have been justified in their origin may become serious evils by being perpetuated long after the causes that gave rise to them have disappeared. Such a situation now confronts the Christian church. The two hundred and more denominations in the United States are a manifest scandal. There is no rational justification for such a large number. They confuse the public mind with respect to the essentials of the Christian faith. They divide and weaken the Christian forces at a time when a united Christian front is imperatively needed to stem the advance of powerful pagan forces such as the current secularism and nationalism. Under existing conditions the world, as Bishop Brent said, is too strong for a divided church. We urgently need a greater degree both of church union and of Christian unity. The Christian ideal demands it, and so also does the religious crisis now confronting the world.

At the same time we must not forget that the history of the church contains a solemn warning against an exaggerated emphasis on the unity of the church and on its identification with an external organization. Such an emphasis led in Roman

Catholicism to what has been called "theocratic imperialism."[7] The church was transformed into a political institution, a vast empire, an autocratic state. This transformation, it is true, was in large measure due to the special conditions that confronted the ancient and medieval church. It also cannot be denied that as an ecclesiastical empire the church rendered important services to Western civilization. But along with these services went great evils. Under a politically minded leadership worship tended to become external and formal. Stress was laid on outward obedience to the church and its regulations rather than on moral inwardness or purity of heart. The latter, to be sure, continued to have a place and an important one in the life of the church. The mystics preached and practiced it with ardor. But in official circles and in the church as a whole it occupied no such central position as it does in the New Testament. The tendency was to lay the emphasis on outward conformity.

Another evil result of the medieval ecclesiastical imperialism was its corrupting influence in the field of church administration. To maintain an institution so elaborate as that required by the imperialistic policy of the medieval church involved necessarily very heavy expenses. To meet these expenses the church could not impose taxes and collect them by force as the state does. It, consequently, resorted to the sale of indulgences, the expropriation of wealthy heretics, and other disgraceful practices that aroused the conscience of the church and of the world and led eventually to the Protestant Reformation. Since then these evils have been to a large degree corrected, but they represent a danger to which an elaborate ecclesiastical institution is almost inevitably exposed.

A further and more serious evil resulting from the medieval emphasis on the organic unity of the church was the persecution of heretics.[8] This persecution is the darkest chapter in the

---

[7] W. R. Inge, *Christian Ethics and Modern Problems*, pp. 140-200.

[8] Cf. H. C. Lea, *A History of the Inquisition of the Middle Ages* (1888) and *A History of the Inquisition of Spain* (1906-7); C. J. Cadoux, *Catholicism and Christianity* (1929), pp. 548-617.

history of the church. It equalled, if it did not surpass, in cruelty the persecution of the Christians by the Roman Empire. People charged with heresy were burned alive or otherwise exterminated by the thousands and much larger numbers subjected to inhuman tortures. That the church resorted to such barbarous measures in its efforts to eradicate heresy was no doubt in large part due to the general cruelty of the age. But back of that lay a deep-seated spirit of intolerance. This intolerance grew out of the belief that there is no salvation outside of the organized church and that the maintenance of the unity of the church is, consequently, a matter of supreme concern to mankind. To punish heresy is, therefore, even more of a duty than to punish crime against the state. "For," as Thomas Aquinas said, "it is a much graver matter to corrupt the faith which quickens the soul, than to forge money, which supports the temporal life. Wherefore, if forgers of money and other evil doers are forthwith condemned to death by the secular authority, much more reason is there for heretics, as soon as they are convicted of heresy, to be not only excommunicated but even put to death."[9]

This spirit of intolerance has greatly moderated in the modern world, but the right of persecution has not been officially renounced by the Roman Catholic Church, as it has been by the Protestant churches. And, in view of its official teaching on the subject, it is not impossible nor improbable that, if favorable conditions should arise in Roman Catholic countries, the persecuting spirit would be revived. It is often said by liberals that persecution is ineffective, that it defeats its own end, that the blood of the martyrs is the seed of the church. But this is far from universally true. It was not true of Christianity in Japan, nor of Protestantism in Spain, Italy, and France. Persecution has often achieved a large degree of success. Its failures have not been sufficiently pronounced to warrant the charge of futility against the policy as a whole.

---

[9] *Summa Theologica,* II-II, Q. xi, art. 3.

The decisive objections to persecution would seem to be these. It does violence to the conscience of the individual, and it stands in the way of intellectual and social progress. These two go together. There may, it is true, be some question as to the sanctity of the individual conscience. Liberty of conscience or freedom of thought may lead to serious error, and to correct such error coercion may at times seem to be necessary. But in dealing with a problem of this kind it is important to distinguish between real error and what we think to be error. This holds true of the church as well as the individual. If the church is unwilling to tolerate in others what it regards as error, it will inevitably suppress truth along with error; and the result will be intellectual stagnation over a wide area. If there is to be true progress, there must be a willingness on the part both of the church and state to permit what they believe to be error and to entrust the eradication of error, if such it be, to educative processes rather than to the use of force.

This does not mean that force may never be used against erroneous and perverse opinion. Liberty of conscience and freedom of thought are not absolute rights. One's moral and other judgments may, if published and acted upon, be obviously detrimental to the public good; and in such instances suppression may be necessary. But just when liberty becomes license and freedom a moral or social peril, is not easy to determine. One may scent peril where there is none. This the church has often done, and the result has been the persecution of the innocent and the erection of barriers to intellectual and social progress.[10]

In promoting the cause of church union it is important to bear in mind the foregoing evils of a theocratic imperialism, which history has taught us, as well as the benefits to be derived from a larger degree of church union than at present prevails. It is also important to recognize the truth in the tra-

[10] In view of this dark side of the church's history note the following remark by Swinburne. "I could," he said, "worship the Crucified, if he came to me without his leprous bride the church." Quoted by Dean Inge, *op cit.*, p. 143.

ditional distinction between the "visible" and the "invisible' church. The unity of the latter does not necessarily imply the unity of the former. True Christian unity may exist without organic church union, though under normal circumstances church union no doubt tends to promote Christian unity.

Ecclesiastical Discipline

Within limits it is obviously the duty of the church to maintain its own unity, both organic and spiritual; and it is also clearly its duty to promote and preserve its own purity and sanctity. To achieve these ends, the exercise of ecclesiastical discipline has seemed necessary. This discipline has been directed against both erroneous teaching and evil conduct; and its aim has been either to reclaim the offender from the error of his ways, or to cut him off from the church and thus to save it from contamination. The penalties imposed have been both spiritual and physical, both ecclesiastical and civil. So long as the church was separate from the state, the penalties were for the most part excommunication, or deprivation of certain church privileges, or some sort of penance. When later the church became more or less of a state institution, the penalties were often the same as those of a criminal court, such as imprisonment, confiscation of property, torture, and death. Discipline of this kind reached its climax in the Papal and Spanish Inquisitions. The primary purpose of these Inquisitions was to suppress heresy and to preserve the unity of the church. But the horrors to which they led produced a profound reaction in the modern world, and the resulting tendency has been more and more to restrict the punitive authority of the church and to limit its discipline to ecclesiastical measures or to purely spiritual means. The Roman Catholic Church, as noted above, has not as yet renounced the right of persecution, although its practice is in abeyance; and it still exercises a strict eccelsiastical discipline. The Protestant churches, however, not only have repudiated the principle of persecution but have more and more sought to secure the legitimate ends of church discipline by appeals to the conscience of ministers and laymen rather than by resorting to church trials.

Discipline apart from persecution, however, has figured so prominently in the history of the church that it calls for at least brief consideration in the present connection. That discipline is essential to such an organization as the church, is evident. No institution with such ideals and tasks as the church has, could fulfill its mission in the world without rules and regulations which its members are required to obey. Obedience to the laws of the church and loyalty to its ideals are at once the uniting bond and the dynamic of the organization. Relatively speaking, a church or other social or political organization is strong and influential in proportion to the degree in which its members are ready to subject themselves to discipline and sacrifice themselves for the common good. The discipline may be misguided, and often has been. It has concerned itself with tithing mint, anise, and cummin rather than with the weightier matters of the law. It has diverted conscience from its normal human channels and fixed attention on certain rules of conduct that may be described as artificial and provincial. It has tended toward a narrow ecclesiastical or sectarian conception of the Christian ethic. But despite these evils resulting from a misdirected discipline the principle underlying disciplinary activities of the church has been a sound one. It has recognized the necessity of guiding and strengthening in a practical way the human will in its struggle with the non-Christian tendencies of human nature; and it has also recognized the fact that the Christian has obligations to the church as an institution, obligations that are of vital concern both to the individual and the church and also to humanity. These facts have through the ages given a more or less distinctive character to the popular Christian morality.

The point at which ecclesiastical discipline has most seriously affected Christian conduct has been its connection with the doctrine of sacramental grace. This doctrine is one with reference to which there is considerable difference of opinion.

But in its more distinctive form it means that the divine grace is mediated through external rites known as sacraments. The mediation is mysterious in nature; but it yields forgiveness, regeneration, and the other blessings of salvation. The sacraments are thus of the utmost importance. As channels of the divine grace, they transcend all purely ethical achievements, and hence in the ancient and medieval church they became objects of primary religious concern. To secure their faithful observance was perhaps the chief task of the priests. Ecclesiastical discipline was largely directed toward that end, and as a result lost much of its earlier moral seriousness.

For sacramental grace is not in and of itself an ethical conception. There is no moral ground for ascribing a saving effect to baptism and the eucharist. The only moral basis for forgiveness is repentance, and the value of repentance is independent of any external rite. To make an external rite essential to forgiveness is to dull the moral sense; and sacramentalism has often had this effect. More or less of moral admonition has, it is true, been usually associated with the administration of the sacraments. But this has been secondary except in the case of the sacrament of penance. Penance is the only sacrament that has a distinctly ethical foundation. It provides for the forgiveness of sins committed after baptism, and from the practical or disciplinary point of view has been the most important of the sacraments. It consists of three parts: contrition, confession, and satisfaction. In so far as these were sincerely fulfilled they provided a moral basis for the priestly absolution. But the sacrament was often vitiated by formalism, and its ethical value destroyed by the sale of indulgences.

The Reformers, consequently, rejected the sacrament of penance and substituted for it repentance and the doctrine of justification by faith. But the idea of faith was in many instances so imperfectly moralized that the Protestant conception of it became hardly less magical than the Catholic conception of sacramental grace. Opposed to this tendency, however, there have been activistic and progressive movements such as Puritanism and Methodism that have laid emphasis on discipline and have given to it a more ethical direction than had previously been customary.[11]

Viewing the history of the church as a whole it is evident that ecclesiastical discipline has often been ascetic, arbitrary, artificial, narrow, and sectarian. In the form of casuistry and probabilism it led to many absurdities and evils.[12] But despite these imperfections it has been a potent factor in the moral education of the race, in the creation of a missionary spirit, and in the unification of the church. Indeed, properly guided, it is essential to the structure of the church and to the fulfillment of its purpose in the world.

The Church and the State

Having considered the nature, unity, and discipline of the church from the ethical standpoint, it remains for us to deal briefly with its relation to the state. This relation has varied both in practice and in theory as conditions have changed. At times the state has been hostile to the church and sought its destruction. At other times and for the most part its relations with the church have been friendly and co-operative, though there have been frequent conflicts between civil and ecclesiastical leaders. These conflicts have usually been due to differences of opinion concerning the respective spheres of authority represented by the church and the state. That these differences should arise was almost inevitable. For there is no sharp line of demarcation between church and state. Their activities necessarily to some extent overlap. The things that are Caesar's belong also to God; and the things that are God's belong also in part to Caesar. There is no way of completely separating the two from each other.[13]

---

[11] The importance of discipline in early American Methodism is illustrated by the following entry in Bishop Asbury's *Journal,* June 29, 1775: "Without discipline we should soon be as a rope of sand; so that it must be enforced, let who will be displeased."

[12] Cf. Pascal, *Provincial Letters.*

[13] Cf. Frank Gavin, *Seven Centuries of the Problem of Church and State* (1938).

Furthermore, the state by its very nature claims supremacy in its own territory. It is "the society of societies." All societies, the church included, are subordinate to its authority. They derive from it the legal right to exist. In this respect the church is under the control of the state; and if its existence should threaten or seem to threaten the security and unity of the state, the state would regard itself as jusified in destroying the church or so restricting its activities as to render it harmless. This is the way in which the more serious persecutions of the church by the state have arisen. They have been efforts on the part of the state to maintain its own supreme authority. On the other hand, the church by its very nature has claimed a certain moral authority over the state or at least the right to pass moral criticism on its acts and policies. It is itself a universal institution. It transcends all national limits and regards itself as representing not only the common human conscience at its highest but also the revealed will of God. As representative of this higher moral standpoint, it is its duty to condemn evil wherever it manifests itself and to seek to raise the standard of both public and private morality. The state, therefore, comes properly under the moral criticism, if not the moral tutelage, of the church.

In view of the foregoing facts, it is not strange that the relation between church and state has often been strained and that at times there have been serious conflicts between them. These conflicts were naturally most serious during the first three centuries when the church was confronted by a pagan state. But since then they have continued in one form or another. The medieval period was one of almost constant conflict between civil and ecclesiastical authorities. The nature of these conflicts underwent more or less of a change as a result of the Reformation and the rise of the great European national states. But they still occurred from time to time and in recent years have threatened the very existence of the church in totalitarian states such as Russia and Germany. In some of these conflicts, especially those of the medieval period, the church may justly be charged with having been the aggressor. But in most of them it has been on the defensive. It has simply tried to protect what it regarded as its rights against the encroachments of the state. For the most part it has been too weak to attempt anything more.

This reference to the rights of the church raises the question as to whether the church has any independent rights over against the state. The tendency among statesmen and lawyers is to deny any such rights. "There are," we are told, "there can be no rights except the right of the state."[14] The state is omnipotent. It is "the society of societies," and from it all other societies, the church included, derive whatever rights or authority they have. This conception of state omnipotence or state absolutism was inherited from the pagan Roman Empire and has profoundly influenced political thought during the centuries that have since intervened. At present it is embodied in powerful "totalitarian" states. But it is not necessarily confined to them. A democratic parliament might arrogate to itself an authority as absolute as that of a dictator. Indeed, "the claim to parliamentary omnipotence," as Figgis says, "was the real cause of the American Revolution."[15]

Opposed to the conception of an absolute and omnipotent state, in so far as it denies to the church any independent rights, is the theory that the church has such rights and that these rights are grounded in their divine origin. The church did not receive them from the state, and the state has no right to take them away. This has been the claim of the church from the beginning. But it is not a claim that necessarily requires the separate existence of the church. After the triumph of the church over the pagan state the two came to be thought of as constituting a single society. They were not regarded as independently existing social entities, each with the same personal constituency. Rather were they looked upon as together form-

[14] M. Emile Combes, as quoted in J. N. Figgis, *Churches in the Modern State*, p. 56.

[15] *Ibid.*, p. 82.

ing a church-state. In such a unified society it was possible to speak of conflicts between church and state; but what was really meant was conflicts between two classes of officials, the ecclesiastical and the civil. The popes and emperors of the medieval period were both "rulers in one society." And they both held the same ideal of an absolute and coercive Christian state. This ideal carried with it the right and duty of persecution, and in this and other respects involved such an entanglement of civil and ecclesiastical prerogatives as made practically impossible a solution of the problem of the relation of state and church to each other.

Neither the church nor the state could assert what it regarded as its full rights without claiming supremacy over the other; and this supremacy neither side would accord the other. The popes would never consent to turn matters of conscience and religion over to the politicians; and the emperors would never allow that the state was dependent for its existence on the sufferance of the hierarchy. So frequent conflicts resulted. This was inevitable so long as membership in the church was bound up with citizenship in the state, and so long as both state and church looked upon their own authority as absolute and as including the right and duty of coercion.

Not until the absolutism of both church and state is surrendered can the problem of their relation to each other be satisfactorily solved. The solution is not necessarily to be found in the separation of church and state. This may at present be the best practical method of handling the problem in view of the religious heterogeneity of the modern state. But under other conditions it is quite possible that a state church might have advantages over so-called "free" churches. In any case the essential thing in the relation of the church to the state is not its legal status but its recognition as a social organization with an inherent and independent right of self-development. This inherent right or power of self-development may belong to an established as well as a free church. The established church may have certain external limitations imposed upon it that the free church does not. But if it is truly a church, it must have the right to be a distinct social entity and to develop according to its own innate spirit. This applies not only to the church but to other social unions such as the family, labor unions, scientific organizations, art clubs, fraternities, and many others that might be mentioned. These social unions have all arisen out of "the natural associative instincts of mankind," and are entitled to a place in a developed civilization. The church may go beyond this and claim for itself a special divine origin and authority, but this claim would hardly be recognized by the modern secular state. The only ground for the existence of the church which would appeal to the modern mind is that it is the social expression of a fundamental human instinct or need. As such it is a natural product of human life and has its independent rights. The state did not create the church any more than it did the family and other basal social institutions represented by labor, commerce, and culture; and it has no right to exercise an absolute control over them. This is the fundamental truth in the doctrine of political pluralism referred to in the preceding chapter.

State absolutism is a theory deduced from the abstract idea of unity. It does not comport with the facts of life. What we have in the world is not simply the state and a multitude of unrelated individuals but also "a vast complex of gathered unions." These unions do not exist merely for their own sake. They are essential to the protection and enrichment of the life of the individual. The unitary absolute state tends to engulf all of human life in its own barren unity. It is a kind of "super-man ruling individuals who are below men." [16] What alone can save human society from its devastating effects is the limitation of its authority by the recognized rights of the church and other social unions. Of all these unions the religious society or societies have done most to restrain the ravages of the absolute state. In doing so they at times came into conflict

[16] *Ibid.*, p. 86.

with each other and by insisting each upon its own rights created a tension for which the only remedy was a new spirit of tolerance and freedom. Ecclesiastical animosities and conflicts thus gave birth to political liberty. But what is of particular moment in the present connection is the fact that the church has an inherent right to develop its own life and that the recognition of this fact is he sole condition on which the relation of the modern state and church to each other can be properly adjusted.

This principle applies also to the relation of other social unions to the state. But there is this important difference. As W. E. Hocking points out, both religion and politics "claim to engage the whole will," while other interests, and the groups that support them, command only "fragments of the human will." [17] In politics and the state man seeks the satisfaction of his whole will in history; in religion and the church he seeks it beyond history. In the one case his interests are temporal and relative; in the other, eternal and absolute. These two interests are not mutually exclusive. They cannot be completely separated from each other. Yet they both demand the loyalty of the whole will. And out of this double demand there inevitably arise situations in which the religious man is forced to ask himself the question whether he will obey God or man. In such cases only one answer is possible. Religion claims precedence over politics, the absolute over the relative. This is the point at which the church differentiates itself most clearly from other social groups within the state, and the reason why in the present world conflict it has defied the tyranny of the state as no other group has done. Einstein, in a frequently quoted statement with reference to conditions in Nazi Germany, said:

> Only the church opposed the fight which Hitler was waging against liberty. Till then I had had no interest in the church, but now I feel great admiration for, and am attracted to, the church which has had the persistent courage to fight for spiritual truth and

---

[17] *Man and the State,* pp. 415 ff.

moral freedom. I feel obilged to recognize that I now admire what I used to consider of little value.[18]

In its history as a whole the church has, in its relation to the state, been guided by two fears: the fear of anarchy and the fear of statolatry or the deification of the state. Of these the former has been the more persistent. As against the peril of anarchy the church has, consequently, for the most part allied itself with the state and re-enforced its will. It has done this even when the state was grossly tyrannical. The result was that it came to be regarded by many modern liberals as the natural ally of the autocratic state and as a deadly foe of freedom. But today the tables have been turned. What the church now most fears is not the possibility of anarchy but the ruthless tyranny of a pagan and deified state—a peril as serious in Germany as that which confronted the church in the Roman Empire during the first three centuries of its history. Against this revival of a pagan autocracy the church has heroically set its face and by so doing has placed itself at the head of all those cultural groups whose very life is dependent on freedom of thought and action. What has made possible for the time being this leadership of the church in the struggle against tyranny has been its profound and unique faith in a spiritual reality beyond time and space.

Culture

What has just been said of the service that the church is at present rendering the higher cultural interests of mankind by its heroic resistance to tyranny in Europe, forms a natural transition to a brief discussion of culture in general. By culture I do not mean what Matthew Arnold understood by it. With him culture was "the study and pursuit of perfection," and the pursuit of perfection was "the pursuit of sweetness and light," or, in other words, beauty and intelligence. These were the "main characters" of the perfection sought, but the per-

[18] Quoted by Basil Mathews, *Pattern for Living*, p. 52.

fection itself was inclusive. It was "the harmonious perfection of our whole being." It was not of the "hole-and-corner" variety. It included religion, morals, and spiritual values in general, and thus became the chief good of life, transcending historical religion and becoming itself virtually a rival religious cult.[19] By some the term may still be used in this transcendent and semi-idolatrous sense; but for the most part the cult of culture, of which Matthew Arnold was the high priest, is now a thing of the past. In any case we are not here concerned with it; nor are we concerned with Arnold's broad interpretation of culture divested of its semireligious associations, common though this view is.

By culture we mean a restricted phase of our higher life, the phase associated directly with our intellectual and aesthetic natures. Morality and religion as such are not included in it. We speak, it is true, of moral and religious culture, but this implies a broader use of the term. As here used the cultural aspect of life is differentiated from the purely moral and religious. It expresses itself in science, art, and education. These forms of spiritual activity do not, to be sure, lie wholly beyond the province of religion and morals, but they are sufficiently distinct to be considered separately under the head of culture.

The words culture and civilization are often used synonymously.[20] But in German there is a well-established distinction between them, and this appears to some extent in English usage. Wilhelm von Humboldt has stated it as follows: "Civilization is the humanizing of the nations in their external organization, and in the spirit and temper to which this is related; to this

[19] *Culture and Anarchy*, pp. 51, 47, xxxiii, xliv. Cf. the remark by Turgenev: "My faith is in civilization, and I require no further creed." Quoted in B. Bosanquet, *The Civilization of Christendom*, p. 63.

[20] So R. T. Flewelling in his able, learned, and timely work *The Survival of Western Culture* (1943). Dr. Flewelling defines true civilization (or culture) as "one that provides the proper environment and inspiration for the highest type of personal achievement and happiness, and at the same time conserves the highest good of all" (p. 10).

culture adds science and art."[21] So far as derivation is concerned, the word "culture," as in "agriculture," would seem more naturally applied to the mechanical side of man's developing life, and the word "civilization" to its more spiritual side. But usage has reversed the meaning of the two words in so far as any distinction is made between them.

In the sense in which we have defined the term, culture may be classed as an order of creation. It does not have the clearly defined social structure of the family, state, and church. It is more of a pervasive spirit, and in this respect has a certain kinship to the "invisible church" of Protestant theology. It has, however, its special representatives in various social groups such as schools, scientific societies, and art clubs. These organizations have as their main task the transmission and dissemination of culture and thus sustain to it about the same relation that the various churches do to religion. The churches on the whole have greater cohesiveness and permanence than the purely cultural institutions. But culture is grounded in the spiritual or rational nature of man as truly as religion is. In the language of the schools, there are theoretical and aesthetic aprioris in the same sense as there is a religious apriori. That is, there is in man a native capacity and desire for knowledge and beauty just as there is a similar capacity and desire for religion. These capacities and desires are inherent in reason itself, so that we may speak of a theoretical reason, an aesthetic reason, and a religious reason. The first two of these lie at the root of, and give rise to, culture. They are divinely implanted within us and hence culture may properly be called an order of creation.

As such it has an independent basis and in this respect is co-ordinate with religion. Neither is derived from the other. Religion is not primitive science, as some have argued, nor is scientific and aesthetic culture a by-product of religion, as others have maintained. The two have grown up together. Their normal relation to each other is friendly and co-operative. Both

[21] Quoted in Brunner, *Divine Imperative,* p. 384.

are ideal interests of the same person or the same community. But it is possible to abstract one from the other and to concentrate attention on one or the other in such a way as to establish a rivalry and even hostility between them. This has not infrequently occurred. Religion has feared and resented the arrogance of culture, and culture has feared and despised the arrogance of religion. In both cases religion and culture have misunderstood and perverted their own true nature and function. There is nothing in culture as such that need exclude or minimize religious faith, and there is nothing in religion as such that need interfere with the pursuit of knowledge and of art. Ignorance may at times have seemed to be the mother of piety, and culture the nursing maid of unbelief and moral laxity. But that neither of these cases represents the normal relation of culture and religion to each other is evident from the many great thinkers and artists who have been devout believers and from the present status of religious belief. A century and a half ago Schleiermacher addressed one of the most famous books written in modern times on religion to its "cultured despisers."[22] Today there is still much unbelief, but it no longer occupies the haughty place in cultured circles that it did in the eighteenth century. The recognition of a kinship between religion and culture is becoming more and more common. Each needs the other. Religion needs culture for its illumination, and culture needs religion for its purification. To promote science and art is, therefore, a religious duty as well as the fulfillment of a natural impulse. No permanent good is achieved by insulating religious faith and ascribing to it an exclusive miraculous character; and still less of value is accomplished by attributing exclusive objective validity to science and relegating religion to the realm of fancy. These extremes have been and are advocated by the partisans of religion and of culture to the detriment of both.

Science is primarily concerned with knowledge, with the

---

[22] *Discourses on Religion* (1799; trans. J. Oman, 1893).

quest of truth. This quest is also the professed concern of religion. But in one case it is the truth of fact and in the other it is the truth of faith in which the human mind is chiefly interested. And these two interests have often seemed to be at variance with one another. The result has been a long conflict between them; and the church, consequently, for a long time seemed by its very nature to be an enemy of science and philosophy. "Until the seventeenth century," says W. E. H. Lecky, "every mental disposition which philosophy pronounces to be essential to a legitimate research was almost uniformly branded as a sin, and a large proportion of the most deadly intellectual vices were deliberately inculcated as virtues."[23] This state of affairs, we now see, was due to a mistaken conception of the relation of religious faith and scientific knowledge to each other. Each has its own sphere. There is nothing in religious faith as such that is inconsistent with the disinterested quest of knowledge. Rather does the ethical spirit of Christianity require the love of truth and truthfulness in all of life. To "live with lies" in the scientific realm is as repugnant to the true Christian spirit as to live with them in our personal relationships. A better understanding of the doctrine of creation and of the divine immanence has made this clear. Much scientific research, it is true, has little, if any, religious value; and one can readily understand why an evangelist like Wesley, after going through the British Museum, should have exclaimed: "What account will a man give to the Judge of the quick and the dead for a life spent in collecting all these!"[24] But the spirit of free inquiry has nevertheless its intrinsic worth. And it has, furthermore, improved in so many ways the material conditions of human life that it manifestly deserves the blessing of the church. The Christian law of love requires such an attitude toward it. Science, both practical and theoretical, is in its ideal an ally rather than a rival of true religion.

---

[23] *Rationalism in Europe* (1873), II, 90.

[24] *Journal*, IV, 301.

Art, which is the other main constituent of culture, has on the whole stood in a more friendly relation to religion than science. This has been due to the fact that art is more idealistic in its content. Science has also its ideal, an ideal of rationality and truth. But this ideal in the natural sciences is implicit rather than explicit. It is the real with which these sciences are concerned. They seek to reproduce a fixed objective order, and are bound by it. Art, on the other hand, is free and creative. It seeks to produce ideal forms and harmonies that transcend the natural order and satisfy the aesthetic nature as the immediate things of sense do not. It creates in imagination a realm of beauty that gives wings to the spirit and eases the burden of our humdrum life, and thus serves a redemptive purpose akin to that of religion. It is not, therefore, strange that for the most part religion and art should have gone hand in hand, that religion should have expressed itself in music, poetry, painting, and sculpture, and that art should so often have found its material in the objects of religious faith.

Art is itself autonomous. It has its own laws. It is not necessarily either religious or moral. It has flourished in corrupt and skeptical ages, as in ancient Greece and in the Italian Renaissance. It has been associated with idolatry, and is sensuous in its tendency. For these reasons there have always been earnest religious people who have looked with suspicion on works of art as aids to worship and have at times resolutely opposed their use. "Images" were condemned in the Old Testament, and Puritanism was on the whole unfavorable to art in general. But there is nothing in historic Christianity, either Catholic or Protestant, that implies hostility to art as such. Art has needed and received from the church moral and spiritual guidance, as applied science has; but it has in turn greatly enriched and refined the expression of the Christian faith. "Art for art's sake" is a false ideal in so far as it implies disregard of moral and other ideal considerations, but it is valid in so far as it affirms for art an independent place in man's spiritual life.

Art and science perpetuate themselves and develop from generation to generation through education; and culture thus becomes a living stream in human history. It is so also with morality and religion and with civilization in general. Education is both receptive and creative. It consists partly in adjustment to one's environment and partly in the quest of an ideal. The latter is the type of education particularly concerned with culture. It aims at self-realization, at the attainment of what ought to be, not at mere conformity to what is. It is the necessary means to the achievement of life's true end. As such it has a place in the divine plan and may be claimed as a human right.

But what kind and degree of cultural training each one should receive is a question that can be answered only in general terms. Some have interpreted the democratic principle of equality as meaning that the same opportunities of a liberal education should be open to all. But it is obvious that many do not have the capacity for advanced training in the arts and sciences, and that some, who have the capacity, are so situated economically or socially that they could make very little use of it. The Duke of Wellington once said to an applicant for an office, after conversing with him for a while: "Sir, you have received too much education for your brains."[25] That is no doubt true of many in our day. A college degree with them is hardly more than a badge of economic or social station. In such cases advanced training is of doubtful value; and this holds also for more capable persons whose external situation does not permit them to put their special training to practical use. Ability and utility should be decisive considerations in determining how much and what kind of education a person should receive.

General education up to a certain point would today be almost universally admitted to be a great boon to mankind. But it may be prostituted to evil purposes. This has occurred

[25] Quoted by F. Paulsen *A System of Ethics,* p. 549.

in recent years in the totalitarian states, and the resulting attitude of the public mind toward other states has become one of the most serious threats to civilization.

In the past much evil resulted from the ecclesiastical control of education, and in many countries this peril still persists. Freedom and autonomy are of the utmost importance in the field of education. Neither culture nor true religion can thrive without them and without a recognition of the fundamental and independent rights of educational institutions.

CHAPTER XIII

THE ECONOMIC ORDER

THE economic order is not a social group or organization as is the family, state, or church. It is more like culture, but less subjective. Culture is in its essential nature intellectual and aesthetic. It has its devotees and its institutions. But primarily it is a thing of the spirit. The economic order, on the other hand, is more objective. It has to do with the needs of the body. It is the process or processes by which the material goods of life are produced, distributed, and consumed. These processes operate to a considerable extent through labor unions and business associations of various kinds, but they are not limited to such groups. They embrace mankind as a whole. They include not only the fields of "industry" and "commerce" but all other activities concerned with "wealth," that is, with material objects which minister to human wants. These economic activities have in the course of human history undergone numerous changes and increased greatly in complexity. But through all these changes they have had a common purpose, that of satisfying human needs; they have involved certain constant factors such as labor, soil, tools, and finished products; and they have also had the task of creating such a surplus of material goods as alone makes possible a truly civilized life. They have thus had more or less of unity, and hence may properly be spoken of as an economic order.

AN ORDER OF CREATION

This order, in view of its human necessity and universality, must from the theistic standpoint be regarded as grounded in the divine will. God has established it as a permanent phase of human life on earth, and because he has done so it is to be accepted as an order of creation. This does not mean that any stage of its development is final, nor does it mean that the "order" is itself self-sufficient. The economic order as an order of creation is instrumental. It points to a good beyond itself. But in this respect as well as in and of itself it has the divine sanction. It is a good in which we are to participate, and participate with a good conscience. There is in it no inherent evil that defies elimination and that stains the soul of every participant. It is in its essential nature God's good gift to us.

But while in the abstract or the ideal such a favorable and optimistic view of the economic order may be warranted, the present reality, we are told by some theologians, is quite different. Between it and the abstract ideal stand the fall of man and his ineradicable sinfulness. However good or perfectible the economic order ought to be in view of its divine origin and its beneficent purpose, it is not such at present. Man's sin has radically altered the situation. It has withdrawn the economic order from moral control and imparted to it a sinful autonomy. Economics has now its own independent laws, and these laws have the right of way in their own field. The attempt "to bring economic activity under ethical discipline inevitably ruins it." "The sinful autonomy of the economic order can never be overcome."[1] A relative improvement, it is true, is possible. Within certain narrow limits the economic order may be humanized or moralized. But fundamentally there is no way of eradicating the evil from it.

There are thus two quite different conceptions of the economic order as an order of creation. According to one the economic order, though an order of creation, is itself inherently and incurably sinful. But despite this fact it serves a divine purpose. It is the divinely appointed means for the preservation of human life. Hence it is our duty to share in it. By so doing we obey the law of love, and to a limited extent may humanize the order itself. But the order in its essence remains sinful, and we necessarily share in its sin. "It is not possible for the individual

[1] Brunner, *op. cit.*, p. 403 (Ger. ed. p. 388).

to engage in economic activity without sin."[2] The fact that the economic order is an order of creation does not therefore furnish a ground for social optimism, but rather the reverse.

Opposed to this pessimistic view is the more optimistic and ethical conception of the orders of creation. According to it, there is no necessary evil in the economic order or any order of creation. Its indefinite improvement is possible. And in "the progressive amelioration of humanity" we may see the coming of the Kingdom of God. This amelioration may be slow, probably will be such, but no limits can be set to it by the myth of man's fall or by a subethical doctrine of original sin. Such doctrinaire barriers to the belief in social and economic progress should not be allowed to block the way to the possible Christianizing of the economic order. This possibility must be kept open as a ground of hope, though the time and the extent of its realization belong necessarily to the unpredictable future.

The foregoing distinction betwen a conservative and more or less pessimistic conception of the economic order on the one hand and a progressive and more or less optimistic conception of it on the other has, as we have seen, a theological basis. But it is also grounded in divergent philosophies of human nature. It is, for instance, maintained by many of a naturalistic turn of mind that man is by nature a selfish being and that his dominant motive in life as a whole, and especially in the economic sphere, not only is but must be self-interest. Benevolence, as Bentham put it, may be of value as a dessert, but only self-regard will "serve for a diet." The constitution of human nature excludes, therefore, the possibility of a radical change in the economic order. The pervasive and controlling motive of this order must be regard for one's own welfare. The economic man necessarily seeks "to gain the maximum of wealth at the cost of the minimum of labor." He is made that way, and there is no reason to believe that in this fundamental respect he will undergo a change. If one is theologically inclined, he may

[2] *Ibid.*, p. 399 (Ger. ed., pp. 384 f.).

identify this native self-interest with original sin. But, however that may be, it is a permanent trait of human nature.

Opposed to this philosophy of human nature is the view that man is an altruistic as well as a selfish being and that his nature is not unchangeable. He has within him a group instinct as well as a self-instinct, and nurture has much to do with determining which will prevail. There is no native selfish spirit in man that necessarily expresses itself in fixed economic laws. What we call economic laws are subject to change. The competitive system of the past has undergone important modifications. Men are learning that "philanthropy pays." Oppression, on the one hand, and rebellion, on the other, are bad for business. Mutual understanding and co-operation are better than conflict of interests. As men generally come to see this, the rules of business tend to change. Economic laws respond in a measure to moral demands. The change may be slow, but there is no necessary antithesis between the economic and the moral order. The former may gradually come under the sway of the latter. This is at least a possibility.

This more optimistic view of human nature and the economic order has on the whole gained in favor both within and without the church during the past century.

Consumption and Distribution

In the economic order, as we have noted, there are three general processes: production, distribution, and consumption. Of these the last has been to some extent the subject of moral regulations in Christian circles. There have been admonitions against gluttony, against excesses in drinking, against undue indulgence in amusements, against excessive finery in dress, and against extravagant expenditures on the external comforts of life. Such indulgences have seemed unworthy of the spirituality and moral seriousness of Christian teaching. At times this moral earnestness has taken a Puritanic turn. Especially pronounced during the past half century has been the movement in favor of the prohibition of the liquor traffic. But in general the economic interest of the church and of Christendom has in modern times been directed more toward the problems of production and distribution than those of consumption.

In connection with distribution or the division of wealth there are two fundamental questions that have engaged Christian thinkers. One has to do with the moral ideal. Does the Christian ideal imply or require economic equality? The other is concerned with the method or means of improving present conditions. In seeking the ideal or a better economic order, should the emphasis be placed on charity or justice as a motive of action? Or, from a somewhat different point of view, should the means adopted be primarly voluntary or compulsory?

In the early church universal equality was accepted by many as the ideal. They did not, however, treat it as an immediate practical goal. They rather looked upon it as belonging to the primitive state of perfection, from which man had fallen. Originally, according to their view, all things were held in common. There was not private property, and no property rights in general. Private rights and the inequalities to which they have given rise were due to usurpation. Nature did not create them. Its law is common right or equality. This is also the law of the New Testament, the law of love. Love bids us give to "everyone according to his needs." This is the divine will. The goodness of God requires that all his children be treated alike. Equality is inherent in the moral ideal.

But while in the abstract this may be true, and while it is true that before God all men are equal and equally dependent on the divine grace, it does not follow that God wills the same economic, social, political and cultural status for all. Such equality does not exist and never did. There have always been inequalities of human ability and of human fortune, inequalities that have obviously not been due to human sin, individual or corporate. They have been grounded in the divine will. Why God willed them, we do not know. There is an incalculable element in his activities. We cannot wholly justify them, certainly not from an equalitarian standpoint. All that we can do is to accept them and adjust ourselves to them as best we can. This is what the doctrine of creation means. It means reverence for the Creator, submission to his will. It does not mean universal equality. Equalitarianism is an abstract doctrine of the schools, not a living doctrine of faith.

Recognition of unavoidable inequalities in the economic order and in the order of creation in general does not, however, imply fatalism nor a hopeless conservatism. Evil social conditions may to some extent be remedied. This conviction has been implicit in Christian teaching from the beginning. But in effecting this improvement, on what should the emphasis primarily be placed? Historically the church placed it on charity. In so doing it followed the lead of the New Testament. It preached the gospel of brotherly love with a zeal and a sustained passion the like of which has not been known elsewhere in human history. In exhorting people to almsgiving it appealed at times to more or less selfish religious motives such as the acquisition of merit and the hope of reward hereafter. But despite defects of this kind its mission to the poor was on the whole actuated by a profound altruistic spirit. A true philanthropy inspired it, and nowhere else do we find so persistent and massive a movement directed consciously or unconsciously toward mitigating the evils of poverty and toward the improvement of existing economic conditions. The key to the movement was its emphasis on charity. This emphasis was of immense value, both ethical and economic. But it did not solve the problem of poverty, "the hugest of all curses, taking the world over." [3]

Its failure at this point was in part due to the assumption that the existing economic order had in its main outlines been providentially established and that in view of all the factors to be taken into account it was not unjust. There were, to be sure, evils associated with it, and these might and ought to be mitigated by the exercise of charity. But they were not evils against

[3] F. J. McConnell, *The Christian Ideal and Social Control*, p. 42.

which revolt was justified. The poor might hope for relief from them through the receipt of alms and through other charitable means, but they were not warranted in demanding a reorganization of the economic system as a right. This system was for them fixed, a kind of external fatality, to which they were in duty bound to adjust themselves. Then, too, the poverty resulting from the system was not regarded as an unmixed evil. It afforded people in general the opportunity of exercising charity and so acquiring merit in the sight of God. Also, as a mode of life voluntarily assumed, it was looked upon as a virtue, as a badge of sainthood. There was thus more or less of a religious justification of it and a consequent acquiescence attitude toward it.

Another reason for the failure of charity to achieve a permanent improvement of economic conditions was the fact that almsgiving on a large scale by encouraging indolence tended to perpetuate the poverty it sought to relieve. Poverty, we now know, is not due wholly nor chiefly to indolence, as is so often assumed by the well-to-do classes. John Wesley was right in denouncing this assumption as "wickedly, devilishly false."[4] But there is, nevertheless, a tendency toward idleness in human nature which needs to be resisted; and this resistance is in danger of being broken down by indiscriminate charity. The failure to see this and to realize the social peril involved in it was undoubtedly a serious weakness in the doctrine of charity as preached and practiced by the early and medieval church. There was no lack of zeal in either the preaching or the practice of the doctrine. Indeed, so zealously was the doctrine practiced as well as preached that, if it had been the correct method of dealing with the problem of poverty, it would probably have met with success. Certainly a fair trial was given it.

---

[4] *Journal*, IV, 52 (Feb. 8, 1753). On the relation of Wesley to social and economic reform see the discriminating and masterly treatment of the subject in Bishop McConnell's *John Wesley*, pp. 233-310; the able and stimulating discussion of it by G. C. Cell, *The Rediscovery of John Wesley*, pp. 363-414; and the scholarly treatise by W. J. Warner, *The Wesleyan Movement in the Industrial Revolution*.

Its inadequacy became more and more evident under the altered social and economic conditions of the modern world. Consequently, there arose an increasing conviction that, while there would always be a place for charity, the major emphasis in dealing with the problem of poverty ought to fall elsewhere. For one thing, the French Revolution and the industrial revolution in England made it clear that human society is more plastic than had been supposed, and that changes in its economic structure are possible that would make the lot of the underprivileged more satisfactory. These changes, it was first thought by social idealists, could be effected by an appeal to the benevolence of the propertied classes. But the futility of such an appeal was soon demonstrated. People then began to insist on these changes as a right to which they were justly entitled. Justice instead of charity became their watchword. But that, too, was soon seen to be insufficient. Voluntary justice in many instances proved to be almost as difficult to secure as voluntary charity. Hence there was a resort to legislation, to the strong arm of the state, and to other uses of force. Compulsory methods supplanted or supplemented the earlier voluntary and persuasive methods.

In this change the church did not as an institution assume the direct leadership. It could not have done so without what would have been regarded as an unwarranted participation in politics and without resort to measures that would have seemed inconsistent with its proper function in human society. Indeed, it at times opposed the methods employed by the leaders of social and economic reform. It condemned not only violence and the idea of class war but also peaceful means by which laborers sought to enforce their will upon their employers. The result was that the church seemed to many a conservative and reactionary, instead of progressive, force in society. But despite these facts it is now clear, as we look back over the reform movement as a whole, that the church, in the words of Lord Stamp, "blazed the trail, it showed the value of social regeneration, it educated public opinion."[5] For centuries it was itself the chief agent of social relief or regeneration. This work it carried out on a voluntary basis, and necessarily inadequately. But in so doing it gradually developed a more general sense of social responsibility, until finally, fifty or sixty years ago, the state began to take over much of what had previously been the special function of the church but which was now increasingly felt to be a common obligation of society. The wealth and power of the state were thus put back of the great socially regenerative movement initiated by the teaching and example of the church.

State support and state control of the movement, however, while greatly expanding and strengthening it, have, as above stated, altered its ethical basis. Individual participation in it has become compulsory instead of voluntary. And the justification of the movement has shifted its emphasis from the duty of benevolence to that of justice. This change resulted naturally from the new relation of the movement to the state, for the state is primarily concerned with the administration of justice. The change, however, has had a wholesome effect both on the ethic of the state and that of the church. It has tended to humanize the ethic of the state by interpreting justice in terms of benevolence and mutual aid; and it has tended to broaden and make more effective the social ethic of the church by interpreting charity in terms of justice and mutual responsibility. In any case the church has come to see that its own economic teaching has in the past been too narrow and too individualistic. It has been too largely concentrated on private and public charity. Something more is needed if the economic evils of the past and present are to be overcome. There must be a new and juster economic order. Only in such an order can self-respect and economic responsibility be adequately cultivated in all classes of society. And such an order, so far as we can see, can be established only through the authority of organized society.

---

[5] *Christianity and Economics,* p. 188.

Of late the church has, consequently, come to lay a new emphasis on social justice and civil law as means of solving the problem of distribution.

Labor

In the field of "production" there are two main factors: labor and capital. Both have given rise to important ethical problems.

In the case of labor the more fundamental questions have had to do with its obligatory character, its dignity, and its worth. There is in human nature a disinclination to work. Children prefer play to work, and many people never get over this characteristic of childhood. They prefer leisure to labor and consider it clever if they can get by with less work than their neighbors. The primary reason why men work is that some work is necessary if they are to live. This is what differentiates human from animal life. Animals do not work in the human sense of the term; they follow their instincts. Work is consciously directed effort and often runs counter to animal impulses. But it is necessary to human life and, consequently, is morally obligatory. Indolence is a vice. There is no place in society for an idle class. On this point Christian teaching has been explicit and emphatic from the beginning. "If any will not work, neither let him eat."[6] This has been the basal and generally accepted rule. Willingness to work is a Christian duty.

But with reference to the dignity of labor opinion has not been so uniform either within the church or without. There has always been a tendency on the part of the "higher" or "intellectual" classes to look down upon manual or industrial labor as more or less degrading. It was so in ancient Greece. The philosopher did not "work." That was the task of slaves and the lower classes generally. Aristotle spoke of "the industries that earn wages" as "vulgar" and as degrading the mind.[7] The mystics in pantheistic religions have taken a similar view,

---

[6] II Thess. 3:10.
[7] *Politics*, 1337, b.

though on different grounds. They have looked upon manual labor as binding the soul to the earth and thus defeating the very purpose of their own lives, which was to emancipate themselves from the world. This derogatory attitude toward common labor also underlay much of the early medieval Christian teaching on the subject. Work was regarded as fundamentally a "curse." It was a penalty imposed on man for his primal sin. As such it had its value. Since the Fall it had been an important means of discipline. It had acted as a curb on vice. From the standpoint of the present sinful life it was, therefore, to be encouraged. Work was better than idleness. But the "contemplative" life was nevertheless higher than the "active" life, and the active life of the secular clergy, as distinguished from the contemplative life of the monastic orders, was higher than the active life of the lay folk. The latter were engaged for the most part in manual and industrial labor. Such work was necessary for the maintenance of life. But for this very reason there was a disposition to assign it to a lower rank. The life of the spirit was regarded as so superior to that of the body that anything having to do primarily with the latter received necessarily an inferior rating.[8]

It was the Reformation that released "work" from the curse of the Fall and of a false spiritualism and represented it as a divine order of creation. Emphasis was now laid on the fact that the biblical command to "subdue" the earth and to "dress" and "keep" the Garden of Eden preceded the primal sin and the resulting condemnation of man to a life of "toil." According to Scripture, therefore, manual labor, at least a moderate amount of it, has its place not only in the present but in the ideal order of man's earthly life. Nature is not automatic. It does not produce unaided what man needs. Labor is necessary. It is a part of the divine plan. In order to realize the divine purpose man and nature must work together. Only thus can civilization be created and the normal possibilities of human life be adequately realized.

---

[8] *T. Aquinas, Summa Theologica,* II-II, QQ. clxxxi-clxxxii, clxxxiv.

A new dignity was thus given to manual and industrial labor by the Reformation. This dignity consisted, on the negative side, in the repudiation of the earlier sharp distinction between lower and higher kinds of work, and on the positive side, in the recognition of three distinct functions that work serves in human life. The first has just been referred to. Human labor supplements nature and brings it to its proper fruition. In nature the lower animals are included. Man has not only the task of subduing the earth. God has "put all things under his feet; all sheep and oxen, yea, and the beasts of the field, the birds of the heavens, and the fish of the sea."[9] He is to "have dominion" over them all, and "over all the earth."[10] This is his divinely appointed task, a task that involves labor. But labor from this point of view is far from debasing; rather does it link man with the divine.[11]

Another function of labor from the Reformation standpoint is that of service to one's fellow men. This is the true test of its worth. It does not matter what the kind of work may be. If it is a real service to the community, it has the divine approval. The older distinction between sacred and secular and between intellectual or spiritual and the "merely usual" is thus obliterated. A mother's work in the home may be as truly spiritual as that of the nun in the cloister, if not more so. It is service that imparts true spirituality to labor. Labor, in other words, is social service. Its aim is not simply to maintain life but to create a civilization, no matter whether the laborer is aware of it or not. This is characteristic of Western civilization. It is animated by the desire to transcend nature and to build a higher and better social order. Machinery is a means to this end. So also are the virtues of enterprise, diligence, and thrift. Puritanism invested these virtues with a supernatural sanction, and by

[9] Ps. 8:6-8.

[10] Gen. 1:26.

[11] Ps. 8:5.

so doing "turned them from an unsocial eccentricity into a habit and a religion." [12]

A third function of labor is self-development. Through work a man disciplines himself; cultivates patience, persistence, and faithfulness; acquires knowledge and skill; and in other ways strengthens, enriches, and perfects his personality. Some types of work no doubt serve this purpose better than others, but all useful work which is properly adjusted to individual taste, training, and ability has this value. Work makes the worker as well as serves the community. It is this double utility that gives dignity to labor and constitutes the true test of its worth in the sight of both God and man.

But while this utilitarian evaluation of labor has to a large degree rescued manual and industrial labor from its unchristian disparagement in the past and won for it a new and higher appraisal, there are still many unsolved ethical problems connected with it, such as unemployment; profitsharing by employees; a minimum wage; limitation of the hours of labor; prohibition of child labor; enrichment of the life and duties of factory workers; better pay for women workers; and larger economic opportunities for racial groups, especially Negroes. Concrete problems of this kind are not easily solved. Their solution can be wrought out only in life itself through the method of trial and error. And when solved, new problems are likely to take their place. Claims and counter-claims seem to be an inevitable phase of human life. But though this be true, much can be done in the way of moderating the bitterness of the struggle and improving existing conditions by continued emphasis on the moral dignity and worth of labor, and by the inculcation of good will and a sense of public responsibility.

CAPITAL AND CAPITALISM

"Capital," the other main factor in production, is often used in the sense of wealth in general. But in works on economics it is commonly limited to "produced wealth used pro-

[12] R. H. Tawney, *Religion and the Rise of Capitalism,* p. 272.

ductively for gain."[13] Thus defined çapital does not include land and other gifts of nature, since they are not "produced"; nor does it include finished or consumer's goods, since these are not "used productively for gain." Within this narrower meaning of the term a distinction is drawn between "commercial capital" and "industrial capital." The latter did not come into extensive use until the modern manufacturing era, while the former was employed on a large scale in medieval and ancient trade and transport.

So far as the New Testament is concerned, no account is taken of the different kinds of material wealth or capital. Wealth is understood in the popular sense as riches or as property of any kind. The possession of property or of riches is not in and of itself condemned. Jesus took it for granted not only that trading and the normal business life of his day were morally permissible but that faithfulness in this field of activity was to be commended.[14] There was no indication of a revolutionary attitude on his part toward the existing economic system.

What Jesus did, was not to repudiate material goods as evil but to warn men against the moral and religious perils involved in the quest and possession of them. He speaks of the "deceitfulness of riches,"[15] and of the danger of "covetousness."[16] In and of themselves, riches may have their value; but they are in danger of blinding men to the highest values of life and leading them to think that their own life consists in the abundance of the things which they possess. It was this peril that Jesus especially feared and that led him to warn his disciples against laying up treasures on earth.[17] Doing so might result in their serving mammon rather than God.[18] But this was not a necessary result. Jesus had some men and women of means among his

---

[13] *Enc. Brit.*, 14th ed., IV, 793.
[14] Matt. 25:14-30; Luke 19:12-27; Mark 12:1-11; 13:34.
[15] Matt. 13:22.
[16] Luke 12:15.
[17] Matt. 6:19.
[18] Matt. 6:24.

immediate followers.[19] It was not, then, wealth but a wrong attitude toward it or the misuse of it that he condemned.

Still, there is little, if any, positive appreciation of wealth in the New Testament. The possession of earthly goods, it was clear, enabled a person to give alms to the poor as he otherwise could not. But people were not exhorted to make money for that purpose.[20] If they had more of it than others, they were to use it that way. But the deliberate attempt to accumulate earthly treasures was regarded as morally and religiously perilous, and was not encouraged. Apart from the satisfaction of immediate human needs, wealth was not thought of as having any particular value. There was no appreciation of its indispensable function in the developments of civilization. Indeed, early Christianity had no long-range outlook into the future and was not concerned, as we are, with the problems of a new and better economic order. The better future to which the early Christians looked forward was already at hand, and for it no material preparation was necessary. Even in the secular economy of their day capital in its modern industrial sense had little place, and no emphasis was put upon it as a condition or means of economic and social progress.

It was this lack of insight into the social value of productive capital that led to the ancient opposition to interest or usury, an opposition that persisted into modern times.[21] Money in primitive societies was lent chiefly to the poor to meet their immediate needs. To exact interest for its use seemed, therefore, to be taking advantage of their unfortunate situation and to be hardhearted. For the lender lost nothing by making the loan. If he did not lend to the poor, his money would lie idle. Money, it was said, is barren; and "time" creates nothing. It has no price; and if it had, the price would belong to God rather than man. Such ideas as these were current in pre-

---

[19] Matt. 27:57; Luke 8:3; 19:8 f.

[20] Contrast Wesley's repeated exhortation: "Gain all you can; save all you can; give all you can." See his Sermon L on "The Use of Money."

[21] See Josiah Stamp, *Christianity and Economics*, pp. 37-47.

Christian times and were taken over by the early Church Fathers, who gave to them the support of Scripture and put back of them the authority of the Church. The chief scriptural basis for the rejection of interest was Luke 6:35: "Lend, hoping for nothing again." On the basis of these words of Jesus and such Old Testament passages as Leviticus 25:36 f and Deuteronomy 23:20, the taking of interest was condemned as "a mortal sin, punishable by excommunication." [22] That this attitude of the church imposed restraints on trade and placed obstacles in the way of loans to the poor was evident, but it remained nevertheless the official ecclesiastical position down to the rise of modern commerce and industry. Under modern business conditions the economic value of money and especially of productive capital became so clear that the traditional arguments against interest gradually crumbled, though it took two centuries or more before they disappeared from Christian ethics.

Pope Clement V (1305-14) declared that anyone who "shall pertinaciously presume to affirm that the taking of interest for money is not a sin, we decree him to be a heretic, fit for punishment." [23] The Reformers divided on the question, Luther and Melanchthon looking to the past and Calvin turning to the future.[24] In England an act was passed in 1552 prohibiting all interest and condemning it as "a vice most odious and detestable, as in divers places of the Holy Scriptures it is evident to be seen." But this act was repealed in 1571. In 1612 Dr. Fenton, one of the translators of the Authorized Version, reaffirmed vigorously the older view, saying that "this hath been the general judgment of the Church for above this fifteen hundred years without opposition." But by the end of the seventeenth century the opposition to interest was practically over among Protestants. In the Roman Catholic Church it continued in abated form till into the nineteenth century.

---

[22] Edgar Salin, *Encyclopedia of the Social Sciences,* XV, 195.

[23] Quoted by Josiah Stamp, *op. cit.,* pp. 45, 40, as are also the parts of two other sentences quoted in this paragraph.

[24] On the economic views of Luther and Calvin see R. H. Tawney, *op. cit.,* pp. 79-132.

With the new evaluation of productive capital and the consequent legitimizing of interest a new era in the economic history of the Western world began. This era is known as the era of "capitalism." The name came into common use during the latter half of the past century. It originated as a term of reproach but has since come to be generally accepted as a designation of the prevailing eonomic system by way of contrast with "socialism." The capitalistic system in its modern "industrial" form has in the main grown up during the past two centuries.[25] That it has a definite and distinctive character is generally recognized. But how to define it has been a baffling question. There is as yet no satisfactory definition of it. There are, however, certain fundamental elements in its creed that may be noted. One is private property; another is free enterprise; a third is industrial capital; and a fourth is the profit motive. When these tenets are geared into high speed, they make of the capitalistic system an extremely efficient instrument of production. Indeed, it has been said that it is the only economic system that has solved the problem of production. But, along with its undoubted merits, there have been serious evils associated with it, such as the degradation of labor and the laborer, the loss of the sense of vocation, gross inequality in the distribution of wealth, strife between labor and capital, excessive competition, overproduction and wasteful production, recurring periods of depression, and unemployment. These evils have led to sharp differences of opinion with reference to the capitalistic system as a whole. Socialists have roundly condemned it, and many Christian leaders have joined in the condemnation. Serious efforts have been and are being made to link Christianity with socialism on the ground that the latter system is in closer harmony with the Christian doctrine of the brotherhood of man than is capitalism.[26]

---

[25] On the relation of its development to religion, especially to Calvinism, the theory of Max Weber is worthy of careful study. See his *Protestant Ethic and the Spirit of Capitalism* and a criticism of his theory by Georgia Harkness, *John Calvin,* pp. 178-191.

[26] Cf. H. F. Rall, *Christianity,* pp. 119-39, on the present social setting of religion, a book of extraordinary ability and value.

The resulting problem is too complex for consideration here. But there are two or three general observations that may be made. One is that Christianity represents no definite economic doctrine and should not be identified with any economic system. It transcends all such systems and warns men against too great preoccupation with earthly treasures. In this respect it condemns both capitalism and socialism in so far as each tends to become a religion of external goods. But this does not mean that one system may not create a more favorable environment for the Christian faith and ethic than the other, nor does it mean that Christianity does not have an obligation to do what it can to transform the economic order into greater conformity with the Christian moral ideal.

A second observation is that the contribution of the church to the improvement or reform of the economic order must in the main be moral and spiritual, not political and technical. Its emphasis must be on principles, not on plans and programs. For the latter its leaders do not for the most part have the necessary training and experience. Their primary task must be to bring existing social and economic conditions under the searchlight of the Christian moral ideal and thus stir the consciences of men both within and without the church to action.[27] Technological leadership is not the function of the church. It may and must, it is true, apply the ideal to concrete conditions. But its distinctive function is not to formulate specific plans of reform but to illustrate and enforce such basic truths in the Christian ideal as respect for the personality of all men and the conception of wealth as a trust and of ownership as stewardship. Where these truths grip the consciences of men, and of political and industrial leaders in particular, the foundation is laid for an indefinite improvement in social and economic relations. Without them no progress is secure.

[27] Cf. G. Bromley Oxnam, *The Ethical Ideals of Jesus in a Changing World* (1941), a series of vivid and dynamic addresses on the practical application of the Christian ethic to the present economic and international situation. See also F. Ernest Johnson, *The Church and Society* (1935), a book of fine practical and ethical insight.

A third and concluding observation is that there are important truths in both capitalism and socialism, and that the road to progress lies in the fusion of these truths rather than in the partisan adoption of one system and the exclusion of the other. We need the capitalistic emphasis on free enterprise, on individual responsibility, and on adequate incentive to creative work. But we need also the socialistic emphasis on co-operation, on social responsibility, and on ethical rather than financial incentives to social service. These two groups of emphases do not necessarily exclude—they balance—each other. And since capitalism is the prevailing system in what has been estimated as six-sevenths of the world, the probability is that the future economic development will take the form of a gradual socializing of the present system and that the outcome will be a modified or reformed capitalism. Whether the new order, however, will be a modified form of capitalism or a modified form of socialism does not matter so long as the fundamental values of both systems are conserved. At present what seems most needed in capitalistic countries is a better balancing of human and property rights. Many employers need still to learn that "where capitalism stakes money, labor stakes life." [28] and that, as between the two, life must in the long run have the right of way.[29] The full recognition of this fact will inevitably mean profit sharing and other forms of partnership in which labor participates in the responsibility of management. Important developments in this direction have already taken place; and as they are carried further and become more general, there is good reason to believe that much of the present friction between capital and labor will cease and that other serious evils of the present system will be mitigated, if not altogether removed.

---

[28] J. L. Garvin in *Enc. Brit.*, 14th ed., IV, 806.

[29] Significant in this connection is the "personalist" movement in France, whose creed is "the primacy of the human person over material necessities and over the implements man needs for the development of his person." See Emmanuel Mounier, *A Personalist Manifesto* (1938).

PART V

CONCLUSION

CHAPTER XIV

THE VALIDITY OF CHRISTIAN ETHICS

THUS far we have been primarily concerned with an exposition of the principles of Christian ethics and their application to the concrete conditions of human life. This has been the chief purpose of the book. Incidentally reference has been made here and there to the question of validity, but there has been no systematic discussion of it. The subject has been reserved for the concluding chapter because one would naturally be better prepared to deal with it after having surveyed the general field of Christian ethics.

It has been our contention throughout the book that there is no proper antithesis between theological and philosophical ethics. There are, it is true, certain types of philosophical ethics that are out of harmony with Christian ethics. They take a skeptical attitude toward the moral life as a whole; they seek to deduce the moral nature from nonmoral elements; and they deny to the moral law any universal or objective authority or validity. But these theories, variously called hedonistic, eudaemonistic, and utilitarian, are not only hostile to Christian ethics; they are equally opposed to other types of philosophical ethics. There are great schools of ethics, described as intuition al, idealistic, rationalistic, or aprioristic, that have grounded the moral life in a native and distinctive capacity of the human spirit. This capacity is not deducible from any simpler nonmoral element. It is an original and constituent factor in human nature. It is as independent and as trustworthy as is the capacity for sense experience, the capacity for aesthetic experience, and the capacity for religious experience. It stands in its own right. It justifies itself and needs no other support.

The Divine Will as the Ground of Christian Ethics

There are some who profess to see in this theory of moral autonomy a fundamental point of contrast between intuitional and Christian ethics. Christian ethics, it is said, looks upon the divine will as the source and ground of the moral law. To be morally good from the Christian standpoint is to be obedient to the divine word and the divine commands. It is divine revelation that lies at the basis of Christian morality. Apart from revelation there can be no true moral insight and no adequate validation of the moral law. It is God alone who discloses to us the true nature of morality and invests it with authority. Neither intuition nor reason can take his place. The moral theories based on one or the other or both may, it is true, have a certain advantage over those of a hedonistic or utilitarian type. They give to the moral life a dignity, independence, and rational foundation that it would not otherwise have. But no merely rational or human grounding will suffice. Indeed, such a grounding gives to the moral life a false anthropocentric or egoistic character. True Christian morality must be theocentric. It cannot find a trustworthy support either in intuitionalism or any other form of apriorism.

This line of reasoning, as we have previously pointed out, rests on a false dualism. It is possible for men to claim for themselves moral self-sufficiency, and this self-sufficiency they have at times interpreted as exempting them from dependence on divine revelation or divine aid of any kind. They have set up their own moral independence or autonomy as a substitute for, or rival of, Christian ethics. And in response Christian apologists have often either rejected the principle of moral autonomy or sought to prove its complete inadequacy. Man, they say, is a sinner, and hence has neither the moral insight nor the moral energy necessary to achieve moral independence.

His only hope is the miraculous intervention of the Divine Spirit, and this means the introduction into human life of a factor distinct from, and alien to, human nature. God and man are thought of as in their essential nature standing apart from each other. This is the view of both the naturalistic rationalist and the traditional Christian apologist. But both are mistaken. Man's native capacity for moral experience is not his own creation. It is a divine gift and hence constitutes no ground for self-sufficiency and pride. It leaves one in dependence on God. On the other hand, the fact that this native capacity is a fundamental endowment of the human spirit and that it is as firmly grounded as the intellectual, aesthetic, and religious aspects of human nature, creates a profound prepossession in favor of its objective validity and justifies the view that it is warranted in claiming for itself divine sanction. The highest in man is a revelation of divine truth and the divine will. This conclusion is implied in the doctrine of creation.

It is no doubt true that if the divine will were objectively communicated to us and if it made known what we ought to do in every circumstance of life, the moral problem would be greatly simplified. But it is obvious that there is no such revelation of the divine will. When it comes to the details of conduct we have in most cases to decide for ourselves what we ought to do. At any rate we have no external revelation to guide us. And the situation is much the same when it comes to the principles of ethics. We have had seers and prophets throughout the ages who have proclaimed what they believed to be the divine will; and in some cases their convictions have, we think, been justified. But in no case did their message have an external credential that guaranteed its truth regardless of its content. In every instance there has been legitimate ground for question as to whether the prophetic word spoken was of divine origin; and the question has been one that could be settled only by an inquiry into the ethical or spiritual character of the utterance.[1]

[1] Deut. 13:1-3.

Its divine source and validity could only be determined by the strength of its appeal to the enlightened conscience. There is and can be no other test of the moral will of God. We cannot, therefore, erect the divine will into a purely objective moral standard, nor can we find in it an authoritative basis for the moral law. Our necessary uncertainty with respect to the content of the divine will makes this impossible.

There is also another reason why we cannot utilize the divine will as an absolute ethical standard. Even if we knew the full divine will with respect to our own conduct, it would not be morally authoritative unless it awakened within us a moral response. Mere compliance with an external command, either human or divine, does not make an act moral. It becomes such only when it has our own moral approval. If a command does not commend itself to our conscience, it has for us no moral authority. The moral law is by its very nature autonomous. A heteronomous law, a law imposed upon us by others without an approving response from within, is not a truly moral law. The moral law must be self-imposed. If it is not, if it is imposed upon us by an external divine will and derives its entire authority from this source, it loses its ethical character. Moral authority necessarily comes from within. It cannot be grounded in an external will, even though this will be divine and our knowledge of it adequate.

The attempt, therefore, to find in the divine will an independent, objective, and authoritative basis of morality must be rejected. Schopenhauer was right in insisting that such an attempt necessarily moves in a vicious circle.[2] It bases morality on the divine will, and then discovers that no revelation of the divine will can be authentic which is not in harmony with the moral law. Morality is thus as necessary to the ascertainment of the divine law as the divine will is necessary to the knowledge and grounding of the moral law. If we make morality dependent on the divine will, we can justify what we regard as

[2] See p. 16.

the divine will only by making it dependent on morality. Thus we end where we began.

Eduard von Hartmann was also right in arguing that an act is not right because God wills it. Rather is it true that God wills it because it is right. If if were not so, right on our part would be mere external obedience; and mere external obedience falls below the plane of true morality. An act is truly moral only when it is freely willed by the actor and willed because it is right. In other words, true morality is autonomous and hence cannot be based exclusively on the will of another, even though the other be God.

But while von Hartmann and Schopenhauer were justified in their criticism of an ethical theory based exclusively on the divine will, they were mistaken in so far as they assumed that such a theory is necessarily implied in Christian ethics. The Christian does, it is true, think of his duties as divine commands; but this does not mean that his duties have no validity for him apart from their relation to the divine will. The prophetic-Christian movement has always recognized a natural moral law. It has given to this morality a new setting; it has imparted to it a new dynamic; it has purified, elevated, and intensified it. But the great historic significance of the movement lay not so much in religionizing morality as it did in moralizing religion. Religion has always been a power in human life, but it has not always been a power for good. It has been concerned with rites and ceremonies, with the maintenance of obsolete, useless, and even harmful customs; it has been narrowly nationalistic; it has been socially and intellectually unprogressive; it has neglected the weightier matters of the law. This was the situation in ancient Israel, and what the prophets did was to detach religion from these more or less evil or useless associations and interests and impart to it a new ethical spirit. They moralized and universalized the idea of God and insisted that the essence of the truly religious life consists in righteousness: in doing justly and loving mercy. They thus linked religion indissolubly with morality and by so doing rendered an immeasurable service to both. But their primary interest was in moralizing religion rather than in giving to morality a religious setting.[3] Religion in their day was in a way taken for granted by people in general; no one questioned it. What they, consequently, needed was not more religion but religion of a new and more spiritual type, a religion grounded in the moral law. It was not more emphasis on the divine will that was needed but more emphasis on the moral character of the divine will.[4]

In the view of the prophets and also of Jesus it was not an arbitrary divine will that established the moral law; it was rather the moral law that defined the divine will. It was man's native moral insight that made possible the prophetic moralization of religion. The fundamental basis of Christian morality is to be found, therefore, not in an undefined and external divine will, but in the moral structure of human nature as it came from the hand of God. In other words Christian morality has the same rational basis as natural morality. Both are grounded in the moral nature of man, and to refer this nature to a divine source and to conceive of it as susceptible of divine guidance is in no way out of harmony with the principle of moral autonomy. Christian ethics is not heteronomous in any sense that would tend to discredit its validity.[5] It is both autonomous and theonomous. Indeed, theonomy may be defined as "an autonomy filled with religion." [6]

---

[3] Under other conditions, such as those which prevail at present, Father Tyrrell was probably right in saying that "the religious interpretation of morality is a greater gain for mankind than the moral interpretation of religion" (*Through Scylla and Charybdis,* p. 20).

[4] See the monumental *Introduction to the Old Testament* (1941), pp. 415-615, by R. H. Pfeiffer; *Old Testament Religion* (pp. 163-235) by E. A. Leslie with its fresh approach to prophecy in the light of its Canaanitic background; *The Beacon Lights of Prophecy* and *The Religious Teaching of the Old Testament* by A. C. Knudson.

[5] Cf. Edward Caird, *The Critical Philosophy of Immanuel Kant,* II, 296 f.

[6] P. Tillich, *The Interpretation of History,* p. 24. See the clear and comprehensive discussion of moral autonomy in Brightman, *Moral Laws,* pp. 256-87.

General Moral Skepticism

We may claim, then, for Christian ethics, at least in its essential nature, as valid a basis as that of philosophical ethics. Indeed, they have a common rational basis. But the validity of both has been questioned and rejected by many. Hence some account needs to be taken of moral skepticism in general.

The skeptical attack has been primarily directed against the idea of duty or moral obligation. That duty is a basal and essential element in the common moral consciousness is generally conceded. But it is argued that the common view of duty is mistaken. Duty is not an ultimate and unique moral sentiment. It does not necessarily imply an absolute distinction between right and wrong, nor does it presuppose the power of contrary choice. It is the outgrowth of fear or social coercion and hence is itself reducible to a form of prudence. The sharp distinction between the moral and the natural thus vanishes. Moral obligation becomes a disguised form of selfishness or a mere reflection of what is socially useful.

In reaching this skeptical conclusion various lines of argument have been employed, three or four of which may be briefly stated. For one thing, it has been argued that man has no real freedom and hence has no real duties. His entire conduct is determined by forces over which he has no control. His consciousness of freedom is an illusion, and so also is his consciousness of duty. For a being who has no power of contrary choice duty has no meaning. And with the elimination of duty the whole moral life collapses.

Another method of discrediting the moral convictions of mankind consists in maintaining that pleasure is the only possible or the only rational aim of action. If we always act with a view to pleasure or if this is the only reasonable motive of action, it is obvious that there are no real moral differences between people. They all have the same motive, either because of necessity or at the behest of reason. In the former case pleasure determines desire and desire determines the will. Everything is necessitated. There is no freedom, and the logical result is that stated in the preceding paragraph—the overthrow of all morality. If, on the other hand, pleasure is regarded as the only reasonable motive, freedom would not be denied. But the moral situation would not be materially improved. To hold that pleasure is the sole rational aim of action would keep the moral on essentially the natural plane. It would not eliminate the sense of duty. But it would leave no place for high moral endeavor and would tend to level life as a whole.

A third line of thought tending toward ethical skepticism has been derived from the theory of evolution. It is argued that man has descended or ascended from an earlier brute state of existence and that he, consequently, in his essential nature is still a brute. His nature has, to be sure, undergone various refinements; but no radical change of structure has taken place. The sense of moral obligation may seem to be wholly new, but actually it is not such. It grew up out of the notion of the socially useful, which in turn was grounded in the animal instinct of self-preservation. Moral obligation is, then, simply a refined and disguised animal instinct and has no other authority than that derived from this source and from social tradition. There is nothing spiritually unique and authoritative in it, and hence the moral life has no such independent foundation as has been claimed for it. It is simply a reflection of social custom or an unconscious deduction from it.

A still further argument in support of moral skepticism has been drawn from the diversity of moral judgments that we find in the course of human history.[7] Moral codes have varied to such an extent that there is hardly a specific commandment on which there has been universal agreement. What the conscience of one community has condemned, the conscience of another community has permitted. So obvious is this fact to students of the history of morals that many have concluded that all moral judgments are relative and

[7] Cf. Westermarck, *Christianity and Morals*, pp. 31-39; *Ethical Relativity*, pp. 3-61, 183-219.

that none of them, either particular or general, have absolute validity. All are conditioned by the circumstances under which they arise, and hence none of them represent a valid objective standard.

The foregoing arguments against the validity of our moral experience and others similar to them have had wide currency. But they have failed to achieve their purpose because they have been based on false assumptions. They have assumed that man has no real freedom. They have assumed that he is for the most part determined in his conduct by pleasures of the passive sensibility. They have assumed that the moral has been developed out of the nonmoral and that the true nature and significance of morality are to be learned from its early and crude beginnings. They have assumed that the wide diversity of opinion and practice in the moral field is inconsistent with the idea of a unique and normative moral nature.

In response to these assumptions it is sufficient to point out that if similar assumptions were applied to our cognitive or intellectual nature, the results would be equally disastrous. The denial of freedom would mean the collapse of reason as well as of conscience. The crude "scientific" notions of primitive men would invalidate modern science. The deduction of the rational from the irrational would deprive reason of its distinctive and authoritative character. The many differences of opinion among philosophers and scientists would be sufficient ground for rejecting the trustworthiness of the human intellect. In a word, the application of the same methods of criticism to the intellectual as to the moral nature would result in an intellectual skepticism quite as thoroughgoing as the general moral skepticism which we are considering.

The fact is that every phase of our developing spiritual life must be judged by its outcome, not by what it came out of. Not its roots but its fruits must furnish the material on which to base our estimate of its worth or its validity. It is our present intellectual insight, our present moral insight, our present religious insight, and our present artistic taste that constitute our standards of judgment. No genetic theory can take the place of our present rational or spiritual convictions. Every institution and every system of belief must be judged by what it now is and by the appeal it now makes to our reason and conscience, and not by its historical antecedents.

For the fundamental justification of our ideal interests we must, then, turn to the human mind. It is there and there only that we can find an adequate basis for the moral life. We have a native capacity for moral experience, and this capacity is self-verifying. We cannot go beyond it. It stands in its own right.[8] It is as independent and as trustworthy as is the capacity for sense experience, for religious experience, and for aesthetic experience. None of these capacities, it is true, can demonstrate its own validity. We accept them all on faith. But on this faith the whole spiritual life of mankind rests. Without it there could be no science, no religion, no art, no morality. It is in this faith that morality along with the other ideal interests of life finds its ultimate basis, and it is here and here alone that we have an effective and decisive refutation of ethical skepticism.

The Ethic of Power

Skepticism is the foe alike of Christian and of idealistic ethics. Both have a common interest in the philosophical justification of the moral law. They also have a common interest in an ethic of love as opposed to an ethic of power. Christian ethics is more emphatic on this point than idealistic ethics, but aside from this difference of emphasis their general attitude is much the same.

Bishop Gore has said that since the time of Jesus no one has propounded a "new standard or moral law for human life that has entered into rivalry with his with any wide effectiveness."[9]

---

[8] See my *Validity of Religious Experience,* pp. 141-85. A criticism of this aprioristic theory will be found in D. L. Scudder, *Tennant's Philosophical Theology,* pp. 188-204.

[9] *The Philosophy of the Good Life,* p. 220.

But while this is so, there has from the beginning been a rival pagan ethic. This ethic is . n ethic of power and pride. It was widely current in the ancient pagan world and in one form or another has persisted down through the centuries. But only in comparatively recent times has it been formulated in such arresting fashion as to command world-wide attention and to be regarded by many as a serious threat to the whole Christian ethic. The most striking formulation of it is to be found in the writings of Friedrich Nietzsche.[10]

According to Nietzsche the Christian ethic is to be condemned for two fundamental reasons. It is, on the one hand, a slave morality, a morality of the common man, a morality of love; and, on the other hand, it is an ascetic morality, a morality that takes a negative attitude toward the present world and that seeks to suppress all natural instincts. Over against these characteristics of the Christian ethic Nietzsche affirms, on the one hand, an ethic of power, an ethic of the superman, and, on the other hand, an ethic of nature, an ethic of the beast of prey, an ethic of animal impulse. Of these two types of ethic, the first was the earlier and more significant phase of Nietzsche's teaching. It is with it that we are here primarily concerned. The second type represents a marked decline from the first, and has no special significance for us except in so far as it illustrates the conclusion to which the first type naturally leads.

Nietzche's ethic of power and his rejection of the Christian principle of love had their immediate source in his own aristocratic temper and inordinate egotism. He looked on men in general with "sovereign contempt." They were to him and to the superman what "the ape is to man." [11] They have no intrinsic worth. "A people is the circuit which nature makes to

[10] Nietzsche was not a systematic thinker. There are many contradictions in his "philosophy." Indeed, he "made a virtue of inconsistency." But fundamentally his ethic was, as above stated, an ethic of power and pride; and it is this aspect of his teaching that has given to it historic significance. On its relation to Nazism see Crane Brinton, *Nietzsche* (1941), pp. 200-31, Cf. G. A. Morgan, *What Nietzsche Means* (1941).

[11] *Thus Spake Zarathustra,* Prologue, 3.

arrive at six or seven great men." "Society has a right to exist not for the sake of society, but only as the substructure and scaffolding on which a select species of beings may rise to their higher mission and, in general, to a higher existence."[12] The only positive function of the rank and file of mankind is thus to serve as "instruments of the great; for the rest, let them go to the devil and to statistics."[13]

In view of this attitude toward his fellow men, it was only natural that Nietzsche should take a hostile attitude toward Christianity and its doctrine of love. This doctrine seemed to him a symbol of weakness and cowardice. It owed its origin to the most craven and worthless members of society. They invented it in their own self-interest and then hypocritically promulgated it as the moral ideal. Christianity, which sponsored the doctrine, is thus the creation of the base, ignoble, and unheroic elements in society. It is "the revolt of all things that crawl on their bellies against everything that is lofty." "I call Christianity the one great curse, the one great intrinsic depravity, the one great instinct of revenge, for which no means are too venomous, too underhand, too subterranean and too mean—I call it the one immortal blemish of mankind."[14]

By such extravagant denunciations of Christianity Nietzsche sought to establish a sharp antithesis between "noble morality" and "Christian morality," between "the morality of the masters" and "the morality of the slaves." He thus represented himself as championing a higher type of morality, a morality "beyond good and evil" in the Christian sense of these terms, a heroic morality, a morality for supermen. What he says of this new and higher morality contains much that appeals to the Christian conscience.[15] He emphasizes, for instance, courageous endurance of hardship, rigorous discipline, an unconquerable

[12] *Beyond Good and Evil*, 258.

[13] Essay on "The Use and Abuse of History," IX, in *Thoughts Out of Season*, II, 84.

[14] *The Antichrist*, 43, 62.

[15] Cf. J. N. Figgis, *The Will to Freedom, or The Gospel of Nietzsche and the Gospel of Christ* (1917), pp. 58-158.

will, and the "spiritualization of sensousness." But he does not do so in the interest of others. His motive throughout is egoistic, the glorification of the superman.

And eventually this leads him to negate the moral element in his ideal altogether. He rails against Christianity as an ascetic revolt against nature and ends by becoming himself an immoralist, an advocate of a cynical naturalism. He conceives it as his function "to translate man back again into nature." "Obligation," he says, "is a stupid old prejudice and misunderstanding."[16] "Remorse of conscience is indecent." The notions of freedom, responsibility, guilt, and punishment he seeks with all his power "to remove out of the world." The true life for him becomes a life "free from any moralic acid." "Everything good," he says, "is instinct—and consequently easy, necessary, free." The pagan ideal of strength and heroic achievement with which he began thus "degenerates into a glorification of mere animalism."[17]

That this took place is instructive. There were two main reasons for it. One was the unwarranted antithesis that Nietzsche assumed and affirmed between the ancient pagan and the Christian moral ideal. The fact is that these two ideals do not completely exclude each other. The cardinal virtues of the Greeks have had a recognized place in Christian ethics throughout almost the whole of Christian history. They have been to some extent transformed and spiritualized by Christian influence, but they have not lost their independent significance. They have been incorporated in Christian morality as a supplement to it. Historic Christian morality has been and is a fusion of biblical and Greek ethics, just as Christian theology is a fusion of biblical teaching with Greek philosophy. As a result of this fusion the Greek or pagan virtues were, to some extent at least, Christianized and lifted to a higher level. But when

---

[16] Compare the statement attributed to Hitler: "Conscience is a Jewish invention; it mutilates man."

[17] A. S. Pringle-Pattison, *Man's Place in the Cosmos* (1902, pp. 312-14). The entire essay on Nietzsche (pp. 254-319) should be read.

detached from their Christian connections, as they were by Nietzsche, they revert to a lower level and lose not only their present moral quality but the moral worth they possessed before the advent of Christianity. When a person is brought up in the Christian ethic and later rejects it in the interest of an earlier pagan ethic, a moral lapse takes place that leads naturally to immoralism.

It was so with Nietzsche. And with him the decline was hastened by his colossal egotism and his "unsparing contempt" for his fellow men. At the root of all morality lies respect for others, and when this is gone the moral nature is blighted and animalism takes the place of morality. This is the natural history of a pure ethic of power, and it is illustrated by the Nietzschean philosophy of the superman. An ethic of power is at bottom no ethic. It is a denial not only of the Christian ethic but of all ethics. This is its fatal defect. It is not a rival moral theory. It is a negation of morality, a form of immoralism. As such it may, as at present, be a serious menace to civilization. But it can itself have no *moral* justification, and hence can never be a substitute for the Christian ethic. From the outset it is doomed by the human conscience.

The Pragmatic Test

In the Nietzschean philosophy of the superman and the allied Nazi and Fascist doctrines it is assumed that the Christian ethic lacks the more manly and heroic virtues. It is pacifistic and effeminate. It preaches patience and humility instead of martial courage and ruthless self-assertion, and hence is unfitted to be the ethic of a military state and a master race. A new set of values must, therefore, take its place—one based on naked power. In this appraisal of the Christian ethic there is no doubt a large element of truth. The Christian ethic is primarily an ethic for the individual, not for the state. What it seeks to do is to regenerate the human heart, to purge human conduct of its selfishness, and to lead men to live as true children of God. That this means an eradication of brutality and a toning down of man's native aggressiveness, and that it ought also mean a humanizing of the processes of government, is obvious. But that it implies weakness, cowardice, and incapacity for government is certainly not warranted by history. No more virile, progressive, and heroic peoples have appeared in human history than those who have professed the Christian faith. This has been true of them both in peace and war. Indeed, they have been pre-eminently the fighting nations of the world—so much so that some have seen in this fact "the most miserable shipwreck" of Christian principles. But however that may be, the fact itself is convincing evidence that the Christian ethic has not weakened human character and made men less stubborn and valiant in their resistance to what they regard as evil. Rather has it increased and strengthened their heroic devotion to the ideal.

Many other criticisms have been passed upon the Christian ethic. To some of these reference has already been made. The more important ones may here be stated or restated in general terms.

1. Objection has been raised to the doctrine of justification by faith on the ground that its ethical implications and actual consequences have in several respects been evil. Faith, it is said, is for most people inadequate as a source of love and the virtues that flow from it. It may suffice for ecstatic converts such as Paul,[18] but not for ordinary believers. With them faith is largely a matter of doctrinal belief and as such lacks creative power. But not only is it defective as a moral dynamic; the belief in its sole saving efficacy leads to moral laxity. There is evidence of this both in the Apostolic age[19] and at the Reformation. "The Lutheran church," said Harnack, "had to pay dearly for turning away from 'legal righteousness,' 'sacrifice' and 'satisfactions.' Through having the resolute wish to go back to *religion* and to it alone, it neglected far too much the moral task,

[18] Gal. 5:6.

[19] James 2:14-16.

the 'Be ye holy, for I am holy.' "[20] And not only did the doctrine of justification by faith lead to moral neglect; it led to a species of antimoralism, a condemnation of "good works" that must have had a demoralizing effect on many.

2. It is pointed out that the church has often stood in the way of independent scientific research and that in this respect there has been in Christianity a pronounced bent toward anti-intellectualism as well as toward antimoralism. The two have gone together. Faith has been placed above reason, and doctrine above life. Intellectual and moral integrity has been sacrificed to doctrinal conformity. The result has been the breeding of intolerance toward all dissent from inherited creeds and frequent persecutions of heretics. Truth has been arbitrarily identified with dogma, and the quest of new truth discouraged. The moral rights of the intellect have been disregarded and at times grossly violated.

3. The Christian ethic, it is said, has been vitiated by sacramentarianism and asceticism. No matter what religious value the sacraments may have, they are not moral acts. And the very high importance attributed to them in the Catholic churches has tended to dull the human conscience. Asceticism, on the other hand, has deflected consicence from its true objectives. It may have had value as a moral discipline. But it has for the most part been self-centered. It has not been primarily a preparation for social service. Its emphasis has been on the contemplative rather than the active life. A false attitude has also been taken toward nature. Its rights have in important respects been disregarded or denied. The natural goods of life have not received a true appraisal; and conscience has, consequently, failed to fulfill its proper function in the life both of the individual and of society. It has been misled by a one-sided and false spirituality.

4. The Christian ethic, it is charged, has been unduly conservative in its adjustment to the changing conditions of human

[20] *History of Dogma,* VII, 267 (Ger. ed., III, 807).

life and has thus stood in the way of social and economic as well as intellectual progress. The intellectual backwardness and even obscurantism of the church have already been noted as one of the major criticisms of its ethic. Parallel to this has been the indifference and opposition of the church to many social reforms and beneficent changes. One may note the abolition of slavery, of excessively long hours of work, and of child labor; the emancipation of women; the legalization of interest; the modification of rigid and injurious laws governing the marriage relation; and numerous other changes or developments conducive to human welfare. "It is disquieting," says Dean Inge, "for Christians to have to admit that the growth of humanity, in the sense of humaneness, does not owe much to the Churches." [21] The conservative and privileged classes have to a large extent given practical direction to the Christian ethic. This fact casts a dark shadow over the moral record of the churches and is largely responsible for the deep cleavage between organized Christianity and organized labor, especially in Continental Europe.

5. It is argued that not only the ethic of the church but also the ethic of Jesus is now outmoded. No matter how valid it may have been for his day, it no longer is such for us. We have outgrown it, and necessarily so, because of the relatively of history. The ethical teaching of Jesus belongs to an age so remote and so different from ours that it cannot be authoritative for us. Social and economic conditions in Palestine in his day were so unlike those of our own time that he could not in the nature of the case give us valid directions for the concrete situations that confront us today. Then, too, he said very little, if anything, about various moral problems that have a vital interest for us, such as war, the strife between labor and capital, the function of the state, the relation of the sexes to each other, the duties of citizenship, the relation of the church to the state, and other similar problems. From our present standpoint the ethics of

[21] *Christian Ethics and Modern Problems,* p. 291.

Jesus is thus not only in large part irrelevant; it is altogether too limited in its scope to meet our needs. We must, therefore, in this twentieth century, turn elsewhere for moral guidance.[22]

The foregoing criticisms are all more or less justified. The doctrine of justification by faith, sacramentarianism, and asceticism have to some extent weakened or perverted the Christian ethic. Orthodoxy and the consequent fear of science and of heresy, on the one hand, and social conservatism, on the other hand, have led to grave evils. But these are all defects of the traditional ecclesiastical ethics rather than of what may be called the normative Christian ethic. In its essential nature Christianity is a prophetic religion. Its fundamental standpoint is ethical; and its conceptions of God, man, and the world are so completely oriented to the moral point of view that the total impact of its ideal upon the world has been morally inspiring beyond that of any other movement that has entered human history. It has, furthermore, had within itself the principle of its own criticism and rectification. It has identified itself so radically with conscience that it has felt within itself an incessant urge to overcome the dead past and to keep pace with the development of the enlightened conscience. It has been self-criticism more than criticism from without that has resulted in Christianity's correcting to a considerable degree the mistaken doctrines and the evil tendencies referred to. It has by virtue of its own inherent nature carried out a persistent self-purging process. This fact has made its ethic a progressive ethic, and such an ethic must be judged by its governing ideal rather than by the imperfect manifestations of it in the course of its development.

As for the charge of irrelevancy made against the ethical teaching of Jesus, it would have to be conceded to be valid and convincing if he were a lawgiver and if his ethic consisted of specific rules and regulations. Such rules would in large part almost inevitably become obsolete in the course of time, and in

[22] Cf. F. R. Barry, *The Relevance of Christianity.*

any case could not be so comprehensive as to apply to new situations that would arise centuries later. But Jesus, as we have previously pointed out, was not a lawgiver. He did not lay down a detailed code of conduct for his disciples. Such rules as we find in his teaching were illustrative rather than prescriptive. They were concrete expressions or symbols of moral principles or basic spiritual attitudes, and derived their significance from this fact. What Jesus was concerned about was not rules but principles, not obedience to commands but purity of heart. It was love to God and man and a transformed and holy will that he required of men; and such requirements as these are timeless. They do not change; they are never outgrown. They are as fresh and obligatory today as ever.

Just how these Christian principles and the Christian spirit should express themselves in concrete action is not always clear. Some guidance we find in Scripture and in the teaching and practice of the church. But for the most part the problem is one that each must solve for himself. And this is one of the glories of the Christian ethic. It sets before us a moral ideal that cannot be transcended, indeed an unattainable ideal, and then imposes upon each one of us the obligation to realize it as fully as we can in the concrete relations of human life. Such an ethic, it is clear, can never be outmoded. It is relevant to every age.

In applying the pragmatic test to the Christian ethic it is, therefore, important to distinguish between the Christian ideal and its imperfect realization in the life of the individual and in human society. The Christian ideal itself is repudiated by many; but when this is done in a thoroughgoing way, the result, as we have seen, is immoralism. From the standpoint of the moral ideal it is either the Christian ethic or no ethic. This is tacitly and perhaps unconsciously assumed by most anti-Christian moralists; and hence their criticisms are for the most part directed, not against the Christian ideal itself, but against perversions of it or failures to put it into practice. Emphasis on practice has not been lacking in the Christian church. "Christianity," says Lord Stamp, "stands in a class apart from all other religions and systems of ethics in the preponderance of practice over precepts under ·ll conditions."[23] But despite this Christian emphasis, practice has admittedly fallen far short of precept. No one would be more ready to acknowledge this than the true Christian. In estimating, however, the moral shortcomings of the past there is need of sympathetic imagination. The historian needs to take into account the extreme difficulties against which the Christian ethic had to contend in its efforts to secure obedience from rude and semibarbarous peoples. He needs also to recognize the importance of the distinction between Christianity and the church. The medieval church was more of a state than a church in the modern and biblical sense of the term. It was not a voluntary organization. It was based to a large extent on the use of force. This accounts in no small degree for the cruel and repressive measures to which it resorted in order to maintain its own unity and integrity. It was the church-state rather than the Christian church that was chiefly responsible for such evils as those of the Inquisition.

So far as the Christian ethic itself is concerned, there may be some question as to the extent of its beneficent influence. It is often difficult to trace the causes of social reform and progress. Many factors are at work, and it is probably true that in some instances undue credit has been claimed for the Christian ethic. But in the history of humane progress as a whole there can hardly be any serious doubt that its influence has been "overwhelmingly important." In almost every phase of human life its humanizing, liberating, purifying, and elevating influence has been felt.[24] There is nothing comparable to this in any non-Christian country. The story of applied Christianity has no parallel elsewhere, except on a very modest scale. In spite of the many and serious ways in which it has been misrepresented by professed adherents, the Christian ethic in its prac-

[23] *Christianity and Economics,* p. 188.

[24] See C. L. Brace, *Gesta Christi; Christ and Civilization,* ed. Paton, Bunting, and Garvie.

tical application is still the high point of man's moral development and its own most powerful apologetic.

Attempts have been made to break the force of this apologetic by attributing the apparent moral and social achievements of Christianity to other sources, such as the Stoic philosophy, Roman law, and the natural intellectual progress of mankind. That these different factors did exercise a very considerable influence on the development of European morals is not to be questioned. But it is not to them that we owe what is highest and best in European civilization, its humanitarian and progressive spirit. This spirit had its manifest source and inspiration in fundamental and more or less distinctive principles or convictions of the Christian ethic: the principle of love, the principle of purity or perfection, the conviction of the sacredness and infinite worth of every human soul, and the conviction of the essentially religious nature of social service. These principles and convictions lie at the basis of the modern democratic, humanitarian, and idealistic philosophy of life.[25] They stand in their own right and justify themselves. But the belief in their validity is greatly strengthened and confirmed by the contributions they have made to social reform and progress in the course of Christian history.

The Religious Basis of the Christian Ethic

There is another phase of the Christian ethic that has a bearing on the question of its validity. This is its religious basis and especially its relation to the belief in a future life. The charge of otherworldliness has frequently been brought against it. For this charge there has been and is some justification. The ethical significance of the belief in the life hereafter has at times and by many been seriously misconceived. It has been made a

[25] See A. D. Lindsay, *The Essentials of Democracy*. Note the statement of Colonel Rainboro, an officer in Cromwell's army, that "the poorest he that is in England hath a life to live as the richest he" (p. 13), and the author's derivation of modern democracy from the Protestant sects that believed in the Inner Light (p. 56).

ground for taking a more or less pessimistic or indifferent attitude toward the life that now is. The life to come has been regarded as so completely transcending in importance the present life that the latter has by way of contrast been thought of as "a vale of tears," devoid of any rich and satisfying content that could command the enthusiastic devotion of men. The result has been that many have directed their gaze in a one-sided way toward the future world and have neglected in one way or another the present earthly tasks that ought to have engaged their chief attention. Their moral life has, consequently, suffered at its very root.

Furthermore, the future life has to a large extent been viewed from the standpoint of reward or punishment. The New Testament represented this point of view, and still more so did the later teaching of the church. To some extent the appeal to future reward or punishment no doubt had a sobering and inspiring effect on people. It imparted a new seriousness and zest to the moral life. But it also gave to it an egoistic direction and thus impaired its ethical purity. It has at times been asserted that the mere desire for a future life is tainted with selfishness; but, as Bowne used to say, it has never been made clear why it is any more selfish to desire to live hereafter than to desire to live tomorrow.

The fact is that the belief in the life to come, despite the many crude expressions it has received in the past, is a profoundly significant ethical belief. What we owe to it is not primarily the assurance of reward or the fear of punishment for deeds done in the body but the conviction that life has meaning, that its destiny is such as to make high aims and strenuous endeavor worth while. What men most need in the moral life is inspiration; and adequate inspiration for the noblest living can be found only in a world view that gives continuity and permanent meaning to life.

Such a view of human destiny, when properly understood, does not tend to make men egoistic but rather the reverse. It does not distract men from the normal duties of the present life. It does not deprive the world and life in it of their value. What it does is to give to the present life a new dignity, a new worth, a new sanctity. It endows the soul with a new strength and makes one all the more eager to play his full part in the world. Instead of acting as a depressant, "the Beyond is in very truth," as Troeltsch says, "the power of our Now and Here."[26]

The religious basis of the Christian ethic, however, is not confined to the belief in the life hereafter. Christian theology as a whole is involved in it, and toward theology in general there is increasing skepticism. The modern mind is antitheological; and because it is such it tends to distrust the Christian ethic also and to look upon it as outmoded, as no longer relevant to our age. This feeling is widespread, and for it there is no doubt some justification. Certainly it is true that the ethic of Jesus had its basis in his religious convictions. Without his faith in God and the life eternal his ethical ideal would be suspended in the air. It would have no metaphysical support. His law of love was grounded in the love of God. His emphasis on the sanctity of human life had its source both in the divine love and in the immortal destiny of man. His high ideal of personal purity and holiness was based on the holiness of God and on the transforming power of his Spirit in human life. Thus the fundamental elements in his ethic were all derived from his religious faith, and apart from it would have no adequate rational basis. Their acceptance through the ages as the highest expression of the moral life has been largely due to the acceptance of the Christian world view.[27]

That this world view is less commonly held at present than in the past and that its decline in popularity has carried with it more or less ethical skepticism, seems clear. But that this means a weakening of the rational grounds of either the Christian faith or the Christian ethic, is an unwarranted assumption. Both are intellectually as firmly grounded as ever. Neither is

---

[26] *The Social Teaching of the Christian Churches,* II, 1006 (Ger. ed., p. 979).

[27] Cf. Brightman, *The Spiritual Life,* pp. 103-41.

in the remotest danger of capitulating to its naturalistic adversaries. The Christian ethic will never be supplanted by "an ethic of power." The only ethic that can permanently commend itself to the human spirit is an ideal ethic, an ethic of love and purity; and if such an ethic implies the Christian faith, as we believe it does, the human spirit will see in this fact, not a ground for renouncing the Christian ethic, but rather a valid reason for continuing to adhere to the Christian faith. The Christian ethic and the Christian faith support each other; and as a result of modern research their common outlook upon life has, in the words of Troeltsch, lost "nothing of its greatness or its inward significance" [28] and, to this we may add, nothing of its credibility.

[28] *Op. cit.,* I, 21.

A BRIEF BIBLIOGRAPHY

I. General

Alexander, A. B. D.: *Christianity and Ethics,* New York: Charles Scribner's Sons, 1914.

Bowne, B. P.: *The Principles of Ethics.* New York: Harper & Bros., 1892.

Brightman, E. S.: *Moral Laws.* New York: Abingdon-Cokesbury Press, 1933.

Brunner, Emil: *The Divine Imperative.* Tr. from Ger. New York: The Macmillan Co., 1937.

A Dictionary of Religion and Ethics. Ed. S. Mathews and G. B. Smith. New York: The Macmillan Co., 1921.

Encyclopedia of Religion and Ethics. Ed. James Hastings. 12 vols. and Index. Charles Scribner's Sons, 1910-27.

Garvie, A. E.: *The Christian Ideal for Human Society.* New York: Harper & Bros., 1930.

Gore, Charles: *The Philosophy of the Good Life.* Gifford Lectures. New York: Charles Scribner's Sons, 1930.

Haering, Theodor: *The Ethics of the Christian Life.* Tr. from Ger. New York: G. P. Putnam's Sons, 1909.

Hall, T. C.: *History of Ethics Within Organized Christianity.* New York: Charles Scribner's Sons, 1910.

Hartman, Nicolai: *Ethics.* Tr. from Ger. 3 vols. New York: The Macmillan Co., 1932.

Lecky, W. E. H.: *History of European Morals.* 2 vols. 3rd ed. rev. New York: D. Appleton & Co., 1879.

Luthardt, C. E.: *History of Christian Ethics.* 2 vols. in Ger. Vol. I tr. W. Hastie. Edinburgh: T. & T. Clark, 1889.

Niebuhr, Reinhold: *An Interpretation of Christian Ethics.* New York: Harper & Bros., 1935.

Nygren, Anders: *Agape and Eros.* Tr. from Swedish. 3 vols. New York: The Macmillan Co., 1932, 1938, 1939.

Osborn, A. R.: *Christian Ethics.* New York: Oxford University Press, 1940.

Paulsen, Friedrich: *A System of Ethics.* Tr. from Ger. New York: Charles Scribner's Sons, 1899.

Rogers, A. K.: *Morals in Review.* New York: The Macmillan Co., 1927.

Sidgwick, Henry: *Outlines of the History of Ethics.* London: Macmillan & Co., 1886.

Smyth, Newman: *Christian Ethics.* New York: Charles Scribner's Sons, 1892.

Stump, Joseph: *The Christian Life.* New York: The Macmillan Co., 1930. (Contains a lengthy bibliography.)

Troeltsch, Ernst: *The Social Teaching of the Christian Churches.* Tr. from Ger. 2 vols. New York: The Macmillan Co., 1931.

Westermarck, Edward: *Christianity and Morals.* New York: The Macmillan Co., 1939.

———: *The Origin and Development of the Moral Ideas.* 2 vols. New York: The Macmillan Co., 1906-8.

Widgery, A. G.: *Christian Ethics in History and Modern Life.* New York: Round Table Press, 1940.

II. Special

Adam, Karl: *The Spirit of Catholicism.* Tr. from Ger. New York: The Macmillan Co., 1929.

Angell, Norman: *The Great Illusion.* New York: G. P. Putnam's Sons, 1933.

———: *Human Nature and the Peace Problem.* London, 1925.

Arnold, Matthew: *Culture and Anarchy.* London, 1869.

Barbour, G. F.: *A Philosophical Study of Christian Ethics.* Edinburgh, 1911.

Barry, F. R.: *Christianity and the New World.* New York: Harper & Bros., 1932.

Begbie, Harold: *More Twice-Born Men.* New York: G. P. Putnam's Sons, 1923.

———: *Twice-Born Men.* New York: Fleming H. Revell Co., 1909.

Brace, C. L.: *Gesta Christi,* or *A History of Humane Progress under Christianity.* New York: Armstrong, 1883.

Bready, J. W.: *England: Before and After Wesley.* New York: Harper & Bros., 1938.

A BRIEF BIBLIOGRAPHY

Brightman, E. S.: *The Spiritual Life*. New York and Nashville: Abingdon-Cokesbury Press, 1942.

Brinton, Clarence Crane: *Nietzsche*. Cambridge: Harvard University Press, 1941.

Brunner, Emil: *Man in Revolt*. Tr. from Ger. New York: Charles Scribner's Sons, 1939.

Bury, J. B.: *The Idea of Progress*. New York: The Macmillan Co., 1920.

Cadoux, C. J.: *Catholicism and Christianity*. New York: Dial Press, 1929.

——: *The Early Christian Attitude to War*. London, 1919.

——: *The Early Church and the World*. New York: Charles Scribner's Sons, 1925.

Calhoun, R. L.: *God and the Common Life*. New York: Charles Scribner's Sons, 1935.

Cell, G. C.: *The Rediscovery of John Wesley*. New York: Henry Holt & Co., 1935.

Dulles, J. F.: *War, Peace, and Change*. New York: Harper & Bros., 1939.

Ferré, Nels: *Swedish Contributions to Modern Theology*. New York: Harper & Bros., 1939.

Figgis, J. N.: *Churches in the Modern State*. New York: Longmans, Green & Co., 1913.

Flew, R. N.: *The Idea of Perfection in Christian Theology*. New York: Oxford University Press, 1934.

Flewelling, R. T.: *The Survival of Western Culture*. New York: Harper & Bros., 1943.

Gardner, Percy: *Evolution in Christian Ethics*. London, 1918.

Groves, E. R.: *Christianity and the Family*. New York: The Macmillan Co., 1942.

Harkness, Georgia: *John Calvin: The Man and His Ethics*. New York: Henry Holt & Co., 1931.

Henson, H. H.: *Christian Morality*. Gifford Lectures. New York: Oxford University Press, 1936.

Hocking, W. E.: *Lasting Elements of Individualism*. New Haven: Yale University Press, 1937.

——: *Man and the State,* New Haven: Yale University Press, 1926.

——: *The Spirit of World Politics*. New York: The Macmillan Co., 1932.

Hopkins, C. H.: *The Rise of the Social Gospel in American Protestantism, 1865-1915*. New Haven: Yale University Press, 1940.

Hough, L. H.: *Free Men*. New York: Abingdon-Cokesbury Press, 1939.

Inge, W. R.: *Christian Ethics and Modern Problems*. New York: G. P. Putnam's Sons, 1930.

Johnson, F. E.: *The Church and Society*. New York: Abingdon-Cokesbury Press, 1935.

Lea, H. C.: *A History of the Inquisition in the Middle Ages*. 3 vols. New York: Harper & Bros., 1888.

———: *A History of the Inquisition of Spain*. 4 vols. New York: The Macmillan Co., 1906-7.

Lee, Umphrey: *The Historic Church and Modern Pacifism*. New York and Nashville: Abingdon-Cokesbury Press, 1943.

Leighton, J. A.: *Social Philosophies in Conflict*. New York: D. Appleton-Century Co., 1937.

Leslie, E. A.: *Old Testament Religion*. New York: Abingdon-Cokesbury Press, 1936.

Lewis, Edwin: *A New Heaven and a New Earth*. New York and Nashville: Abingdon-Cokesbury Press, 1941.

Lindsay, A. D.: *Christianity and Economics*. New York: The Macmillan Co., 1933.

———: *The Essentials of Democracy*. Philadelphia: University of Pennsylvania Press, 1929.

———: *The Two Moralities*: Eyre & Spottiswoods, 1940.

McConnell, F. J.: *The Christian Ideal and Social Control*. Chicago: University of Chicago Press, 1932.

———: *John Wesley*. New York: Abingdon-Cokesbury Press, 1939.

Mitchell, H. G.: *The Ethics of the Old Testament*. Chicago: University of Chicago Press, 1912.

Moffatt, James: *Love in the New Testament*. New York: Harper & Bros., 1930.

Morgan, G. A.: *What Nietzsche Means*. Cambridge: Harvard University Press, 1941.

Mounier, E.: *A Personalist Manifesto*. Tr. from French. New York: Longmans, Green & Co., 1938.

Niebuhr, Reinhold: *Moral Man and Immoral Society*. New York: Charles Scribner's Sons, 1932.

———: *The Nature and Destiny of Man.* Gifford Lectures. 2 vols. New York: Charles Scribner's Sons, 1941, 1943.

Nock, A. D.: *Conversion.* New York: Oxford University Press, 1933.

Oxnam, G. B.: *The Ethical Ideals of Jesus in a Changing World.* New York and Nashville: Abingdon-Cokesbury Press, 1941.

Paton, Bunting, and Garvie, eds.: *Christ and Civilization.* London, 1910.

Peabody, F. G.: *Jesus Christ and the Christian Character.* New York: The Macmillan Co., 1905.

Pfeiffer, R. H.: *Introduction to the Old Testament.* New York: Harper & Bros., 1941.

Rall, H. F.: *Christianity: An Inquiry into Its Nature and Truth.* New York: Charles Scribner's Sons, 1940.

Scott, E. F.: *The Ethical Teaching of Jesus.* New York: The Macmillan Co., 1924.

Scott-Craig, T. S. K.: *Christian Attitudes to War and Peace.* New York: Charles Scribner's Sons, 1938.

Scullard, H. H.: *The Ethics of the Gospel and the Ethics of Nature.* New York: Doubleday, Doran & Co., 1928.

Slosser, G. J.: *Christian Unity: Its History and Challenge in all Communions in All Lands.* New York: E. P. Dutton & Co., 1929.

Sorokin, P. A.: *The Crisis of Our Age.* New York: E. P. Dutton & Co., 1941.

Stamp, Josiah: *Christianity and Economics.* New York: The Macmillan Co., 1939.

Tawney, R. H.: *Religion and the Rise of Capitalism.* New York: Harcourt, Brace & Co., 1926.

Treitschke, H.: *Politics.* Tr. from Ger. 2 vols. New York: The Macmillan Co., 1916.

Tsanoff, R. A.: *The Modern Ideals of Our Civilization.* New York: E. P. Dutton & Co., 1942.

Uhlhorn, Gerhard: *Christian Charity in the Ancient Church.* Tr. from Ger. New York: Charles Scribner's Sons, 1883.

Underwood, A. C.: *Conversion, Christian and Non-Christian.* New York: The Macmillan Co., 1925.

Webb, C. C. J.: *Contribution of Christianity to Ethics.* New York: Longmans, Green & Co., 1932.

Weber, Max: *The Protestant Ethic and the Spirit of Capitalism.* Tr. from Ger. New York: Charles Scribner's Sons, 1930.

Westermarck, E.: *The Future of Marriage in Western Civilization.* New York: The Macmillan Co., 1936.

——: *The History of Human Marriage.* 3 vols. New York: The Macmillan Co., 1921.

Whitchurch, I. G.: *An Enlightened Conscience.* New York: Harper & Bros., 1941.

Williams, N. P.: *The Ideas of the Fall and of Original Sin.* New York: Longmans, Green & Co., 1927.

Workman, H. B.: *The Evolution of the Monastic Ideal.* London, 1913. 2nd ed., 1927.

——: *Persecution in the Early Church.* New York: Jennings & Graham, 1906.

Wright, R. F.: *Medieval Internationalism.* London: Williams & Norgate, 1930.

York, Elizabeth: *League of Nations, Ancient, Medieval, and Modern.* London: Swarthmore Press, 1919.

INDEX

INDEX